ALLYSON COOPER

Cricut For Beginners

4 books in 1: All You Need To Know About Cricut, Expand On Your Passion For Object Design And Transform Your Project Ideas From Thoughts To Reality

Copyright © 2020 Allyson Cooper

All rights reserved

© Copyright 2020 - All rights reserved.

The content contained within this book may not be reproduced, duplicated or transmitted without direct written permission from the author or the publisher.

Under no circumstances will any blame or legal responsibility be held against the publisher, or author, for any damages, reparation, or monetary loss due to the information contained within this book. Either directly or indirectly.

Legal Notice:

This book is copyright protected. This book is only for personal use. You cannot amend, distribute, sell, use, quote or paraphrase any part, or the content within this book, without the consent of the author or publisher.

Disclaimer Notice:

Please note the information contained within this document is for educational and entertainment purposes only. All effort has been executed to present accurate, up to date, and reliable, complete information. No warranties of any kind are declared or implied. Readers acknowledge that the author is not engaging in the rendering of legal, financial, medical or professional advice. The content within this book has been derived from various sources. Please consult a licensed professional before attempting any techniques outlined in this book.

By reading this document, the reader agrees that under no circumstances is the author responsible for any losses, direct or indirect, which are incurred as a result of the use of information contained within this document, including, but not limited to, — errors, omissions, or inaccuracies.

CRICUT FOR BEGINNERS

Introduction 8

Chapter 1. Cricut Machine Models 18

Chapter 2. Cricut Tools And Accessories 31

Chapter 3. Materials That Can Be Used For Cricut 63

Chapter 4. Design Space Application 68

Chapter 5. Cricut Projects For Beginners 84

Chapter 6. Making Money With Cricut 100

Conclusion: Tips For Start In The Best Way 104

CRICUT MAKER FOR BEGINNERS

Introduction 110

Chapter 1: What Is A Cricut Machine And How Does It Work? 116

Chapter 2: Cricut Explore Air 2 Vs. Cricut Maker 121

Chapter 3: Insights Of Explore Air 2 Machine 124

Chapter 4: Tools And Accessories Needed To Work With Explore Air 2 Machine ... 132

Chapter 5: Insights Of Cricut Maker Machine 136

Chapter 6: Tools And Accessories Needed To Work With Cricut Maker Machine ... 143

Chapter 7: How To Use Design Space 148

Chapter 8: Design Space Software Secrets And The Design Space App 154

Chapter 9: Best Projects You Can Do With Cricut Maker 161

Chapter 10: Best Projects You Can Do With Explore Air 2 170

Chapter 11: Tips And Tricks To Make Cricut Machines Easier And Efficient 177

Chapter 12: Best Software To Use With Cricut And Create Super Design Templates *181*

Conclusion *186*

CRICUT DESIGN SPACE

Introduction *190*

Chapter 1: The Platform Design Space: Getting Started *194*

Chapter 2: Tools And Functions *201*

Chapter 3: Projects: How To Start A New Project *218*

Chapter 4 Advanced Tips And Techniques *243*

Chapter 5 Other Tips & Tricks *259*

Chapter 6 Common Problems And How To Solve Them *265*

Conclusion *273*

CRICUT PROJECT IDEAS

Introduction *276*

Chapter 1. Cricut Design Space Project Ideas *280*

Chapter 2. List Of Materials That Can Be Used With Compatible Cricut Machines *285*

Chapter 3. Materials For Cricut Machines *292*

Chapter 4. Easy Cricut Project Ideas *297*

Chapter 5. Paper-Based Projects *304*

Chapter 6. Cricut Projects With Vinyl *310*

Chapter 7. Project To Create Fabric Cuts (Part 1) *318*

Chapter 8. Project To Create Fabric Cuts (Part 2) *332*

Chapter 9. Project With Glass *338*

Chapter 10. Other Ideas For Advanced Level *343*

Chapter 11. Other Projects Using Cricut Design Space *349*

Chapter 12. Other Projects Using Cricut Design Space (Part 2) *358*

Conclusion *380*

CRICUT FOR BEGINNERS

Introduction

What is a Cricut?

The Cricut machine is a fantastic creation. This helps you cut paper, cloth, and vinyl sheets to whatever pattern you would like. These actual production designs may be achieved via software tools like the Cricut Layout Studio or via Capsules using pre-engineered structures assembled into them. Therefore, if you're an enthusiastic scrapbooker, this system is a must-have.

What Can I Make With This?

There are several one-of-a-kind problems for you to use a Cricut. While you know what type of task you want to perform, and at the same time considering what kind of decoration and supplies you need to use the machine, please take a look at the rest of the other projects and parts that Cricut has just started. Demand (and what are basically "decent possessions" that you can spend when you need them) Scrapbooking and Card Making.

There are loads of scrapbooking thoughts and scrapbook designs than you can discover for your Cricut!

Or, once you don't want the opportunity to make cards yourself, there are some pointers and special effects for making cards quickly.

Weddings and Gatherings

Cricut machines are great for making custom stylistic themes for weddings and gatherings!

Occasions

Utilize your Cricut to make an occasional stylistic layout for any event!

Home Stylistic Theme

You can make loads of various undertakings to improve your home!

Everything from cushions and divider craftsmanship to big business thoughts!

Clothing and Extras

One of my preferred things to make with my Cricut is shirts, onesies, and tote sacks. You can put warmness switch vinyl on exceptionally much any material surface. However, you can likewise utilize a Cricut to make adornments, headbands, and then some!

Vinyl Decals and Stickers

Our assortment one intrigue is lessening vinyl decals and stickers, and you can do this with the Cricut Maker.

It can cut through any vinyl in no time easily—you should simply make your format in Cricut Design Space, teach the PC to begin cutting; at that point, weed, and change the arrangement to your picked surface.

Texture Cuts

One of the essential selling elements of the Maker is the truth that it comes outfitted with the new product Turn Cutting edge.

On account of uncommon coasting and moving movement—by and large with the gigantic 4kg of power at the back of the Cricut Maker—this ability that the work area can lessen unmistakably any texture.

The truth is out. Denim? Check. Overwhelming canvas? Check. Silk? Check. Chiffon? Check. We've continually constrained using a particular texture shaper sooner, than as the registering gadget lessening machines essentially weren't compelling to deal with more massive textures. We cherish the truth that the Maker is an across the board machine.

It comes furnished with a texture-cutting mat so that you can lessen bunches of textures aside from the utilization of any support. Astonishing!

Sewing Examples

Another key prepared of the Maker is the gigantic Sewing Test Library that you'll get passage to when you've purchased the machine.

It comprises of earnestly many examples—some from Effortlessness and Riley Blake Designs—and capacity you can genuinely pick the model you like, and the Maker will remove it for you.

No additional removing designs physically yourself (and not any more human blunder ruins!)

Additionally, secured is a launder-able texture pen that will call attention to the spot the example parts intend to stable together.

Balsa Wood Cuts

On account of the incredible 4kg of weight and the Blade Sharp Edge (sold independently,) the Cricut Maker can slice using substances up to 2.4 mm thick. That limit thick texture that had before been beyond reach with the Cricut and Outline machines is currently open to us. We can hardly wait to start cutting wooden with it!

Thick Cowhide Cuts

In a similar vein as factor #4, thick cowhide can cut with the Maker!

Natively Constructed Cards

Paper crafters aren't forgotten about with the Maker either.

Paper and card cuts will be less complicated and snappier than at any other time because of the machine's vitality and exactness. Your Scratchpad playing cards just went up a level.

Jigsaw Riddles

We comprehend that the Cricut Maker can cut through significantly thicker substances with the Blade Edge than any time in recent memory.

The central perspective we give it a shot? Making our special jigsaw confound. We'll save you, refreshed!

Christmas Tree Adornments

The Revolving Cutting edge that vows to lessen through any texture is the ideal gadget for designing occasion improvements. Scour the Sewing Design Library for Christmassy designs (we've purchased our eye on the gingerbread man adornment!) lessen out the example utilizing felt, or whatever texture you want, and after that, sew it all in all independently.

Blankets

Cricut has collaborated with Riley Blake Designs to give various sewing designs in the Sewing Design Library.

This capacity, that you can utilize the Maker to remove your sewing correctly, divides before sewing, them aggregately independently.

Felt Dolls and Delicate Toys

One of the Effortlessness designs we have our eye on in the Sewing Design Library is the "Felt Doll and Garments" example. We understand a couple of little women and young men who'd love a natively constructed dish to add to their collections. Just pick the bar, cut, and sew. Simple peasy!

Shirt Moves

You need to arrange the switch in Design Space, load the glow switch vinyl to the manufacturer (or flash it drastically on the HTV if you may feel timid;) it recommends that the PC start cutting, and ironing your switch the shirt. Or, on the other hand, you should utilize the fresh-out-of-the-box new Cricut Easy Press to switch the vinyl—it's everything, the solace of an iron meets the adequacy of a warmness press!

Texture Appliques

Additionally, available to get individually, is the Fortified Texture Sharp Edge in lodging, which will allow you to lessen additional unpredictable material designs, similar to applique.

In contrast to the sharp rotating edge, the Fortified Texture Edge requires reinforced sponsorship on the material to diminish adequately.

Calligraphy Signs

The Cricut Maker's significant selling element is its Versatile Apparatus Framework. It is the element that will verify that you keep up your Maker until the end of time. In reality, it's a gadget machine that exclusively suits every one of the instruments and sharp edges of the Explore family. However, it will fit as a fiddle with every future device and cutting edges made using Cricut.

The vitality of the Cricut Maker limit that you can cut thicker substances than sooner than that is appropriately perfect for intricate gems designs.

And keeping in mind that you aren't in any way, shape, or form, to cut gold, silver, or jewel on there, at whatever point soon, an excellent pair of cowhide rings are just inside reach.

Wedding Solicitations and Spare the Dates

As a whole, we know about how "little" costs like welcomes and sexually transmitted diseases can add to the super price of a wedding.

As makers, we also know how to counter-balance a portion of those costs using making matters like ourselves.

The Cricut Maker is perfect for making staggering welcomes—presently, not exclusively, would you remove confusing paper designs, anyway that calligraphy pen will come in reachable once more.

Wedding Menus, Spot Cards, and Support Labels

You're nearly no longer compelled to creates before the wedding function—you can likewise utilize your Maker to adorn for the gigantic day itself. The sky is just the confinement directly here; however, in all reality, make menus, region playing a card game, and lean toward labels. Attempt, and ensure you utilize a practically identical arrangement for all your stationery to protect the subject upfront.

Shading Book

Do you know these "careful shading" books that are extremely popular at present? And after that, the Maker's total direction is to make your own unique, unquestionably extraordinary, shading book utilizing the Fine-Point Pen device.

Liners

Another part we can hardly wait to make with our new Maker is liners.

The world you claim, as far as substances go—whatever from cowhide to sew, to steel sheets, and everything in the middle.

There are likewise some fabulous liner designs in the Sewing Library to investigate as well.

Texture Key-Rings

Something different that got our attention in the Sewing Test Library was, at one time, a couple of simple designs for fabric key-rings.

Once more, the Maker makes it advantageous—totally decrease out the example, and after that, sew it together.

Headbands and Hair Adornments

Presently, Cricut has propelled a registering gadget that is lessening through thick calfskin; we are fearless thought for mind-boggling, steampunk-motivated hair designs, and even headbands.

Who realized the Maker ought to be so convenient for significant pattern articulations?

Cut-Out Christmas Tree

We know, we know, every individual needs a real Christmas tree eventually of the get-away season. In any case, just on the off chance that you don't have space for a transcending tree in your residence room or, God prohibits, you're hypersensitive to pine, you may need support to make your tree. As the Cricut Maker successfully decreases thick substances like wood, we guess an interlocking wood tree is an incredible task to check with this year. No laser is required when the Maker is available to you no matter what!

How Does It Work?

When you see the finished product from a Cricut machine, you will definitely be blown away. The neatness and appealing look of a typical project done with the Cricut machine will take your breath away. However, only a few people understand the process involved in the creation of such amazing designs.

Curious to know how the Cricut machine is able to cut out materials effectively? There are three major steps involved when using the Cricut machine:

Have a Design

If you have a PC, you can access the Cricut Design Space to access the library of designs. If you have a Mac, you can access the same platform to select a huge variety of designs. In case you don't have any of these two, but possesses an iPhone or iPad, you can use the Design Space for iOS.

If what you have is an Android, you are covered as well. This is because you can take advantage of the Design Space for Android. These are online platforms where you can select any design that best suits your taste.

You can also customize a ready-made design to suit your needs. For example, you can resize it, or modify the shape. You can also add a text or image as you wish, till you have the design just as you want it.

Prepare the Machine

Having selected the design you intend to cut out with the machine, you are ready for the next step. The machine needs to be prepared by turning it on. Once you switch on the machine, you actually don't need to do anything.

You don't have to press any button unless you are using the machine for the first time. In that case, the machine will give you instructions on what to do. It is that simple.

That is why both beginners and experts can make use of the Cricut machine without issues. Your Computer or Phone will have to be paired with the machine via Bluetooth for the first time. However, this will not be needed subsequently because the machine will remember the pairing.

Hence, once the machine is switched on, the pairing between the phone and the machine becomes automatic. The implication of this is that once the machine is switched on, the machine is ready. The next step is to send the design to the machine.

Send the Design to the Machine

This is the last stage of the process of cutting with the Cricut machine. Once the machine is powered on, at the top right corner of the screen, you will see the "Make It" button; this is a big green button on the Cricut Design Space

The first thing the software does is to preview the various mats you have. A mat represents a sheet of material; hence, having two different colors in your project implies two mats. There are times that your project can be a combination of fabric and paper. During such occurrences, you will have a mat representing each material utilized for the project. Once you have prepared the machine, you need to decide the dimension with which the machine will do the cutting. If you intend to make two cards, the machine has to be instructed to make two project copies.

You will find this option at the top left of the Cricut Design Space. Most of the materials you will be cutting will be cut at 12″ × 12″ size. This is because this is the standard size that is the most prominent on the Cricut machine. However, if you prefer a different dimension, you can always alter it. The mirror switch has to be flipped to mirror the design you want in case you want an iron-on design. This has to be done to guarantee that the alteration is reflected by the finished project.

Once you are set to send the design to the Cricut, you will click "Continue." This option can be seen at the bottom right corner of the Cricut Design Space. It is easy to continue at this point because the software will prompt you to take you through what ought to be done.

Don't get what-up about how to set up different projects of different materials and colors. This is because the instructions you need will be displayed on the screen, and you can easily follow through. Once you follow the instructions presented to you by the machine, you are guaranteed top-quality cuttings.

The machine will request that you pick the particular material you want to use for the first mat. Simply choose whether it is paper, vinyl, fabric, leather, or any other material. Once you do this, the machine will automatically adjust pressure, speed, and the brush blade as necessary. Hence, just ensure you do your part of instructing the machine to do your bidding as desired. You can trust the Cricut machine from that point to do all that is needed for a perfect project. After the machine has adjusted itself to cut, you will put the material into the Cricut cutting mat. At this point, you will then load the machine with the mat. What if I am using different materials for my project? That is also not an issue worth disturbing yourself about. This is because the software will take you through how to go about loading different materials. Once you are done loading the machine with the mat containing the material, you are good to go. This is because you will be prompted by the machine, concerning setting the dial cutting, drawing, or scoring.

The machine will proceed to cut out the mat. The pieces that have been cut out can then be gathered by you and used as desired. This is how the Cricut machine works, and it is basically the same principle for every project.

It is obvious that you don't have to be a genius before you are qualified to use the machine. The instructions are simplified such that anyone who can understand basic English language can use it. Therefore, if you have been thinking that you might not be able to operate this machine, you are wrong.

So, go ahead, try Cricut, and begin your crafting journey!

Chapter 1. Cricut Machine Models

Cricut Explore One

Because of its efficiency, it is still being purchased today although this is the oldest present-day Cricut machine and first in the Explore line.

Photo credit: amazon.com

Explore One is ideal for beginners and inexperienced users who want to get into die-cutting, craft cutting, and plotting. The machine isn't advanced like the other Explore models, and it is also the cheapest Cricut machine you can get.

Capability

The machine is also highly capable, even if it's an old model. The system can also handle scoring, and writing smoothly.

Materials

Photo credit: amazon.com

Regardless of the simplicity and the inexpensive nature of the machine, it is still highly capable. You can use this system to cut a range of 60 materials and more. This includes light materials like vinyl and thick materials like felt.

Cutting Force

The machine comes with a top-notch German Carbide Premium Blade, which can cut through light and thick materials alike, cleanly and neatly. Even if Explore One is recommended for beginners, it is very professional. The blade is also highly durable.

As for the cutting width, the Explore One can cut sizes that range from 23 ½" tall and ¼ to 11 ½" wide.

Even though the Explore One seems excellent, there are some activities that you can't do on the Cricut Design Space if you're using this model.

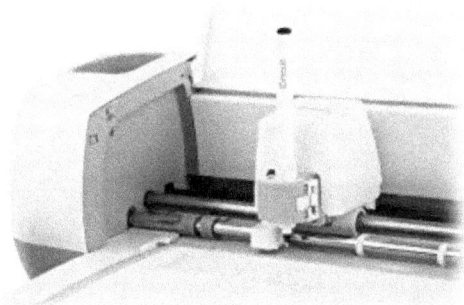

Photo credit: amazon.com

Cricut Design Space is very user friendly when using it for Explore One. It accepts the format files: .jpg, .png, and .bmp.

Also, the Cricut Explore One cannot function wirelessly. If you want to add convenience to it, and you don't mind the cost, then you can buy a Bluetooth adapter and use it to transfer images, or files wirelessly.

The Explore One also comes with one head clamp or carriage only. Because of this, if you want to draw and cut at the same time, you have to buy an adapter.

These are the tools that are in a newly purchased Explore One box:

- 24 x 9.5 x 9.5 sized Cricut Explore One machine.

- German Carbide Premium Blade.

- Over 50 free images.

- Over 25 free one-click projects.

- 12" x 12" Standard Grip cutting mat.

- USB and power cords.

- Vinyl sample.

- Welcome guide.

Cricut Explore Air

Photo credit: amazon.com

While this is quite similar to the Explore One model, it also comes with some additional features. The main difference between them is the presence of the inbuilt Bluetooth adapter. If you don't enjoy seeing cables and wires all around your workplace, especially with the danger of tripping over them, then this model solves that problem.

Capability

The Explore Air is also different from Explore One because it features a double carriage. This means that you can draw, write, or score while you cut because it has two clamps to hold both tools. This saves you money because you don't have to purchase a tool adapter.

Materials

Explore Air is quite liberating when it comes to materials. It features a dial that can allow you to choose the material that you're about to cut. That way, you don't have to guess the blade depth and mess up the material.

The machine will know how deep it will have to cut for felt, and how gentle it has to be for paper or vinyl. This feature is especially great for beginners who are not well versed with the blade depths.

For experienced users, the Cricut Explore Air also features several custom settings that allow the user to customize the cutting of their design.

This model can cut more materials than the Explore One, including fabric, poster board, vellum, and about 70 more.

Cutting Force

Photo credit: businesswire.com

The system is more powerful than the older model when it comes to the cutting force. It features a Cut Smart technology made by Cricut, which enhances the blade control of the system, and gives your creations a more professional look. It can cut anything that is as wide as 23.5 inches accurately and precisely.

It also has the Smart Set Dial, which increases the control you have over the cutting of your project.

The features of the Cricut Design Space are very similar. But, when using Explore Air, you get more freedom, and you are allowed to use .svg, .gif, and .dxf files, in addition to the standard files allowed with Explore One.

Sadly, Explore Air does not have either a knife or a rotary blade. Because of these two types of blades, the Explore Air is recommended for more light crafts and scrapbooking. It does have an inbuilt blade, though.

A brand new Explore Airbox comes with these tools:

- A 25.4 x 10 x 9.2 inches Cricut Explore Air machine with inbuilt Bluetooth technology.
- It has an inbuilt accessory adapter.
- Inbuilt blade.
- USB and power cord.
- Metallic silver marker.
- Iron-on sample.
- Cardstock sample.
- Over 100 images.
- Over 50 ready-to-cut projects.
- 12" x 12" Standard Grip cutting mat.
- Welcome guide.

Cricut Explore Air 2

This is the youngest sibling of the Cricut Explore line. It is the best of the machines in this line. The Explore Air 2, as efficient as the other ones, works even better. It even has a better design, and it comes in different colors than you can do.

Photo credit: amazon.com

Capability

The model features a fast mode that speeds up the cutting process, primarily if you work with deadlines.

It also has the features in the other systems like the German Carbide Premium Blade, inbuilt Bluetooth adapter, dual carriage, and auto-settings.

The great thing about the Explore Air 2 is that it is ideal for both beginners and advanced users.

Materials

This machine can cut through a hundred materials, or even more. This includes, and is not limited to cotton, silk, tissue paper, corkboard, foil, foam, aluminum, leather, clay, chipboard, burlap, and even birch wood.

It also has the Smart Dial, which helps you manage the cutting width depending on the materials.

Cutting Force

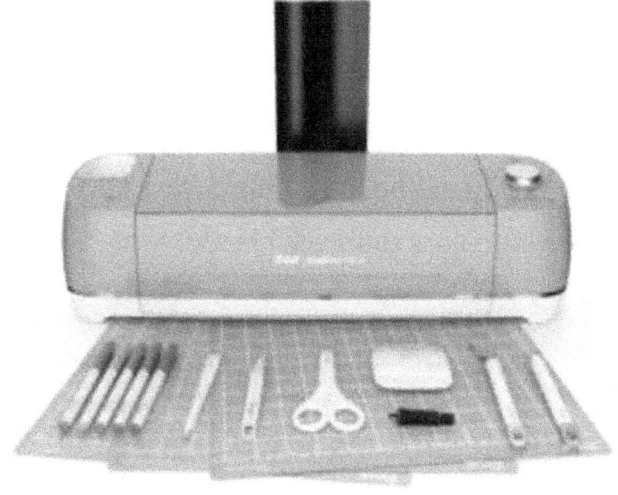

Photo credit: cricut.com

The model is highly potent, and it makes use of the German Carbide Premium Fine-Point Blade, which comes with precision and speed. It is also able to cut any material with a width of 11.5 x 23.5 inches.

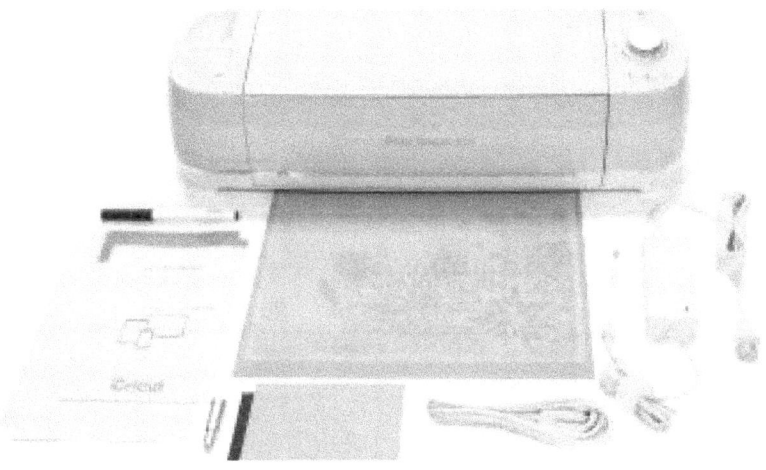

Photo credit: heatbusiness.com

When you first purchase a Cricut Explore Air 2, you get a three months free subscription with access to premium features offered by Cricut.

The Cricut Design Space is also cloud-based for those using iOS devices. With this, you can work offline.

The only downside in this model is the slightly increased noise level, but this is expected because it works two times faster than the previous models.

Your shiny, new Cricut Explore Air 2, will look like this:

- Cricut Explore Air 2 machine.

- Adapter.

- Power and USB cord.

- German Carbide Premium Blade.

- Machine software and application.

- Built-in projects and images.

- Standard Grip cutting mat.

- Cardstock Sample.

- A pen.

- Welcome guide.

Cricut Maker

Photo credit: amazon.com

The newest Cricut die-cutting machine is the Cricut Maker. If you thought that the Explore Air 2 was a great model, then you should get ready to be blown away.

The Cricut Maker is a rare unit amongst other die-cutting machines. The rotary blade is already enough to attract experienced users. And, for beginners, it provides an avenue for improvement and unlimited creativity.

Capability

The Cricut Maker, as an updated version of others, is very powerful and flexible. It comes with a tool kit that includes a rotary-blade, knife blade, deep-cut blade, and fine-point blade. It also comes with a single and a double scoring wheel, as well as a collection of pens. The pens include a fine-point pen, a washable-fabric pen, a calligraphy pen, and a scoring stylus.

Photo credit: amazon.com

The machine also improves its efficiency by adding some unique features. We have the adaptive tool system, which means that the device can adjust the angle of the blade and the pressure of the blade automatically depending on the material. It doesn't need the Smart Dial feature because the Cricut Maker determines your cutting force for you, and its decisions are usually accurate.

It has two clamps, one for the pen or scoring tool, and the other for the cutting blade. This system is also unique because of its fast mode and precise mode. This works for any paper, cardstock, and vinyl.

Materials

As expected, the Cricut Maker will be able to handle more and thicker materials than the machines in the Cricut Explore series.

From light materials to basswood and leather, this machine will exceed your expectations.

Cricut Design Space also provides a lot of benefits for Cricut Maker users. It allows the format files: .jpg, .gif, .png, .svg, .bmp, and .dxf.

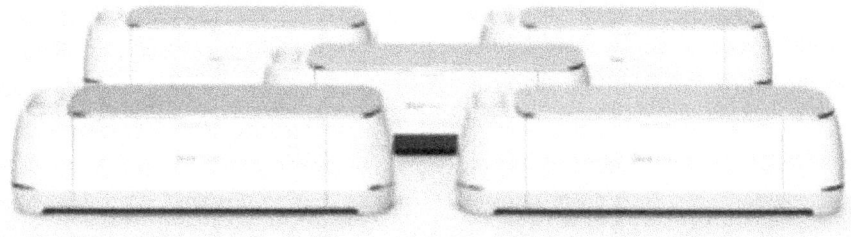

Photo credit: cricut.com

The system also supports a wireless Bluetooth adapter. You can also enjoy the Sewing Pattern Library if you own a Cricut Maker. The library contains 50 ready-to-cut projects, and it is a result of a partnership between Cricut and Riley Blake Designs.

Another great benefit you get when using Cricut Maker with Design Space is that you get free membership of Cricut Access for a trial period.

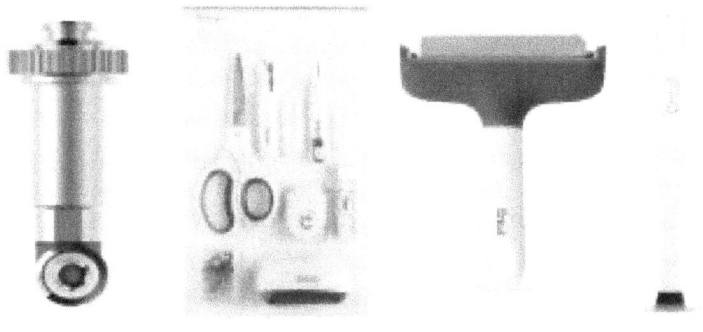

Photo credit: heyletsmakestuff.com

The only downsides to this model are that it is quite slow when working with very thick materials, although that is expected.; and that it also produces a lot of noise because of the fast mode.

This is what comes in the new Cricut Maker box:

- Cricut Maker machine.
- Fine-Point pen.
- Premium Fine-Point pen and housing.
- Rotary blade and drive housing.
- USB cable.
- Power adapter.
- LightGrip Mat 12" x 12".
- FabricGrip Mat 12" x 12".
- 50 ready-to-cut projects, which includes 25 sewing patterns.
- Materials for the first project.
- Welcome guide.

Which Cricut Model Should You Use?

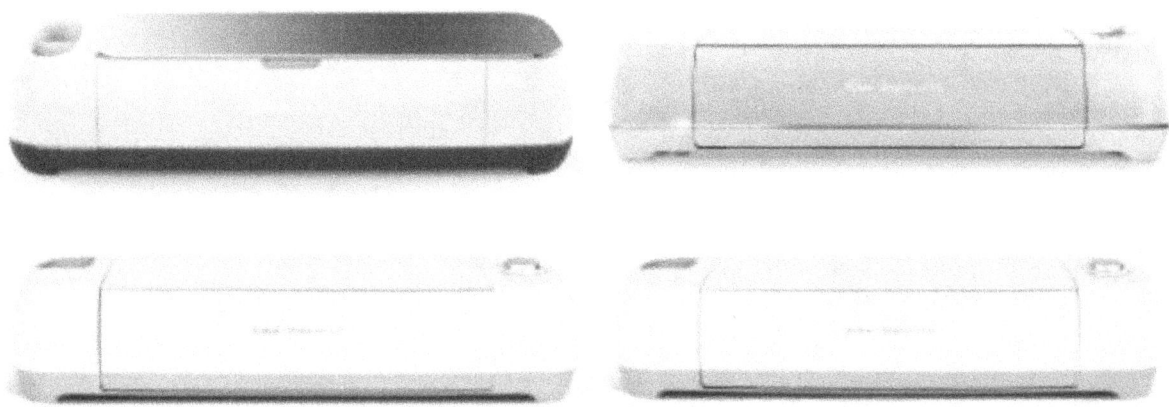

Photo credit: heyletsmakestuff.com

Although all Cricut models are great, the Cricut Maker or Explore Air models are highly recommended, whether you're a beginner or an advanced user. These two machines are usually ideal for most people, no matter the type of craft you use.

For the person who is looking to go into serious crafting, woodworking, sewing, and quilting, then the Cricut Maker is highly recommended. It is highly professional, and it can work for any craft that you're getting into. The system has a lot of benefits, especially on Design Space.

If you're a beginner who is looking to go deep into crafting, then you should also get the Cricut Maker because it will make no sense to purchase an old model, and then buy a new one when you have gained some experience.

You might be planning on using your Cricut machine for business purposes. This will mean that you will be repeating the same action occasionally. For this use, you can use the Cricut Explore Air 2 because it has a fast mode and many other advantages.

Beginners, leisurely crafters, and those who have a tight budget will work better with the Cricut Explore One and Explore Air.

Chapter 2. Cricut Tools And Accessories

Cricut Accessories

Cricut cutting machines come with quite a few accessories that you can purchase to add to the functionality of your machine. There are some accessories that most of the machines can use, and others that are designed only for a specific machine.

The following list of accessories will explain what the items are used for, and what machines they can be used on.

Cricut BrightPad

The Cricut BrightPad is a very handy device for serious crafters, as it illuminates projects to help with weeding, tracing, quilt blocks, paper piecing, and more. It can even help with jewelry making or model building.

The price is approx. $100.

The BrightPad is compatible with all of the Cricut machines and crafting materials.

- Cricut BrightPad Is Compatible With:

- All makes and models of Cricut Cutters.

- Cricut Bright Pad Is Not Compatible With:

- There are no Cricut machines whose device cannot be used alongside.

Cricut Cartridges

Cricut Cartridges are small cartridges that fit into the slots of some of the older Cricut machines (the Explore Air 2 still has a slot for them.) These cartridges were filled with images for purchase in order to expand a crafting image library.

You no longer need cartridges with current machines, and that is why Cricut has discontinued them. You can purchase digital cartridges from the Cricut craft shop website.

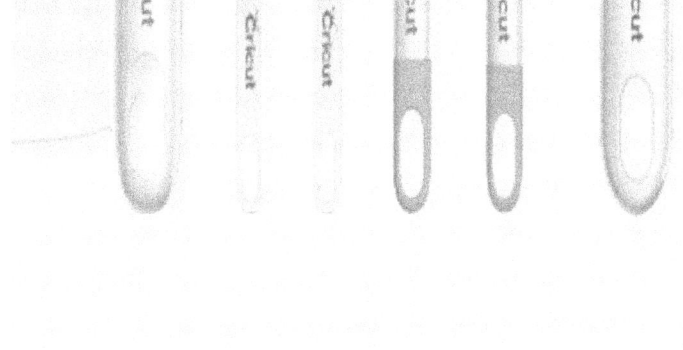

Like the physical cartridges, digital cartridges are sold in batches, which means you have to buy what comes with the pack. However, Design Space has thousands of images, projects, and more, that you can buy as individual items when you are creating your projects.

For those who already have cartridges, they are still able to be used. Design Space still supports them by letting you link cartridges once they have been loaded into the machine.

Although the Cricut Maker does not have a slot for cartridges, you can buy the Cricut USB cartridge adaptor for use with your purchased cartridges.

The Cricut Joy does not use cartridges and you cannot use the Cricut USB cartridge adapter with it.

- Cricut Cartridges Are Compatible With:
    - Cricut Explore.
    - Cricut Explore Air.
    - Cricut Explore Air 2.
    - Most older and legacy Cricut cutting machine models.
- Cricut Cartridges Are Not Compatible With:
    - Cricut Joy.
    - Cricut Maker (it needs an adaptor.)
    - Cricut Cuttlebug.

Cricut Craft Tools

The Cricut Craft Tools have been specifically designed to make crafter's tasks a lot easier. As they are designed around the Cricut cutting machines, they make tasks like extra cutting, weeding, tweezing, tracing, etc., a breeze.

Each one of these tools, cutters, rulers, pens, knife blades, and so on can be purchased individually, or in various toolsets/bundles.

Most Cricut Tools come in standard colors such as cream or grey. There are exceptions and special promotions that may change the colors of the tools.

- Cricut Tools Are Compatible With:

All makes and models of Cricut Cutters.

- Cricut Tools Are Not Compatible With:

    There are no Cricut machines that the tools cannot be used alongside. The only tool that is not compatible with every cutting machine is the Cricut Stylus pen.

- Cricut Tool Colors:

Cricut Tools come in different colors that include:

- Blue.
- Mint.
- Gray.
- Lilac.
- Rose.
- Pink.
- Peach.

It should be noted that not all of the tools come in these colors, and the coloring can differ depending on the tool type.

Cricut Brayer

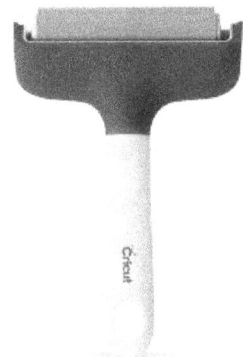

The brayer tool looks a bit like a lint roller. Although it does not remove lint, fluff, etc., it does help with sticking material firmly and smoothly to cutting mats.

The brayer helps the user to smooth the material, and press it firmly down onto cutting mats. It easily gets rid of wrinkles, kinks, bubbles, and can link blocks.

The price is approx. $20.

Cricut Distresser

This tool looks like the Cricut Scraper tool, except that it has two slits on either side of it. The distresser is used to give the paper a textured edge.

Cricut Fabric Shears

Cricut Fabric Shears cut through most fabric with ease, and this includes layered fabrics. The Fabric Shears are extra sharp with precision blades made from stainless steel.

They come with both right and left-handed comfort grip handles.

Cricut Leather Thimble

Cricut has cute leather thimbles to protect fingers when sewing.

Cricut Pin Cushion and Pins

Cricut Pin Cushion is soft and durable with a set of matching pins to help with sewing crafts.

Cricut Precision Piercer

This tool usually comes standard as part of the paper crafting toolset. You will need it if you are working with paper crafting for making flowers, swans, etc. The Precision Piercer allows crafters to put cuts, tiny holes, and other embellishments in the paper.

Cricut Quilting Tool

The Quilting Tool is one that most scrapbookers find incredibly useful. This tool creates professional look spirals and twirls that add extra polish to a project.

Cricut Measuring Tape

The Cricut Measuring Tape measures up to 60". It is a standard fabric measuring tape with the same measurements that you will find on the Design Space screen. This makes it easier to get the designs right for professional-looking craft finishes.

Cricut Rotary Cutter

The Cricut Rotary Cutter comes in two different sizes which are 45 mm and 60 mm. They have a carbon alloy steel rotary blade that slices through fabric like a knife through butter.

This is an excellent tool for precision slices of vinyl, leather, and most fabrics. The blade is replaceable. As the head can slide from left to right, it suits both left-handed and right-handed crafters.

Cricut Rulers

To make crafting more precise and professional, Cricut has a few different sized cutting rulers to make crafter's lives easier.

The cutting rulers sizes include:

- 18" x 24" ruler with a stainless steel straight cutting edge, non-slip base, and a protective grip.
- 12" x 24" clear acrylic design ruler.
- 6" x 26" clear acrylic design ruler.
- 3" x 18" clear acrylic design ruler.

Cricut Scissors

The Cricut Scissors are sharp 5" scissors that are ideal for any material, and they come with a protective case to protect the blades. They easily cut through vinyl, faux leather, paper, cardstock, and more.

They come with a left-handed or right-handed comfort grip handle.

Cricut Scoring Stylus Pen

The Scoring Stylus Pen is used for making fold lines in gift boxes, envelopes, and gift cards.

The Cricut Scoring Stylus Pen can be used by hand to create folds. It can also be used in the following Cricut cutting machines to create folds with a cut:

- Cricut Explore.
- Cricut Explore Air.
- Cricut Explore Air 2.
- Cricut Maker.

Cricut Scraper

The Cricut Scraper comes in a few different sizes: small, medium, and large. It is designed to help prolong the life of the Cricut cutting mats as it scrapes unwanted material off the surface.

This is also a good tool to use if you do not have a Brayer Tool, as it is a good burnishing tool. If you need to make sure that vinyl sticks down securely, run the scraper over it before pulling off of the transfer sheet.

Cricut Seam Ripper

This little tool allows for easy and effective removal of tiny stitches and seams without causing damage to the fabric.

Cricut Spatula

This little tool is a savior when you want to pick up an intricate cut. The tool allows a person to gently get under the image and lift it without tearing it. It is also a handy tool for getting off pieces that have become stuck on the mat, or backing sheet.

Cricut Thread Snips

The Cricut Thread Snips are sharp little snipping tools that quickly snip thread, or end pieces to neaten them up.

Cricut Trimmer

The Cricut Trimmer is a portable 12" trimmer with a precision blade and a 15" swing-out arm. The swing-out arm makes it easy to measure any type of material while the blade cuts effortlessly with precision through the materials.

There are blade replacements available in case the trimmer becomes blunt.

Cricut True Control Knife

The True Control Knife works pretty much the same as a carpenter's knife does. It has a lock-in adjustable blade for more material cutting control, and interchangeable blade sizes.

This knife can cut through a host of different materials including:

- Vinyl.
- Cardstock.
- Canvas.
- Fabrics.
- Leather.
- Paper.

Cricut Tweezer

There are a few kinds of tweezers offered by Cricut and these include:

- Cricut Broad tip Tweezers: The Cricut Broad tip Tweezers are ideal for material crafting, and to lift stubborn material from the cutting board. They are also useful for lifting up delicate cuts that the spatula may not be able to lift.
- Cricut Fine tip Tweezers: These Tweezers have a very fine edge that is needed for small intricate cuts that need to be cleaned up, or stuck down.
- Cricut Hook Tweezers: The Hook Tweezers can get into those awkward bends and twirls of some craft cuts. They are also good for removing larger craft pieces.

Cricut Weeder

The weeder looks like a little hook and is ideal for weeding out (neating) cut image designs. There are two different styles of weeders: the classic weeder and hook weeder. Although the classic weeder is a great starter weeder, and one that all crafters really need, more serious crafters will find the hook weeder really useful for those intricate designs.

Cricut Basic Tool Kit

The Cricut Basic Tool Kit includes the following tools:

- Cricut Scissors.
- Cricut Fine tip Tweezers.
- Cricut Classic Weeding Tool.
- Cricut Scraper (small.)
- Cricut Spatula.

Cricut Fabric/Sewing Tool Kit

The Cricut Fabric/Sewing Tool Kit includes the following tools:

- Cricut Fabric Shears.
- Cricut Seam Ripper.
- Cricut Leather Thimble.
- Cricut Measuring Tape.
- Cricut Snipper.
- Cricut Pincushion.
- Cricut Pins.
- Cricut Brayer Tool.
- Cricut Broad tip Tweezers.

Cricut Starter Tool Kit

The Cricut Starter Tool Kit includes the following tools:

- Cricut Classic Weeding Tool.
- Cricut Scraper (small.)
- Cricut Spatula.

Cricut Precision Cutting Kit

The Cricut Precision Cutting Tool Kit includes the following tools:

- Cricut True Control Knife.
- Cricut True Control Blades. (x 5)
- Cricut Blade Storage Cartridge.
- Cricut 18" x 24" Ruler.
- Cricut 12" x 12" self-healing crafting mat.

Cricut Paper Tool Kit

The Cricut Paper Tool Kit includes the following tools:

- Cricut Piercer.
- Cricut Quilting Tool.
- Cricut Edge Distresser.

Cricut 5" x 6" self-healing crafting mat

Cricut Essential Tool Kit

The Cricut Essential Tool Kit includes the following tools:

- Cricut Fine-Point Tweezer.
- Cricut Classic Weeding Tool.
- Cricut Spatula.
- Cricut Portable Trimmer.
- Cricut Scraper (small.)
- Cricut 5" Scissors for crafting.
- Cricut Stylus Scoring Pen.

Cricut Weeding/Vinyl Tool Kit

The Cricut Weeding/Vinyl Tool Kit includes the following tools:

- Cricut Piercer.
- Cricut Quilting Tool.
- Cricut Edge Distresser.
- Cricut 5" x 6" self-healing crafting mat.

Cricut Scraper and Spatula Kit

The Cricut Paper Tool Kit includes the following tools:

- Cricut Scraper (small.)
- Cricut Spatula.

Cricut Brayer and Remover Tool Kit

The Cricut Brayer and Remover Tool Kit include the following tools:

- Cricut Brayer Tool.
- Cricut Broad tip Tweezers.

Cricut Rotary Cutting Kit

The Cricut Rotary Cutting Tool Kit includes the following tools:

- Cricut Rotary Cutter (45mm.)
- Cricut 12" x 24" Acrylic Ruler (oversized.)
- Cricut 18" x 24" self-healing double-sided crafting mat.

Cricut True Control Knife Kit

The Cricut True Control Knife Tool Kit includes the following tools:

- Cricut True Control Knife.
- Cricut True Control Blades. (x 5)
- Cricut Blade Storage Cartridge.

Cricut Pens

There are two types of Cricut craft pens: the Freehand Pens and the Infusible Ink Pens. They come in different colors and sizes. Not all pens work with all Cricut machines.

Cricut Explore One Pen

The Cricut Explore One Pens come with the Pen Accessory Adapter that can be used with the Stylus Scoring Pen.

- Cricut Explore One Pens Are Compatible With:
    - Cricut Explore One.
- Cricut Explore One Pens Are Not Compatible With:
    - Any other Cricut machines.

Cricut Ultimate Gel Pens

The Cricut Ultimate Gel Pens come in different colors and pen sizes.

- Cricut Ultimate Gel Pens Are Compatible With:
    - Cricut Maker.
    - Cricut Explore Air family.

- o Cricut Explore One (these pens require an adapter for the Explore One.)
- Cricut Ultimate Gel Pens Are Not Compatible With:
  - o Older Cricut machines.
  - o Cricut Joy.

Cricut Extra Fine-Point Pens

The Cricut Extra Fine-Point pens come in different colors and pen sizes.

- Cricut Extra Fine-Point Pens Are Compatible With:
  - o Cricut Maker.
  - o Cricut Explore Air family.
  - o Cricut Explore One (these pens require an adapter for the Explore One.)
- Cricut Extra Fine-Point Pens Are Not Compatible With:
  - o Older Cricut machines.
  - o Cricut Joy.

Cricut Milky Gel Pens

The Cricut Milky Gel Pens come in different colors and pen sizes.

- Cricut Milky Gel Pens Are Compatible With:
  - o Cricut Maker.
  - o Cricut Explore Air family.
  - o Cricut Explore One (these pens require an adapter for the Explore One.)

- Cricut Milky Gel Pens Are Not Compatible With:

    - Older Cricut machines.

    - Cricut Joy.

Cricut Glitter Gel Pens

The Cricut Glitter Gel Pens come in different colors and pen sizes.

- Cricut Glitter Gel Pens Are Compatible With:

    - Cricut Maker.

    - Cricut Explore Air family.

    - Cricut Explore One (these pens require an adapter for the Explore One.)

- Cricut Glitter Gel Pens Are Not Compatible With:

    - Older Cricut machines.

    - Cricut Joy.

Cricut Infusible Ink Freehand Markers Pens

The Cricut Infusible Ink Freehand Marker Pens come in watercolors and normal marker pens. They come in different colors and pen sizes.

- Cricut Infusible Ink Freehand Markers Pens Are Compatible With:

    - EasyPress.

    - EasyPress 2.

    - EasyPress Mini.

- Cricut Infusible Ink Freehand Marker Pens Are Not Compatible With:
    - These pens cannot be used with any Cricut cutting machine.

Cricut Joy Pens

The following pens are not compatible with any of the other Cricut cutting machines. These pens are only for use with the Cricut Joy:

- Cricut Joy Infusible Ink Pens in different colors and point sizes.
- Cricut Joy Gel Pens in different colors and point sizes.
- Cricut Joy Glitter Gel Pens in different colors and sizes.
- Cricut Joy Metallic Markers in different colors and sizes.
- Cricut Joy Extra Fine-Point Pens in different colors.

Cricut Craft Mats

Cricut has self-healing craft mats designed specifically for crafting. It must be noted that these mats are NOT for use as cutting mats. They are purely for cutting and working with material out of the cutting machines.

They are called self-healing mats because they close up when you cut through them. The Cricut mats have twice the self-healing power than most self-healing craft mats on the market.

These mats come double-sided with useful gridlines, numbers, and angles for 30°, 60°, and 90° angle markings on them. These craft mats come in an array of colors. Depending on the type and style of the mat, colors may include:

- Rose.
- Lilac.

- Blue.

- Mint.

- Gray.

- Patterned.

- Black.

The self-healing mats come in sizes that include:

- 12" x 12".
- 18" x 24".
- 24" x 36".

As they are not to be used in a Cricut cutting machine, you can buy these mats for use with your crafts, no matter which cutting machine you have.

Cricut Cutting Mats

All of the latest Cricut cutting machines, except for the Cricut Joy, use cutting mats to cut material. There are four standard mats that are used in these machines. The Cricut Joy does not need mats for some cuts, but there are cuts where that do require a cutting mat. The Cricut Joy needs special mats due to its size and is not compatible with the standard mats used by other Cricut cutting machines.

Standard Cricut Cutting Mats

There are four standard Cricut Cutting Mats; each mat has a different purpose and comes in one or more sizes. These mats are as follows:

- LightGrip mat—Blue.

    - Sizes: 12" x 12", 12" x 24", and 6" x 12".

- Material Weight: Lightweight materials.
- Materials: Washi tape sheets, wrapping paper, thin cardstock, printer paper, vellum, and scrapbook paper (thin sheets.)

- Standard Grip mat—Green.
  - Sizes: 12" x 12", 12" x 24", and 6" x 12".
  - Material Weight: Medium weight materials.
  - Materials: Cardstock textured paper, embossed cardstock, vinyl, and iron-on vinyl.

- StrongGrip mat—Purple.
  - Sizes: 12" x 12", 12" x 24", and 6" x 12".
  - Material Weight: Heavyweight materials.
  - Materials: Poster boards, faux leather, faux suede, corrugated cardboard, chipboard, metal, stiff fabrics, leather, thick cardstock, glitter cardstock, and mosaic vinyl.

- FabricGrip mat—Pink.
  - Sizes: Sizes: 12" x 12", 12" x 24", and 6" x 12".
  - Material Weight: Fabrics, as well as layered fabrics.
  - Materials: Fabric.

Cricut Joy Cutting Mats

The Cricut Joy has its own specific cutting mats that do not work with any other Cricut cutting machines. It should be noted that none of the standard cutting mats work with the Cricut Joy.

The Cricut Joy Cutting Mats include the following mats:

- Cricut Joy Card Mat—Blue.
  - Sizes: 4.5" x 6.25".
  - Materials: Cardstock, paper, and materials to make greeting cards.
- Cricut Joy Standard Grip Mat—Green.
  - Sizes: 4.5" x 12" and 4.5" x 6.5".
  - Material Weight: Medium weight materials.
  - Materials: Cardstock textured paper, embossed cardstock, vinyl, and iron-on vinyl.
- Cricut Joy LightGrip Mat—Blue.
  - Sizes: 4.5" x 12" and 4.5" x 6.5".
  - Material Weight: Lightweight materials.
  - Materials: Cardstock, paper, and other lightweight materials.

Cricut EasyPress Mats

For heat transfers, the EasyPress Mats are the better option to choose over an ironing board. Even if you do not have the EasyPress or one of the new EasyPresses, if you are crafting and using iron-on or heat transfers, you should invest in one of these mats. Their flat, durable surface is what makes getting the transfer on correctly a lot easier than a conventional ironing board.

The Cricut EasyPress mats come in four sizes and are compatible with all EasyPress irons and mini irons.

EasyPress Mat Sizes:

- Extra-large sized mat: 20" x 16".
- Large-sized mat: 14" x 14".
- Medium-sized mat: 12" x 12".
- Small-sized mat: 8" x 10".

Cricut Machine Tools

The Cricut machine comes with blades and blade housings that are used for different cutting purposes as well as materials. While the larger Cricut cutting machines have a few blades and blade housings that are universal to them, there are a few blades that are specific to that machine.

Cricut Cutting Machine Blade

The cutting machine's cutting blade has two to four parts to it and these are:

- Blade: The blade looks similar to a nail or thick pin. There are a few types of blades that are used for the cutting of different materials. Blades can be replaced as they can become blunt through a lot of continuous use. The blade has a plastic protective tip at the top that extends into the blade at the bottom.

- Blade Housing: The blade is inserted into the housing. The housing fits into the accessory clamp inside of the cutting machine. The clamp holds and guides the blade.

- Drive Housing: The Cricut Maker has more specialized blades that use the Cricut Adaptive Tool System. The drive housing is what helps to drive the gear that sits on top of the various Cricut Maker blade housings. The blade housings, for some of the Cricut Maker blades, look a lot different than more standard blades. They can be identified by a gold wheel on top of the silver blade housing.

- Blade Tips: The QuickSwap drive housing comes with interchangeable blade tips instead of nail type blades.

Bonded-Fabric Blade

This blades' color is pink, and should not be used on any other materials except bonded fabrics.

- The blade works with the following Cricut cutting machines:
    - Cricut Maker.
    - Cricut Explore family.
    - Cricut Explore Air family (Air and Air 2.)

- The material that can be cut with this blade includes the following:
    - Burlap.
    - Cotton.
    - Denim.
    - Felt.
    - Oil Cloth.
    - Polyester.
    - Silk.
    - Faux Leather.

- Housing for the blade:
  - Pink Bonded-Fabric blade housing.
  - Silver or gold Fine-Point blade housing.
- Cutting mat(s):
  - FabricGrip mat (pink.)
  - Standard Grip mat (green.)

Deep-Point Blade

This blade's color is black and it can be used for cutting materials that need deeper cuts.

- The blade works with the following Cricut cutting machines:
  - Cricut Maker.
  - Cricut Explore family.
  - Cricut Explore Air family (Air and Air 2.)
- The material that can be cut with this blade includes the following:
  - Aluminum Foil.
  - Craft Foam.
  - Corrugated Cardboard/Paper.
  - Leather.
  - Metallic Leather.
  - Magnetic Sheet (up to 0.6mm).
- Housing for the blade:
  - Black Deep-Point blade housing.

- Cutting mat(s):
  - Standard Grip mat (green.)
  - StrongGrip mat (purple.)

Fine-Point Blade

This blade's color is white. It is the standard blade and housing that comes with all Cricut cutting machines. The Fine-Point blades with the white caps are for the newer machines, while the ones with the gray caps are for older Cricut cutting machines.

- The blade works with the following Cricut cutting machines:
  - Cricut Maker.
  - Cricut Explore family.
  - Cricut Explore Air family (Air and Air 2.)

- The material that can be cut with this blade includes the following:
  - Canvas.
  - Cardstock.
  - Fine Faux Leather.
  - Glitter Vinyl.
  - Holographic Vinyl.
  - Heat Transfer Vinyl. (HTV)
  - Iron-on Vinyl.
  - Light Chipboard

- Outdoor Vinyl.
- Parchment Paper.
- Printable Vinyl.
- Tattoo Paper.
- Vellum.
- Washi Tape.
- Window Stick.

- Housing for the blade:
  - The pink Bonded-Fabric blade housing.
  - Rose, silver, or gold Fine-Point blade housing.

- Cutting mat(s):
  - LightGrip mat (blue.)
  - Standard Grip mat (green.)
  - StrongGrip mat (purple.)

Knife Blade

This knife blade is silver and comes with the wheel gear housing.

- The blade works with the following Cricut cutting machines:
  - Cricut Maker.

- The material that can be cut with this blade includes the following:
  - Balsa wood that is either 1/16" or 3/32".

- - Basswood that is either 1/16" or 1/32".
  - Heavy chipboard up to 2.0mm.
  - Matboard 4 ply.

- Housing for the blade:
  - Silver gear wheel housing.

- Cutting mat(s):
  - Standard Grip mat (green.)
  - StrongGrip mat (purple.)

QuickSwap Debossing Tip

This blade tip uses the QuickSwap housing which is silver. Debossing is the process of creating indented imprints in materials. This tip makes beautiful intricate designs effortlessly.

- The blade works with the following Cricut cutting machines:
  - Cricut Maker.

- The material that can be cut with this blade includes the following:
  - Balsa Wood that is either 1/16" or 3/32".
  - Chipboard (heavy) up to 2 mm.
  - Chipboard (light) up to 0.37 mm.
  - Cardstock (heavy and light).
  - Faux Leather (very thin).

- o Foil Acetate.
- o Glitter Cardstock Craft Foam.
- o Kraft Board.
- o Leather.
- o Matboard (4 plies.)
- o Poster Board Foil, normal, and metallic.
- o Tooling Leather.
- o Vellum.
- Housing for the blade:
  - o QuickSwap housing with gold gear.
- Cutting mat(s):
  - o Standard Grip mat (green.)
  - o StrongGrip mat (purple.)

QuickSwap Engraving Tip

This blade tip uses the QuickSwap housing that is silver. The engraving tip takes the Cricut Maker to a different level, as with this you can actually engrave certain materials with the cutting machine.

- The blade works with the following Cricut cutting machines:
  - o Cricut Maker

- The material that can be cut with this blade includes the following:
    - Acetate.
    - Anodized Aluminum.
    - Brass.
    - Bronze.
    - Faux Leather.
    - Foil Acetate.
    - Leather.
    - Stainless Steel.
    - Tooling Leather.
    - Vellum.
- Housing for the blade:
    - QuickSwap housing with gold gear.
- Cutting mat(s):
    - Standard Grip mat (green.)
    - StrongGrip mat (purple.)

QuickSwap Perforation Blade

This blade tip uses the QuickSwap housing which is silver. The Cricut Maker gives crafters a professional edge with unique blades like the perforation blade. This blade allows the crafter to create perforated materials for items like tear-off raffle tickets, journal pages, booklets with tear-out pages, and so on.

- The blade works with the following Cricut cutting machines:
    - Cricut Maker.

- The material that can be cut with this blade includes the following:
    - Acetate and Foil Acetate.
    - Craft Foam; normal and glitter craft foam.
    - Cardstock; heavy and corrugated.
    - Faux Leather (very thin).
    - Felt.
    - Iron-on materials.
    - Poster board normal and metallic.
    - Plastic.
    - Tooling Leather.
    - Vellum.

- Housing for the blade:
    - QuickSwap housing with gold gear.

- Cutting mat(s):
    - Standard Grip mat (green.)
    - StrongGrip mat (purple.)

Quick Swap Wavy Blade

This blade tip uses the QuickSwap housing which is silver. This handy wheel makes wavy lines on the material and it can cut your material in wavy lines as well.

- The blade works with the following Cricut cutting machines:

  - Cricut Maker.

- The material that can be cut with this blade includes the following:

  - Cardstock; heavy and glitter.
  - Cotton Denim.
  - Corrugated Cardboard.
  - Flannel.
  - Fleece.
  - Kraft Board.
  - Poster Board.

- Housing for the blade:

  - QuickSwap housing with gold gear.

- Cutting mat(s):

  - Standard Grip mat (green.)

  - StrongGrip mat (purple.)

Scoring Wheel

The scoring wheel is much like the Stylus Scoring Pen, except it makes an edgier line, and comes in two different point sizes: 01 and 02. The tip chosen will depend on the material you are using.

- The blade works with the following Cricut cutting machines:

  - Cricut Maker

- The material that can be cut with this blade includes the following:

  o Tip 01: Lighter materials like those used with the blue LightGrip mat or green Standard Grip mat.

    - Cardstock.

    - Paper.

    - Vinyl.

  o Tip 02: This tip is better suited to heavier or coated materials that require the StrongGrip mat (purple) or Bonded-Fabric mat (pink.)

    - Glitter Cardstock.

    - Bonded Materials.

    - Poster board like the metallic version.

    - Chipboard (light.)

- Housing for the blade:

  o Silver gear wheel housing.

- Cutting mat(s):

  o LightGrip mat (blue.)
  o Standard Grip mat (green.)
  o StrongGrip mat (purple.)

Cricut Joy Fine-Point Blade

The Cricut Joy uses a Fine-Point blade that is not interchangeable and can only be used with the Joy.

- The blade works with the following Cricut cutting machines:

  - Cricut Joy

- The material that can be cut with this blade includes the following:

  - Cardstock.

  - Cardstock Glitter.

  - Copy Paper.

  - Corrugated Cardboard.

  - Insert Cards.

  - Smart Iron-on Materials.

  - Smart Materials.

  - Poster Board (foil.)

  - Vinyl and Writable Vinyl.

- Housing for the blade:

  - Sliver housing with a white cap.

- Cutting mat(s):

  - FabricGrip mat (pink.)

  - Standard Grip mat (green.)

Cricut Storage Bags

In order to keep your machine safe and in good shape, there are a lot of good storage bag options for the machines. Some of these bags also make it easy to transport the Cricut machine without causing damage.

If you need to use your machine on the go, there are some good options to take your materials, tools, and accessories too.

Cutting Machine Totes

Cricut offers some beautiful tote bags to store the Cricut machines in. These totes come in various colors, and there are a few different sizes.

There is a standard size for larger machines such as the Explore family including the Explore Air and Explore Air 2. These totes are also compatible with the Cricut Maker, and some of the older model cutting machines.

The Cricut Joy has its own protective tote in grey and teal to match the machine.

EasyPress Totes

The EasyPress tote makes it easy to store and protect the Cricut EasyPress. There are two different-sized totes: the 9" x 9" for the smaller EasyPress machines, and the 12" x 10" for the larger EasyPress machines.

Rolling Craft Tote

The Cricut Rolling Craft Tote is not designed for the actual machine, but it is a really handy solution to store all of your crafting materials and tools in. Plus, it has wheels which make it easy to move around, and make it portable. The Rolling Craft Totes come in various colors and provide a wonderful space to neatly organize your crafting materials.

Chapter 3. Materials That Can Be Used For Cricut

The Cricut materials range has grown over the years, and with the introduction of the Cricut Maker, it can now cut even more materials such as metal, leather, and even wood.

Infusible Ink

This is a relatively new type of material for the Cricut range, and it has become really popular with crafters, but it is only available for use with the Cricut Maker and Cricut Joy at the moment. It gives smooth prints onto a fabric that make it look like they have been professionally dyed.

The Infusible Ink range does not only stop at the magnificent inks but comes with a lot of blanks that can be used with the ink. These include:

- T-Shirts.

- Baby Onesies.

- Canvas Tote Bags.

- Coaster Rounds.

- Coaster Squares.

The infusible ink itself comes in the following forms:

- Pens.
- Transfer Sheets.
- Cricut Joy Transfer Sheets.

Iron-On

Iron-On is one of the most popular Cricut materials as it can be used on cushions, clothes, bedding, towels, and so on. Cricut has hundreds of different colors and types, which include:

- Everyday Iron-On.
- Heat Transfer Vinyl.
- Glitter Iron-On.
- Foil Iron-On.
  - Printable Iron-On.

Leather

There are a few different types of leather that some of the cutting machines can cut, and this includes the following leather types:

- Faux Suede.
- Genuine Leather.
- Pebbled Faux Leather.
- Soft Metallic Leather.
- Tooling Leather.

Metal

The new engraving tool and the Knife Blade make it possible to cut metal, which includes:

- Aluminum Sheets.
- Bronze.
- Copper.
- Gold.
- Silver.

Others

There are a lot of different materials that can be cut with the Cricut cutting machines besides the obvious ones. These materials include:

- Party Foil.
- Chipboard.
- Balsa Wood.
- Wood Veneer.
- Window Cling.
- Felt.
- Foam.
- Fabric.
- Bonded Fabric.

Paper

There are more than 11 types of paper, each with at least 5, or move different variations of each type. Cricut cutting machines paper materials include:

- Adhesive-Backed Deluxe Paper.
- Insert Cards.

- Cardstock.
- Glitter Cardstock.
- Corrugated Cardboard.
- Foil Embossed.
- Kraft Board.
- Scrapbook.
- Pearl.
- Poster Board.
- Sparkle or Shimmer Paper.

Vinyl

There are many types of vinyl that can be cut with the Cricut cutting machines, and these include:

- Cricut Joy Smart Vinyl.
- Everyday Vinyl.
- Glitter Vinyl.
- Mosaic Vinyl.
- Holographic Vinyl.
- Party Foil.
- Premium Vinyl Range.
- Premium Outdoor Vinyl.
- Sticker Material.
- Tattoo Material.
- Stencil Vinyl.
- Linen Vinyl.
- Removable Vinyl.
- Permanent Vinyl.
- Metallic Vinyl.

- Textured Vinyl.
- Textured Metallic Vinyl.

Chapter 4. Design Space Application

Design Space On Mobile Device

The Cricut Design Space is cloud-based, and you can pick up your project across various platforms. Here's how you can download the latest version (v 3.18.1) of this application on your mobile devices:

- Apple App Store (iOS): Simply search for "Cricut" on the App Store from your iPhone or iPad, and select "GET" to begin the download. You can then easily login with your registered Cricut ID to continue working on your projects on your phone.

- Google Play (Android): You can search for "Cricut" on Google Play from your Android Phone or Tablet. Then select "Install" to begin the download. Once completed, use your Cricut ID to login, and pick up your projects and ideas where you left off.

How to Install/Uninstall Design Space?

Let us tackle how to install/uninstall on these platforms including Windows, Mac, iOS, and Android devices.

Install on Windows/Mac

- Click on your browser and navigate to www.design.cricut.com.
- If you are a first time user, you need to create a Cricut ID, otherwise, sign in with your Cricut ID. Ensure that the page is fully loaded before carrying out this activity in order to avoid an error.
- Select "New Project."
- Select "Download Plugin" from the prompt.

- Wait for the download to finish, and then select the downloaded file to Open/Run it.
- Click "Next" when the Cricut installer opens.
- Read the "Terms of Use," and accept the agreement.
- Click "Install" to begin the installation.
- Click "Done" at the end of the installation.

Install the Cricut Design Space App on iOS

- Tap on the App Store icon on your device.
- Search for Cricut Design Space.
- Tap the "Get" button to download. Please confirm the download with your iTunes password if prompted. The app will launch and display the necessary options that will be used to complete the process.

Install the Cricut Design Space App on Android

- Tap Google Play Store App on your device to open it.
- Search for Cricut Design Space.
- Tap on the "Install" button.
- Tap on the Cricut Design Space icon to open it when the installation is complete.
- Sign in, and start designing your project.

Uninstall Cricut Design Space on iOS

- Press and hold the Design Space icon on your iOS device till it vibrates
- Press the "X" button to delete it from your device. This is very easy, right?

Uninstall Cricut Design Space App on Android

- Go to "Settings."
- Tap on "Apps" or "Applications."
- Swipe to the "Download" tab or "Application Manager."

- Search for the App you intend to uninstall.
- Tap the "Uninstall" button to finish and the App is gone for good.

Uninstall on Mac

- Move to Finder and open the "Applications" folder.
- Search for Cricut Design Space.
- Drag it to "Trash."
- Right-click on the "Trashcan" and select "Empty Trash" to remove the Application.

Uninstall on Windows

- Click on the "Start" button.
- Select "Settings."
- Select "Application."
- Look for Cricut Design Space and choose "Uninstall."

How to Center Your Designs to Cut in Cricut Design Space?

- Sign in to the Cricut Design section. Click on the "New Project."
- Click "Download."
- Click "Upload Picture."
- Click "Browse."
- Save your picture.
- Select the saved image, and insert an image.
- Select the picture. Click on it.
- As you can see, the picture is automatically moved to the upper left corner.
- To prevent this, you can fool the software by placing the image in the center of your design area and the mat. This is useful if you want to create openings in the middle of a page.
- Click on the shape tool.

- Create a shape of 11.5 x 11.5 inches.
- Select the square and change the setting to cut it in the drawing.
- The square now appears as an outline.
- Click "Align" and "Center" with the selected pattern and square.
- Click the arrow of the size of your square and resize it without moving the top left corner to reduce the size of the square.
- Select the square and pattern, then click "Attach." Click on it.
- As you can see now, the design is centered.

How to Write with Sketch Pens in Cricut Design Space?

- Sign in to the Cricut Design section. Create a new project.
- Click "Download."
- Select upload a picture.
- Click "Browse."
- Open your file, then save. To get a good effect, use a file with thin lines and no large spaces.
- Click on the pattern, and paste it.
- Select the pattern.
- Change the drawing to a drawing.
- You will now see the drawing as an outline drawn.
- Click on it.
- Your drawing will now be displayed on the cutting screen. Click on "Continue."
- If you change your drawing to draw, the software automatically selects the pen tool. Insert the pen or marker into the recommended clip. Insert paper and click on the start icon.
- The pen now draws your pattern.

How to Upload PNG File?

After you've converted your PDF document to PNG file format, there are some ways to clean up the file before printing, and then crop it with Cricut Design Space.

- Click "Create New Project."
- Click "Upload Picture."
- Click on the image to upload.
- Click "Browse."
- The "Open File" dialog box opens. Select the PNG file you want to upload and click.
- An example of a picture can be found in Cricut Design Space. Since we want to edit this file, we select "Complex Image" and click "Next."
- The PNG file is loaded into Cricut Design Space. Select and Delete.

How to Convert a PDF to PNG Format?

- After downloading the PDF document to your computer, open your browser and go to png2pdf.com.
- Click on the upload files.
- The "Open File" dialog box starts. Locate the PDF file to convert (probably in the "Downloads" folder,) click the PDF file, and then the file is uploaded. You should see a progress bar. Once the file has been uploaded and converted, a "Download" button appears below the small image of the uploaded file.
- Click on "Download." The file is going to be downloaded as a ZIP file and should appear in the status bar at the bottom of the screen. Just click on the filename to open the ZIP file.
- The "Open File" dialog opens, and the downloaded file should be displayed. Since the file is still in ZIP format, you must first unzip, or unzip it. Just click "Extract All Files."
- The "Open File" dialog opens, and your newly converted PDF file should be displayed in a PNG file. You can open the file with a double-click if you only want to see what the file looks like. Close the window now by clicking on the red "X."

- After you have converted your PDF file to PNG format, you must upload the PNG file to Cricut Design Space so that you can use the "Print" and "Cut" functions.

Working with Edit Bar in Cricut Design Space

Here are important terminologies to help our understanding of the Design Space Edit Bar, that will have to be defined. A word of caution though is that some of the terms used here are common tools for everyday use on the computer so it shouldn't be difficult to understand but our level of computer literacy is not the same. Therefore, pardon me if you already know many of them. This has been done for the sake of those who do not know. The terms are as follows:

- Undo/Redo: Refers to undoing any change made to the layer, or redo any priorly taken undone action.

- Linetype: Refers to how the machine will interact with the material on the mat including cut, draw, and score as described below.

- Cut: Refers to a cutting layer with the aid of a blade from your material.

- Draw: Refers to drawing the layer with the aid of a Cricut pen.

- Score: Refers to scoring the layer using a Scoring Stylus or Scoring Wheel.

- Linetype Swatch: Refers to choosing additional attributes that your layer will use. There are different types of options you can select from based on the selected Linetype (cut, draw, and score.)

Working with Fonts in Design Space

The ability to personalize a project with the use of distinct fonts and text is one of the unique features of the Cricut Design Space. Why is this unique? Because it gives you the freedom to express the creativity of your mind. This creative ability is innate in us, and there is this satisfaction accompanied by a great sense of accomplishment that is felt whenever the projects are delivered to taste.

The Cricut Design Space has another amazing feature which is the ability to change the font after ungrouping or isolating the letters, you can use the Cricut fonts or the one installed on your computer or device.

How to Select Font?

If you have ever worked with the Image Edit Tool before, then you will definitely be at home with the Text Edit tool in Cricut Design Space. This is because the two tools are similar in their mode of operation in rotating, sizing, and positioning of text. The similarity of the tools will excite you because it makes the job simpler when editing the text and locating the right font. With this, you can personalize projects easily.

How to Edit Fonts?

The Edit bar in Cricut Design Space grants you access to edit the features of particular images or text. These features include Linetype, Size, Rotate, Fill, Position, and Mirror. There are additional options in the Text layers including Line Spacing, Font Styles, and Letter Spacing. So how do you edit the font? Here, I will show you.

Select the text object you want to edit on the Canvas, or you can insert text from the design panel, or select a text layer from the Layers Panel. Once it is selected, the Text Edit Bar will pop up directly below "Standard Edit Bar." Note that the "Standard Edit Bar" will be hidden when you are not interacting with the text.

When the "Text Edit Bar" pops up, you can begin to manipulate the font using the options described below. Simple right?

How to Add Text to Cricut Design Space?

Navigate to the left-hand side of the Canvas and select the Text tool. When the Text tool is selected, the font list will open if you are using iOS/Android, or the Text bar and text box will pop up for users with Windows/Mac.

Select the desired font size and the font type you intend to use, and then input your text. If you intend to start on a new line of text on the same textbox, use the "Return" key after the prior line of text. Do not freak out when you did not choose the font setting before typing the text, with Cricut Design Space, it is possible to type the text before selecting the font on a Windows/Mac computer.

- Click or tap on any area outside the text box to close it.
- To edit the text is pretty simple. Double click on the text to display available options.
- The Edit bar is found at the top of the Canvas for Windows/Mac users, and at the bottom of the Canvas for iOS/Android users.

How to Troubleshoot Error Codes in the Cricut Design Space?

Every electronic device pops up error when there is a conflict with its program. The Cricut Design Space is no exception because it is also a program running on your device, and will also complain if something is missing from its chain of command. As a user interface, it will report this error to you for correction in order to complete its current task.

Let us describe some of these errors and how to troubleshoot them. If you still cannot solve the problem after going through these steps, or the error is not treated here, please feel free to contact Customer Care.

Error (0)

- Restart your computer and machine.
- If your device is short of that then, ensure that your computer or device satisfies these minimum requirements, or try to use another computer or device that meets the requirements.
- Clear your cache, browser history, cookies, and ensure that your browser is updated to the current version.
- Recreate the project if only one and not multiple projects is affected.
- Use another computer or device if the above troubleshooting options fail.

Error (-11): "Device Authentication" Error

- Close all background programs on your computer or device, and then try again.
- Check to see that your browser is updated to the current version.

Error (-18): "Device Timeout" Error

- Switch off your computer or device.
- Close Design Space.
- Restart the Design Space.
- Power on the Cricut Maker, and then try to cut again.
- If no solution, contact Member Care.

Error (-21): "Data Transmission" Error

- Clear your cache, browser history, and cookies.
- Close your browser, re-launch it again, and then try cutting.
- Use a different browser to try cut.
- Check your internet speed, and ensure that it meets the minimum requirement.
- Contact your Internet Service Provider (ISP) for assistance.

Error (-24): "Ping Timeout" Error

- Recreate the project because it is possible that the project file is too large, or is not properly saved.
- Try another USB port on the computer, or make use of Bluetooth.
- Use a different USB cable.
- Check your internet speed.
- If nothing works, try a different computer.

Error (-32): "Firmware Not Available" Error

- Since this error pops up only when there is a compatibility problem, check the connectivity of your device to the Cricut machine.
- If you are 100% sure that the connectivity is correct, then contact Member Care for assistance.

Error (-33): "Invalid Material Setting" Error

- Check the Smart Set Dial. This error appears when there is no selected material from the Design Space and the Smart Set Dial is set to "Custom." Therefore, ensure that the material is selected from the Design Space material drop-down menu.
- Try a different material setting.
- Contact Member Care for assistance.

Design Space Canvas

Purchasing a Cricut is futile if you don't learn exactly how to master Style Room, since you will always require this software to cut any kind of job. In my opinion, Cricut Style Room is an exceptional device for newbies, and also if you have no experience with any other Layout programs like Photoshop or Illustrator, you will certainly discover that although it looks overwhelming, it's quite simple.

Layout Space it's mainly to touch up your projects and create marginal designs with forms and fonts.

If you desire something a lot more innovative, you are most likely to need your own designs or Cricut Accessibility. That's a subscription where you obtain access to their supergiant library. Find out more about it in this write-up and also the guide I create.

When you log into your Cricut Design Area account and also intend to start or modify a new project, you will certainly do every little thing from a window called Canvas. The Canvas Location in Cricut Style Space is where you do all of your modifications prior to you cut your tasks. I get it!

There are numerous switches, options, and points to do that you might feel shed. Do not worry, I am below along the way, applauding you up and motivating you to maintain going. In this publication, you are about to learn what each and every single symbol on the Canvas area is for. To keep every little thing in order as well as easy to understand, we are going to divide the canvas into 4 areas, and also 4 colors:

- Top Panel Yellow: Modifying Area.
- Left Panel Blue: Insert Location.
- Right Panel Purple: Layers Panel.
- Green: Canvas Location.

<u>Pointer</u>: This is not a short message, so I encourage you to get a cup of coffee with some donuts or cookies if possible.

Top Panel Cricut Design Space

The top panel in the Style Space Canvas area is for editing, enhancing, and preparing aspects of the Canvas area. From this panel, you can pick what type of font style you'd like to use; you can transform dimensions, straighten styles, as well as extra! This panel is divided into 2 subpanels. The very first one permits you to save, name, and finally reduce your jobs; and also the second one will enable you to regulate, and also modify points on the Canvas area.

Sub-Panel #1: Name Your Project and Cut it

This sub-panel enables you to navigate from the Canvas to your account, projects, as well as it additionally sends your completed projects to cut.

- **Toggle Menu:** When you click on this button, one more entire menu will move open. This menu is a useful one. However, it's not part of the Canvas, and that's why I won't be entering into a lot of detail. Primarily, from here you can most likely go to your profile, and also transform your photo.

    There are various other useful and technological points you can do from this Menu like calibrating your maker blades; additionally, updating the Firmware (Software) of your tool. Furthermore, you can manage your memberships from Cricut Accessibility, your account details, and also more. I suggest you to click on every web link to make sure that you discover every little thing that Cricut Style Room has for you.

    Note: On the settings chosen, you can transform the visibility as well as measurements of the Canvas; this is explained much better at the end of this article when I describe everything about the canvas area.

- **My Projects:** When you click "My Projects," you will certainly be rerouted to your collection of points you have currently developed; this is excellent because often you may wish to re-cut a previously developed job. So, there's no need for you to recreate the same job over and over.

- **Save:** This option will certainly turn on after you've placed one component on your canvas area. I suggest you save your project as you go. Although the software program is on the cloud, if your browser accidents, there goes your hard work with it.

- **Maker—Explore (Machine):** Depending upon the sort of Cricut you have you will certainly require to select either the Cricut Maker or the Cricut Explore Machine; this is really crucial because on the Cricut Manufacturer you will discover choices that are only readily available to that specific Cricut. So, if you have a Maker, and you are making with the Explore alternative ON, you won't be able to turn on the tools that are for the Maker.

- **Make It:** When you are done posting your files, and also ready to cut, click on "Make it." Your tasks are separated by mats according to the colors of your task. From this home window, you can likewise boost the variety of projects to cut; this is excellent if you are planning on developing greater than one cut.

Sub-Panel # 2: Modifying Font Selections

It's incredibly useful, and also it will certainly help you to modify, prepare, and also organize font styles as well as pictures on the Canvas Location.

- **Undo & Redo:** Occasionally while we work, we make blunders. These little buttons are a great means to correct them. Click "Undo" when you develop something you do not like, or make a mistake. Click "Redo" when you inadvertently remove something you didn't wish to erase or modify. (If only there were something comparable forever itself lol.)
- **Line Type and Fill:** This option will inform your equipment what tools as well as blades you are going to utilize. Bear in mind that relying on the Maker you have actually picked on the top of the home window (Manufacturer or Discover,) you will have different choices.
- **Line Type:** This alternative will inform your device when you are cutting your job, what device you will certainly be using. Right now, there are seven choices (Cut, Draw, Score, Engrave, Wave, Deboss, and Perf.) If you have a Cricut Maker, all options will certainly be readily available, although if you have an Explore, you will only have the Cut, Draw,

and the Score choice. Right here is a much more comprehensive description of each tool:

- **Cut:** Unless you published a JPEG or PNG photo to the Canvas; "Cut" is the default line type that every one of your elements on your canvas will certainly have; this means that when you press "Make It," your maker will certainly cut those designs.

    With the Cut choice chosen, you can transform the fill of your components, at the end of the day, this converts into the different shades of materials you will certainly utilize when you cut your jobs.

- **Draw:** If you intend to create on your layouts, you can do it with your Cricut. When you appoint this line type, you will certainly be prompted to choose any one of the Cricut Pens you have (You require detailed pens, unless you have a 3rd event adapter.) When you select a specific layout, the layers on your Canvas area will certainly be outlined with the shade of the pen you picked. With this tool, when you click "Make It," rather than reducing, your Cricut will certainly create or draw. Keep in mind: This option doesn't tint your styles.

- **Score:** Score is an extra powerful version of the "Rating Line" situated on the left panel. When you appoint this attribute to a layer, every one of the designs will certainly show up scored or rushed. This time, when you click "Make It." Your Cricut won't cut, yet it will score your products. However, keep in mind the wheel just collaborates with the Cricut Manufacturer.

- **Engrave, Deboss, Wave, as well as Perf:** These are the newest tools that Cricut has released for the Cricut Maker, and with them, you will have the ability to create incredible results on various sorts of products. I do not have these tools yet due to the fact that they will certainly be coming out in a number of weeks, once I have them on my hands, I will certainly offer you a quick upgrade.

- **Fill:** The Fill option is primarily to be used for printing as well as patterns. It will only be triggered when you have "Cut" as a "Line Type." Do not fill in forms that you will not print anything. The print is by far, one of the best functions Cricut has due to the fact that it enables you to print your styles, and then cut them; this is remarkable, and also truthfully, it's what motivated me to obtain a Cricut in the first place. When this "Load" alternative is active after you click "Make It;" first, you'll send your data to your home printer and afterward have your Cricut do all the hefty training (cutting.) One more excellent choice for the print kind is patterns. You individuals, this is so trendy. Usage Cricut's options, or publish your own; you can include a pattern to practically any kind of layer. Let's claim it's Valentine's Day, you can make a stunning card with a currently developed pattern from Cricut Access (Subscription, not totally free,) or your own; after that print as well as cut at the same time.

- **Select All:** When you need to relocate all of your components inside the Canvas area, you may have a hard time to select them individually. Click "Select All" to pick all of the elements from the canvas.

- **Edit:** The "Cut" and also "Copy" option will certainly be turned on when you utilize a choice of several elements from the Canvas area. The "Paste" choice will certainly be made it possible when you duplicate or cut something.

- **Align:** If you have previews experience with various other visuals style programs, more than likely you'll recognize just how to utilize this font selection. If you aren't aware of the Align Equipment, let me tell you something; the Align Font selection is something that you intend to understand perfection.

Here's what every Align feature means:

- Align: This function permits you to align all of your layouts, and also it's turned on when picking two or even more elements.

- Line Up Left: When utilizing this setting, all of the aspects will certainly be lined up to the left. The furthest aspect to the left will certainly determine where all of the various other components will certainly move towards.

- Align Right: When using this setting, all of your components will certainly be straightened to the right. The outermost aspect to the right will certainly dictate where all of the various other elements will certainly relocate.

Chapter 5. Cricut Projects For Beginners

If you have just bought your Cricut, you must be pretty eager to get started with some simple DIY designs. The following designs are simple and will help you to manage/work with various materials that can be used with the Cricut machines.

They will also assist you in becoming familiar with some of the tools you will use when creating your designs.

All the projects below assume that you are familiar with Design Space, the materials that can be used with the Cricut, and the various tools you will need for cutting, etc.

Project 1: A Simple Birthday Card

One of the simplest projects to start with is a greeting card. You can use this process to make any type of greeting card you need to make. You can make birthday cards, sympathy cards, milestone cards, and so on.

For this project, we are going to make a birthday card. If you have a milestone birthday coming up, then your Cricut is going to serve you well.

Project Tools, Materials, and Accessories:

- Textured cardstock: light olive-green (or color of your choice).
- Glossy or glitter cardstock: navy blue (or color of your choice).
- Green Standard Grip Cricut mat.
- Cricut Fine-Point Blade.
- Scoring stylus.
- Cricut spatula.
- Pair of scissors for cutting the material to size.
- Glue.

Directions:

1. Login into Design Space and choose "New Project."
2. Once you have logged into Design Space, you will need to choose "Images" from the bar on the left-hand side of the screen.
3. When you are on the "Images" screen, you will need to choose "Cartridges" from the top menu.
4. As you will be making a simple card, in the "Search in Cartridges" box, type in "Simple Cards" as the search criteria. Click the magnifying search button to begin the search.
5. There are 50 images, but only a few will appear on the screen. Click on the "View all 50 images" button next to the box.
6. Scroll through the images until you find the card that reads "Happy Birthday to You." Select the card and insert the image.
7. You will find that this birthday card comes with an envelope design. Highlight the envelope and hide it.
8. Change the size of the card so that it fits into a standard-sized envelope you can get at the store. Change the width to 10" and the height to 7".

9. Now is a good time to save the project. Choose a name you will recognize as you may want to use this project at a later stage. You should remember to save at important stages of the project as you progress through it.
10. Be careful with the stock board when you position it at the top of the mat. It has a tendency to peel back a bit when the Cricut starts to cut. Position the card mid-way to the bottom of the mat in Design Space.
11. When you put the actual cardstock onto the mat, you must put it with the textured side down. There will be a written message on the inside, which will be the smooth side.
12. In Design Space where you are setting the design, click "Mirror" to flip the card correctly.
13. Select a font you like and type "Happy Birthday" positioned in the center of the card on the right-hand side.
14. You will need to choose "Score" to get a line down the center where you will be folding the card. You do not need to use this, but it is handy. You can just as easily fold the card by hand if you do not have the scoring stylus.
15. After you click "Continue," the next step is to set up the material.
16. As the pattern is quite intricate, use the "Cardstock" (for intricate cuts.) Check your dial to make sure it is set correctly (use the custom setting.)
17. Load the scoring stylus and the fine-point blade. Make sure they are loaded in the Cricut and selected in Design Space.
18. Place the olive-green cardstock on the mat with the rough side down.
19. Position it in the Cricut.
20. Load the mat into the Cricut, and press the "Load/Unload" button.
21. Press the "Go" button when you are ready, and let the machine cut out the card.
22. Once the card has been cut, peel the mat away from the card. Use the spatula to carefully peel the card away, trying not to break the fine cut of the card.
23. Use two-sided tape or glue around the inside of the front of the card.
24. Cut the navy blue glossy or glitter cardstock to match the size of the card. Make it a tiny bit smaller.
25. Glue it or stick it down onto the card.

26. Your card is now ready to use.

Project 2: "Welcome to Our Happy Home" Sign

A nice "Welcome to Our Home Sign" can warm up any entry hall. Choose a nice piece of wood, paint it a happy color, then use your Cricut to make an awesome sign to put on it. Use a chalk finish paint to paint your board, and use a bit of sandpaper to make it a little rough to help the vinyl stick. You can customize the sign to say anything you want, but for this exercise, we are going to use "Welcome to Our Happy Home."

Project Tools, Materials, and Accessories:

- A square wooden board the size you want your sign to be.
- Baby blue paint with a matte or chalk finish (paint the wood before making the sign.)
- Permanent outdoor vinyl (black.)
- Green Standard Grip cutting mat.
- Cricut Fine-Point Blade.
- Pair of scissors for cutting the material to size.
- Weeder tool.
- Spatula.
- Brayer for smoothing out the material.

Directions:

1. Take the measurement of your board the width and length.
2. In Design Space, select "Shapes" from the left-hand menu and choose a square.
3. Resize the square by typing in the dimensions of your board.
4. You will need to zoom the shape in to be able to see it on the screen.
5. You can have the background of the shape in any color. If your text is going to be white, you may want to consider making the box black.
6. Next, you will need to choose a font for the writing on your sign.
7. Click on the "Text" option on the right-hand side menu bar.
8. Type "Welcome to Our Happy Home."
9. Position the text onto the box frame on the screen mimicking where you are going to position the writing on your signboard.
10. For this project, choose Aaron Script single-layer cutting font. It is a nice curly font for a sign.
11. Choose the color you want the writing for your sign to be. For the sake of this exercise, we are going to make the font black.
12. Drag the corner of the text box to size the font to how big you want to make it. It must fit comfortably on your signboard.
13. Remove your template box as you no longer need it and it is not going to be cut.
14. Now is also a good time to save your project and give it a name you will recognize for future similar projects.
15. Make sure you have the correct size cutting board.
16. Cut the vinyl to the size you need. If you have made your fonts to fit completely across your sign, make sure the piece is big enough to fit your signboard.
17. Place the vinyl on the Cricut cutting mat. Here is a tip for you: If your mat is losing its stickiness, you need a bit of tape to anchor it firmly to the mat.
18. In Design Space, click "Make It" in the top right-hand corner of the screen.
19. Set the material to vinyl.

20. You do not need a pen or accessory in the first holder, but you will need to use the fine-point blade in the second holder.
21. Load the cutting board with the vinyl and press the "Load\Unload" button.
22. When the light flashes, the Cricut is loaded and ready to press "Go."
23. Gently peel back the vinyl. You may need to use the spatula to help peel the back vinyl off.
24. Use the weeder tool to hook away any vinyl from the middle of the words, for instance, the V-indent on top of the M. Try not to let any vinyl you have hooked fall back down as it may land crookedly and mess up your letter.
25. Once you have cleaned the vinyl from the words, use the transfer tape and ease it over the letters. Smooth it over the letters as best you can as you pull the back sheet of the transfer tape off. Try not to get bubbles in the tape by using the brayer to smooth the tape out.
26. Once you have the transfer tape on the letters, position it where you want to lay it out on your signboard.
27. If you feel you need guidelines, draw them out with a pencil.
28. Gently peel the white side of the transfer tape from the writing. Then position the top part of the sign where you want to start it on your signboard. Smooth out the rest of the sign.
29. Once the letters are positioned and stuck down with the top part of the transfer tape, give them a rub to ensure they are stuck down.
30. Gently pull the top of the transfer tape off the wording and your sign is ready.

Project 3: "Queen B" T-Shirt

T-Shirts are one of the top items to make with the Cricut, and you will soon find yourself being inundated by friends and family asking you to make them, especially once you have mastered the art and are making extra trendy designs.

For this project, we are going to make a T-Shirt that says "Queen B" with a cute bee hovering over the B.

Project Tools, Materials, and Accessories:

- Plain cotton T-Shirt in the color of your choice.
- Iron-on vinyl also called heat transfer vinyl (HTV)—gold.
- Green Standard Grip mat.
- Cricut Fine-Point Blade.
- Weeding tool.
- Pair of scissors for cutting the material to size.
- Brayer.
- Iron or the Cricut EasyPress Iron.
- Cricut heat press mat to iron on.

Directions:

1. Start a new project in Design Space.
2. Choose "Templates" from the left-hand side menu.
3. Choose the "Classic T-Shirts" template.
4. From the top menu, choose the type of T-Shirt (kids short sleeve.)
5. From the top menu, choose the size of the T-Shirt (small.)
6. The back and the front of the T-Shirt will appear on Design Space in the workspace.
7. From the top menu, select the color of the T-Shirt you are using (pink.)
8. Select "Text" from the left-hand menu and type in "Queen B."
9. Set the font; a great free font for this project is Bauhaus 93.
10. Position the text on the T-Shirt, then set the size and change the color to gold.
11. Choose images and find a bee picture. There is a nice free image or some really cute images you can buy.
12. Position the bee above the B and set the color to gold. You can rotate it into a tilted position.
13. Click on the "Make It' button, and you will be prompted with another screen showing the design on the cutting board. This is because, for iron-on vinyl, you need to mirror the image. You mirror the image in order to iron it on with the correct side up. Click the "Mirror" button on the left-hand side of the screen. You will see your writing and image look like it is back-to-front. You may want to move the bee over a bit giving a bit of space between the image and writing.
14. Reset your dial on the Cricut to custom.
15. In Design Space, choose the everyday iron-on for your material setting.
16. You can set the pressure to a bit more if you like.
17. You will see a warning letting you know that mirroring must be on for iron-on vinyl. It reminds you to place the vinyl facedown as well.
18. Check that you have the fine-point blade loaded in cartridge two of the Cricut. Nothing is needed for cartridge one.

19. Cut the vinyl to the space that is indicated by the Cricut Design Space.
20. Place the shiny side of the iron-on vinyl down onto the cutting mat. Use your brayer to smooth out the vinyl onto your mat.
21. Load the cutting into the Cricut, and when the Cricut is ready, click "Go" for it to cut.
22. Unload the cutting mat when it has been cut. Remove the design from the mat, and gently remove the mat side of the vinyl from the carrier sheet (matte side of the vinyl.)
23. Use the weeding tool to pick out the areas of the letters like the middles of the B.
24. Place your T-Shirt onto the Cricut pressing mat with the middle section where you want the transfer to be.
25. If you are using the Cricut EasyPress, you can go to the Cricut website to find the heat transfer guide and the settings you will need for the press. Follow the instructions with the Cricut EasyPress.
26. For a normal iron, preheat the iron.
27. Place the Cricut heat press mat inside the shirt.
28. Heat the surface of the T-Shirt for 15 seconds with the iron.
29. Put the design on the shirt where it is to be ironed on with the carrier sheet up.
30. Place a parchment sheet over the vinyl to protect the iron and the design.
31. Place the iron on the design and hold the iron in place on the design applying a bit of pressure for up to 30 seconds.
32. Turn the shirt inside out and place the iron on the back of the design for another 30 seconds.
33. When it is done, turn the shirt right side out and gently pull the carrier sheet off.
34. Don't wash the shirt for 24 hours after the transfer has been done.

Project 4: Personalized Paper Bookmark

Make a personalized paper bookmark for textbooks and reading books.

Project Tools, Materials, and Accessories:

- Cardstock 8 ½" by 11" (color and type of your choice.)
- Green Standard Grip mat.
- Cricut Fine-Point Blade.
- Weeding tool.
- Spatula.
- Pair of scissors for cutting the material to size.

Directions:

1. Create a new project in Design Space.
2. Choose "Shapes" and select the square.
3. Unlock the square by clicking on the little lock at the bottom left-hand corner of the square.
4. With the square selected, change the shape to 6" wide and 2" high.
5. With the square still selected, click on "Duplicate" in the box on the right-hand side.

6. Select the copy you have made of the rectangle, unlock it, and set the width to 5.5" by 1.5" height.
7. Move the smaller box into the middle of the larger box.
8. Select both of the shapes and click on "Slice" at the bottom right-hand corner of the screen.
9. Remove the box in the middle of the rectangle and delete it.
10. In the middle of the larger box, you will see another smaller rectangular shape. Select it, move it out of the larger box, and delete it.
11. Select text from the left-hand menu. Choose a font. A good one for this is Bauhaus 93 or Cooper Black.
12. Type the name for the bookmark (Chloe.)
13. Move the name to the middle of the rectangle box, centering it, and then stretching it so it fills the hollow middle of the rectangle.
14. Select the rectangle and the name, click on "Copy," and make another three. You can make around four to five bookmarks on an 8 ½" by 11" cardstock.
15. Change the names on the other three bookmarks. Highlight each one separately and then click on "Weld" in the bottom right-hand corner (this must be done to each bookmark separately.)
16. Save your project.
17. Place your cardstock onto the cutting mat and load it into the Cricut.
18. Click "Make It" in Design Space.
19. Select the materials, which will be the cardstock you have chosen.
20. Check that all the cartridges are loaded in the Cricut and you have the fine-point blade loaded.
21. When the Cricut flashes ready, press "Go" to cut out your cards.
22. When the printing is finished, remove the cardstock from the cutting mat, and use the spatula to ensure it comes off without ruining the cut.
23. Clean up the letters with the weeding tool.
24. Your bookmarks are ready for use

Project 5: Fancy Leather Bookmark

Personalized leather bookmarks make really nice gifts. They are also very easy to make with the Cricut.

Project Tools, Materials, and Accessories:

- Cricut metallic leather.
- Cricut holographic iron-on (red for a gold effect.)
- Purple StrongGrip mat.
- Cricut Fine-Point Blade.
- Weeding tool.
- Pair of scissors for cutting the material to size.
- Brayer or scraping tool.
- Cricut Knife Blade.
- Thin gold string or ribbon.

Directions:

1. Cut the leather to the size you want it to be.
2. Each leather holder is approximately 2" wide by 6" high.
3. Cut the holographic paper to the size you want it to be; this will depend on the size of the font and wording you choose for the bookmark.
4. Create a new project in Design Space.
5. Select "Shapes" from the left-hand menu.
6. Choose the square, unlock it, and set the width to 2" with a height of 6".
7. Choose a triangle from the "Shapes" menu, and set the width to 1.982" and the height to 1.931".
8. Position the triangle in the rectangle at the bottom. Make sure it is positioned evenly as this is going to create a swallowtail for the bookmark.
9. Select the circle from the shapes menu, and unlock the shape. Set the width and height to 0.181".
10. Duplicate the circle shape.
11. Move one circle to the top right-hand corner of the bookmark and the other to the left. These will be the holes to put a piece of ribbon or fancy string through.
12. Align the holes and distribute them evenly by using the "Align" function from the top menu with both circles selected.
13. Select the top left hole with the top of the rectangle and click "Slice" in the bottom right menu.
14. Select the circle and remove it, then delete it.
15. Select the top right circle with the top of the rectangle and click "Slice" from the bottom right menu.
16. Select the circle and remove it.
17. Select the bookmark and move it over until you see the other two circles.
18. Select the two circles and delete them.
19. Select the triangle and the bottom of the rectangle, then click "Slice" from the bottom right-hand menu.

20. Select the first triangle, remove it, and delete it.
21. Select the second triangle, remove it, and delete it.
22. Save your project.
23. You will now have the first part of your leather bookmark ready to print.
24. Place the leather on the cutting mat, and use the brayer tool or scraper tool to flatten it and stick it properly to the cutting mat.
25. Position the little rollers on the feeding bar to the left and right so they do not run over the leather.
26. Set the dial on the Cricut to custom.
27. Load the knife blade into the second Cricut chamber.
28. In Design Space, click on "Make It."
29. Set the material to Cricut metallic leather.
30. Load the cutting board and leather into the Cricut and hit "Go" when the Cricut is ready to cut.
31. Unload the cutting board when the Cricut is finished printing and use the spatula to cut the leather bookmark form out.
32. Use the weeding tool to remove any shapes that should not be on the bookmark.
33. Place the holographic paper on the cutting mat, and put the wheels on the loading bar back into their position.
34. Create a new project in Design Space, and choose a nice fancy font. Do not make it any bigger than 1.5" wide and 3" high.
35. Save the project.
36. Click on "Make It," and choose the correct material.
37. Mirror the image.
38. Switch the blade in the second chamber back to the fine-point blade.
39. Load the cutting board and click "Go" when the Cricut is ready to cut.
40. Gently peel the back off the design, heat the leather, and place the name on the bookmark where you want it positioned.
41. Use the same iron-on method as the method in the "Queen B" T-Shirt project above.

42. Your bookmark is now ready to use or give as a personalized gift.

Project 6: Personalized Envelopes

Making personalized envelopes for those personalized greeting cards adds that extra touch.

Project Tools, Materials, and Accessories:

- Envelope 5.5" by 4.25".
- Cricut pens in the color of your choice.
- Green Standard Grip mat.
- Spatula.

Directions:

1. Create a new project in Design Space.
2. Choose the square from the "Shapes" menu.
3. Unlock the square, set the width to 5.5" and the height to 4.25".
4. Choose "Text" from the right-hand menu.
5. This will be the name and address the envelope will be addressed to.
6. Choose a font and size it to fit comfortably in the middle of the envelope.
7. You can choose a different color for the font.
8. Move the text box to the middle of the envelope.
9. Select the entire envelope and click "Attach" from the bottom right-hand menu.
10. When you move the card around the screen, the address text will move with the envelope.
11. Load the envelope onto the cutting board and load it into the Cricut.
12. In Design Space, click "Make It."
13. Choose a material like paper.
14. Check to see if the pen color you need is loaded into the first compartment of the Cricut.
15. When the project is ready, press "Go" and let it print.
16. Flip the card over and stick it onto the mat.
17. Use a piece of tape to stick the envelope flap down.
18. Load it into the Cricut.
19. Change the text on the envelope to a return address or "Regards From."
20. Change the color of the pen if you want the writing in another color.
21. When you are ready, click on "Make It."
22. Make sure the material is set to the correct setting.
23. When you are ready, press "Go."
24. Once it has finished cutting, you will have a personalized envelope.

Chapter 6. Making Money With Cricut

Just as the Cricut machine can be used in a million and one ways (figuratively speaking,) the ways to generate money from it is also numerous.

Some of the ways to generate money from the Cricut machine are highlighted below:

Make and Sell Leather Bracelets

Bracelets are fashionable items, especially leather bracelet. The Cricut machine can easily cut real or faux leather easily giving you less work to do. If you decide to cut, make, and sell leather bracelets, know that the materials needed are just snaps: your Cricut machine, leather, and probably card stock.

If you are interested in selling this craft, you can also create room for preordering, where a buyer can order for a particular design to be created by the designer.

Sell Iron-On Vinyl

This is another money-making opportunity that the Cricut machine provides. You make a design with the iron-on vinyl and sell out to people. The iron-on vinyl can be in the form of text or design. It can also be made for each season or celebration, be it Valentine, Halloween, Christmas, or Easter. Buyers may also order for what they want.

Sell Stickers

This idea is targeted at kids. You can make money by designing educative and entertaining stickers for toddlers and other age groups. Stickers of the alphabet, or map of a locale can be made. Stickers are also used in decorating places like the wardrobe or closets.

Make and Sell Party Decorations and Buntings

There is always a celebration in our day-to-day lives as human beings. It can be a milestone celebration, or simply a fun-seeking escapade. Party decorations made with the Cricut machine can be sold on these occasions.

Other Ideas To Explore

The following are other income generating ideas with the Cricut machine:

Window Decals: Everyone has a peculiar image, an object we are practically obsessed with. Getting a vinyl window decal of one's favorite image will go a long way in giving your decor a boost. Making and selling window decals is quite easy and profitable.

Make and Sell Canvas Wall Art: Customized wall art would generate quick and easy money. Get inspirational sayings or designs, and make them into wall arts for sale.

Design and Sell Onesies: Onesies or bodysuit are generally cute cloth which can be better with amazing artwork. Onesies for babies can be made with a lot of other text apart from "Daddy loves you" or "Momma's baby." Other mushy word art can be used in designing onesies for kids.

Become a Cricut Affiliate: This entails being paid to make tutorials video by the Cricut company. These videos are uploaded to the internet for the netizen to make use of. To become a Cricut affiliate, you need to have a strong internet presence. You must also have a tangible amount of followers on your social media accounts.

Post Tutorial Videos on Your Vlog: This has nothing to do with being an affiliate; rather, you create a blog for videos and upload tutorial videos, and get paid through the generated traffic.

Use of Social Media: You can make any of the craft you find easy and post pictures of it online, announcing to those on your list that it is for sale. This works better because whoever is buying gets to see the picture of whatever he is getting before ordering for it. Personalized crafts should also be included in your order of business.

Design and Sell T-Shirts: A T-Shirt is a clothing piece that is always in vogue. Most especially for college students, a designed tee would be a great fashion item. Creating a designed T-Shirt would generate income.

Design and Sell Hoodies: Hoodies are great wear for cold seasons. A designed one would roll better with the youth. The design can be preordered too.

Design and Sell Leather Neck Piece: A leather pendant can be designed for a necklace and sold out to interested buyers. An all-leather neck piece can also be made and sold.

Design and Sell Banners: Banners can be made for celebrations, festive periods, camping, parties, religious activities, or sporting activities. All these can be made and sold.

Design and Sell Window Clings: Window clings with the design of the seasons can be made and sold. Other designs or images can also be used for creating window clings.

Design and Sell Stencils: Stencils can be created and sold for those that want to hand-paint a post or sign. It would also generate a nice amount of money.

Design and sell safari animal Stickers: Stickers of safari animals are attractive items. They can be made and sold to animal lovers. The sticker is easy to make, and will also be a source of income generation.

Design and Sell Labeling Stickers: Labeling stickers can be made for labeling things in the house. Things in the kitchen, pantry, playroom, classroom, and other places can be labeled with labeling stickers.

Design and Sell Labeling Vinyl: Labeling adhesive vinyl can be made for labeling things in the house. Things in the kitchen, pantry, playroom, classroom, and other places can be labeled with labeling vinyl.

Design and Cut Appliqués: Fancy fabrics can be made into appliqués to design or decorate a place or object.

Design and Sell Christmas Ornaments: Christmas is a period when people celebrate and decorate their workplace, abode, and religious settings, among others.

Design and Sell Wall Decals: Different designs of wall decals can be made and sold for a cheap and affordable price.

Design and Sell Doormats: Beautiful doormat can be made with the machine and sold to customers. It can be designed with either text or images. Customized doormats can also be sold.

Design and Sell Kitchen Towels: Towels used in the kitchen can be designed and sold at affordable prices. The towels can be designed with text or images of delicacies.

Conclusion: Tips For Start In The Best Way

There are a lot of things which you can achieve by making the correct use of your machine. However, it is not just enough to know these, you need to know easier and more improved ways to make use of the machine you have acquired. To make the most out of your newly-acquired machine, here are a few things you should do:

1. **Test out your machine first.** This is a no-brainer, and you should do it as soon as the machine arrives. It is always a safe idea to start by testing out the components of your machine and double-checking to ensure that your machine has all the accessories that were promised. If at this stage, you discover that your machine is missing a few things, you may want to reach out to membership support immediately and get the issues rectified.

2. **Keep the components of your machine (especially the cutting mat) clean.** This is one of the parts of the machine that is constantly subjected to wear, tear, attack by dirt, and spoiling. In order to make sure that your machine remains in the best of conditions, take out time to clean your mat frequently. Best practices when you are trying to get this done is to make use of a lint roller to wipe down the mat after every use and to also scan over the mat once you are done with it to make sure that you take out all the little pieces that may remain from the materials you just cut. Also, be sure to frequently replace the plastic protective sheet that came with the mat, and it is not entirely unheard for you to wash the mat frequently too. However, washing the mat can be a tricky business. Considering the fact that the mat is meant to be in a specific way, you need to make sure that you wash it in such a way that you do not compromise the

integrity of the material the mat is made of. For best practices, wash with lukewarm water and mild dish soap. With these, scrub gently in circular patterns, rinse and allow the mat to drip dry.

3. **Cutting certain materials require that your mat be a bit sticky so that it can hold the material you are looking to cut in place.** Due to some factors like prolonged use, and continuous subjection to heavy work, there may be times that you would need to cut something that requires that the mat has a firm grip on the material, but you may not have access to a good mat that has not lost its stickiness at that time. As a way around this, you can resort to using masking tape or painter's tape to hold the material you are looking to cut in place. However, take this as a cue to change mats because this option won't work forever.

4. **In order to prevent the confusion that can come as a result of having to deal with many blades that you will need for your different projects, it can be safe to adopt the pattern of storing up your blades in such a way that you can tell almost instantly what blade is used to cut what material.** In essence, it is vital for you to learn to separate your blades. Let there be blades that you use to cut vinyl, then the ones you use to cut paper, and wood, and all the rest of them. This will ensure that your blades last for much longer and that you don't use the wrong blades for the wrong projects, thereby creating troubles for your new machine. You can get started by finding small jars to hold the blades, and then labeling each jar to signify which blades go into it. This way, you do not run the risk of making a mistake with your blade placement.

5. **You do not always have to have the right color of vinyl for you to embark upon your projects.** Let's assume that you are about to get started with a project and you need some green vinyl, but all you have is pink-colored vinyl, you must not get dressed and go off to the mall to get the green-colored ones because there is a way around it. Instead of running off to the mall every time you need a different color of

vinyl, why not get some Rustoleum Metallic Spray paint for the future. With this, you can give your un-cut vinyl some spraying and color-over without having to spend money every time. Just for a few bucks, you can get this over with.

6. Dafont.com **and** 1001freefonts.com **are amazing websites where you can find tons of fonts that you can make use of to create even more epic designs.** If you have searched through the Design Space and you have not been able to see something that piques your interests, or you just need to try out something new, you may want to visit those platforms and see what they have in store for you. Also, you will find a lot of support groups on Facebook where you can find a lot of helpful information as regards your creative journey with the machine you have just acquired. Join these groups, and be sure to be an active member of them. You will see that there are some things that may bother you that can be a walkover for another person. All you need to do is reach out. Furthermore, these platforms serve as hosting sites for a ton of helpful tools that can even unclog your creativity even more. Find them as pinned documents, helpful DIY tips, post and comment threads, and in all other formats as they come. The goal is to make sure that you do not try to do this on your own.

7. **Want to do some stenciling, but you are not sure where and how you can get started?** There's no need for you to be confused when you can make use of freezer paper to create custom stencils for your projects. With the Cricut Explore Air 2, you can get to cut the paper and fashion it into some custom-design stencils for your projects.

8. **Make use of tin foils to sharpen your blades.** Notwithstanding how careful you are with the blades, and how you do not mistake them for cutting different materials, it is not possible for your blades not to get to a point where they become blunt and weak. When your blades get blunt, a great way to get them up and running once again is by making use of tin foils to sharpen them. By sharpening with tin foil, you can extend the life of your blade, almost by x3. Sharpening is very simple. All you need to do is to unclamp the blade and run the tip of the blade through the tin foil between 10-15 times.

9. **Using pens other than the Cricut pens to write.** Next to the Cricut pens, there are a ton of other brands that you can make use of, even with your machine. They include:

- Uni-ball Signo UM-153.

- Tombow Dual brush pens.

- Sakura gelly roll.

- Bic marking and Bic crystal.

- Pilot precise.

The list is basically endless. The best part is that for all these pens, you can find them online, and with just a few dollars, you can have them added to your bucket list of pens to work with. However, to make use of these pens with your machine, you need a pen adapter. Pen adapters work for the Explore Air 2, or newer models of the Cricut machine. With these, you can connect any brand of Cricut pens and draw/write away.

10. **Increase your image options by learning how to make your own SVG files online.** While the Design Space and the internet provide you with endless numbers of images, you will agree that there are those times when even the most intricately designed picture does not quite cut it; it does not do justice to what you want to create. Under these circumstances, you need to learn how to bring your inner genius to life.

Using Inkscape, you can create your own SVG files from scratch, or convert your boring pictures to two-layered SVG files. Inkscape is a free tool that you can make use of, and making use of it is relatively easy.

11. **The following step is to make the best use of all the craft creation related wisdom in the context of Cricut cutting machines to embark on your own**

creative journey and make a whole lot of money while doing so. You are now equipped with all the tools and understanding required to create your own unique craft projects that will serve as a medium to channel your creativity. All the Cricut devices are uniquely designed to help you create real-life crafts stemming even from the most unlikely to manifest craft ideas. The results are professional looking with a high finish that you can not only use for your home décor but potentially sell to others with a similar creative wavelength. To help you accomplish this, all the nuances of the Design Space application have been explained in exquisite detail, along with information on a variety of free design resources such as images, fonts, and projects. This guidebook has utilized and presented a variety of beginner-friendly projects that can be accessed through the Cricut library on the Design Space application, so you can enhance your craft skills or learn to be a craftsman without heavily investing in machines and tools.

CRICUT MAKER FOR BEGINNERS

Introduction

What is a Cricut Machine?

A Cricut machine is a cutting machine; it has the unique functionality of being able to cut different materials which you will need for your crafts and DIY projects. Some of these materials include paper, vinyl, and materials as thick as wood. Although they are hardware, Cricut machines are dependent on their connection with your devices like mobile phones and computers.

Cricut machines are a very fun tool to make use of because they allow you to create art from materials you may not have known existed, and they allow your creativity to take flight. With the use of Cricut machines, you are able to create new materials to aid your work, and these materials you create may not be found otherwise.

In a nutshell, you create designs and templates using the device to which your machine is connected (the phone or computer system). These designs are preloaded into the device which your Cricut is connected to, and you can make a lot of changes or modifications with these designs. These designs are what you pre-load into the Cricut and make use of them to cut/print the material you are looking to use, just the way you want it to be.

When it comes to how a Cricut works, there are a lot to be learned about it, but having access to your own Cricut machine is like opening yourself up to a whole new world. There is literally no limit to the number of awesome crafts you can make with the use of the Cricut machine.

How the Cricut Works?

Considering the kind of magic the Cricut performs, you may be tempted to ask how it is able to achieve all these. Before you really begin to ask these types of questions, let us take you on a tour of the answer.

The Cricut works by printing out already-defined designs on a piece of material that will be fed into the machine. What this means is that if you are going to make use of a Cricut to create a design on any material, you have to go through these processes to make the most out of your experience.

Popular Cricut Machine Models - Which is the Best to Go For?

These models all have their characteristics, which make them advantageous over the next and a few setbacks that would make you want to go for the next one above the other one. In this portion, we will take a closer look at these and this will help guide you into the exact Cricut you can get for yourself the next time you are looking to make a purchase of the machine.

Cricut Explore One

The Cricut Explore One is a fun and relatively easy-to-use tool that is most suited for a range of DIY hobbies. This machine is meant for everyday-home applications to cut regular materials and is not really built to take on heavy materials or to be used at an industrial scale. This model of the Cricut machine is easy to be mastered following the ton of guidelines that can be found with it or even over the internet. It can cut through materials of up to 12 inches width and is meant for cutting, scoring, and writing on materials.

The Cricut Explore One comes without the double tool holder feature, is relatively slow with the execution of tasks (when compared against other more recent Cricut models), and has a limited amount of power it can accept to pass through it beyond which it will get faulty. It can be connected to the device that will be used for programming the design onto the machine using a host of options, including the USB functionality, and wirelessly using the Bluetooth feature.

If you are new to the world of Cricut designing and you are looking for a quick tool that comes with the basic functionalities of cutting, printing, and writing, which you can wrap your head around almost immediately, and it is relatively cheaper (especially if you are strapped for cash), then you may want to go for this option. For use, this model of the Cricut is compatible with the free iOS, Android, Windows, and Mac operating systems, and this implies that you can basically make use of it across a number of devices, including your phones and PCs.

This is what this model of the Cricut looks like:

Cricut Explore Air 2

This model of the machine comes with a few more functionalities than the one discussed above. For one, it can cut through a host of materials that the other one mentioned earlier cannot cut through, and it comes with many more perks since it appears to be an improvement of the former model.

The Cricut Explore Air 2 is an equipment that allows its user to create more designs and permit his creative genius to surface even more than if he were using the former one. This is because this model of the machine comes with the ability to flawlessly and perfectly cut through at least 100 different material types, including those that are not easily cut through, like vinyl, iron-on, and the likes of these.

In addition to just cutting materials, this model allows the user to personalize his projects by branding them with designs that he so chooses to, it also helps him to create home-made gifts and even custom-design apparel. Built to last, this machine comes with the special ability of durability. It has the ability to withstand a lot of wear and tear, and this is justifiable since it has to be subjected to a lot of pressure every time it has to cut through a material. Despite all the nuances of this machine, one of its most redeemable qualities is that it is easy to learn. Because of the vast array of materials this Cricut can cut through, it is most suited for a wide range of DIY hobbies; it can cut through materials of up to 12 inches in width. This model of the Cricut is faster than the Cricut Explore One and has the print and cut capability, which makes working with it even more fun than it ordinarily should be.

As it is the case with the Cricut Explore One, this model is also compatible with the free design application that is obtainable on the iOS, Windows, Android, and Mac platforms. Connecting the machine to your internet-enabled device can be achieved using wireless connections like

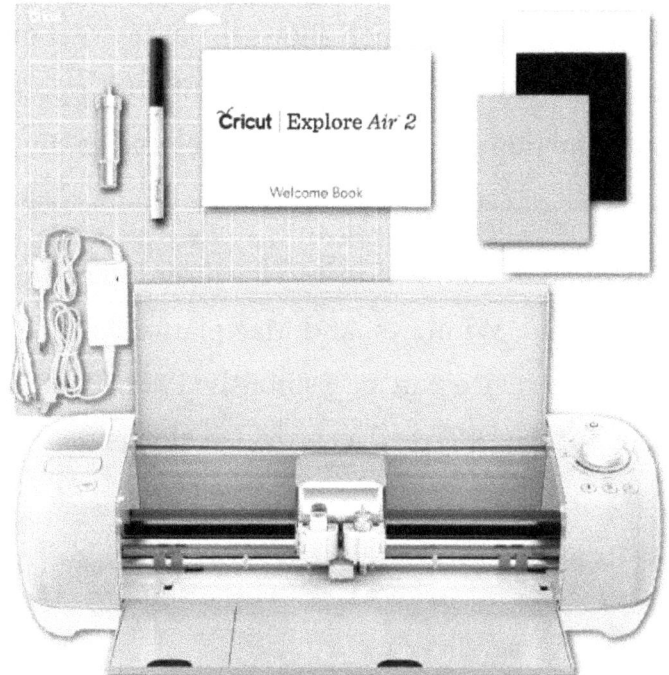

Bluetooth, and also the USB connection feature that is available.

Cricut Maker

This is another model of the Cricut machine. This model is considered to be among the top-ranking Cricut machines and is used for more demanding and professional DIY tasks and performances. Suited to take on materials of up to 12 inches in width, the Cricut Maker can cut up to 300 and above materials, which include the more-difficult-to-cut materials like wood. The Cricut Maker has a high durability level and, considering the usability of this machine, it is easy to be learned following the guide that the Cricut machines come with, or with explainer content scattered across the internet.

The Cricut Maker has a wide range of adaptability as it can be used for a host of tasks, including cutting, writing, scoring, and other professional effects that need a more detailed machine that possesses extra features. This model of the machines comes with a double tool holder and possesses the ability to perform tasks at a rate that is faster when compared to other Cricut machines that have been discussed earlier; up to 2 times as fast. The Cricut Maker supports the print and cut feature, which allows the user to get more creative with the tasks at hand, and opens up the doors to a wider range of craft opportunities. The Cricut Maker is 10 times more powerful than other Cricut machines and so can make a lot of designs and DIY crafts.

Just like the others, it is operated by connecting it to the design space application that is free and available on the iOS, Android, Windows, and Mac platforms. The connection between the machine and the powering device can be established wirelessly using the Bluetooth connection, or by making use of the USB cord as provided alongside the machine.

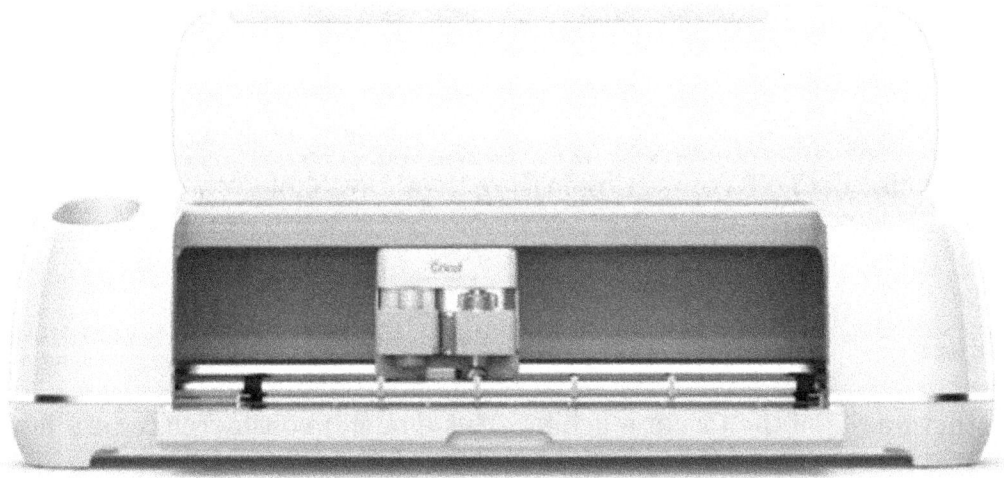

Cricut Joy

It is the last model of the Cricut machine we will be discussing. First off, this is a little machine that permits you to cut, draw, and make designs out of numerous materials, counting vinyl, cardstock, paper, and a few more materials. One of the redeeming qualities of this machine is its size, which makes it easy to be transported and easy to use as well.

As opposed to other Cricut machines, this particular model seems to be able to hold up its own forte, although the small size will usually make people tend to roll their eyes and dismiss it as being the last option to choose when faced with options. This, however, is not the case of the Cricut Joy as it possesses some features that make it a great choice, especially for those that uphold the practice and lifestyle of minimalism. Here are a few of them;

- This machine can create cards in record time. This is as a result of the CardMat feature that it comes with.
- With a weight of approximately 3.9lbs and dimensions (in the sealed box) of about 8.4x5.4x4.2 inches, it is amazing that this machine can cut up to 50 different materials and makes very precise cuts because of the built-in cutting technology.
- Even without the Cricut Mat, which is an integral part of the other Cricut machines, this machine is able to make very precise cuts. This machine supports the continuous cut feature, which allows the user to make cuts that are up to 20ft long.
- This machine comes with access to the free design space app that is available across all platforms and software operating systems. Connectivity is usually established using a wireless component like the Bluetooth connection.

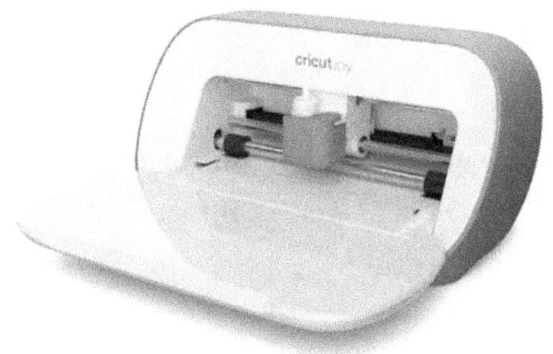

Chapter 1: What Is A Cricut Machine And How Does It Work?

Basic Information about a Cricut Machine

While the brand envelops a few distinct items, including heat presses and embossers, the word Cricut has gotten synonymous with kick-the-bucket cutting machines. So, in case you're wondering, what is a Cricut machine? The appropriate response is a home pass on cutting machines utilized for papermaking and different expressions and specialties.

Basically, it's a savvy cutting machine known as the "flawless passage point to the universe of exactness making."

It's imperative to realize that these machines are not just utilized for cutting paper. They're made to cut a wide assortment of material in astonishing manners. Vinyl is another material that is related to kick-the-bucket cutting machines, just as felt, cardstock, thus numerous others. They can even cut wood!

Notwithstanding cutting a wide range of materials, the machines that are presently accessible can likewise draw with pens, compose with pens, and score material for fresh, easy collapsing.

Setting Up Step by Step

    Opening the Box

When you purchase a bundle from Cricut, you will receive a few boxes, but the most significant box amongst them will hold the Cricut Maker. To recognize it, you'll see the picture of the Maker on the box.

When opening the Cricut box, the first thing you see is the welcome package placed on the machine. This contains a welcome manuscript, a rotary blade with cover, a fine point pen, a USB cable, and a packet with your first project.

When you take the Cricut machine out of the box, the power cord will be underneath along with the cutting mats. You will also see half of the settings on the dial between the fabrics. This is for when you need a little less or a little more force than is given by the programmed settings. If you cut a light cardstock, for example, but the knife doesn't completely cut the design, you can pick the half setting between Light and Cardstock. Or if you cut a poster board and the blade exerts too much pressure by slicing your pad, simply select the arrangement between the cloth and the poster board. If you use another product and face it, you can use this tool well over a hundred different materials, so why wouldn't you? All you need to do is just to change the dial to the setting "Custom". You can then pick the exact product you are using from the massive drop-down list in Design Space. And again, the Cricut changes its blade settings automatically so that you don't have to.

Unwrapping

The Cricut machine is wrapped with a layer of cellophane and a protective wrapper. Before setting up the device, you have to remove the wrappings.

Some Styrofoam protects the in-housing of the machine, and that has to go too.

Your Cricut Maker will also come with some supplies; you should unwrap them and check them out. Lucky for you, the fine point blade is already installed in the Cricut Maker, so you don't have to bother with that.

Visit Cricut /setup

The following step in setting up your machine lies in the technical aspects. Cricut has a webpage dedicated to walking you through this process, which makes it super easy.

Open Cricut /setup on your device. You can use any device that is compatible with Cricut like a smartphone, tablet, or computer. When you do that, you will be asked to install Cricut Design Space and also sign up. Then, you'll be given your Cricut ID.

If you have been using a former Cricut machine before, then you can carry on with your former ID.

Plugging It In

Then, you need to take your USB cord and the power cord to power up your Cricut machine.

This will be shown on the setup wizard of the webpage.

For the USB cord, you connect the square end to the Cricut Maker device and the other end to the computer and, the power cord is easy to connect from Cricut Maker to the power outlet.

Claim Your Bonus

After plugging in your Cricut, you will be able to claim a free welcome bonus from Cricut, which is a free month of Cricut Access. This means that you get to enjoy access to projects, fonts, and Cricut Cut Files.

Begin Your Project

If you need a little something to practice with before starting on your intended project, Cricut Maker machines usually come with a little project in the welcome pack to help you get acquainted with the tools.

The Maker comes with all the tools that you need to complete the project, which is usually the task of making a little card.

After this, you can begin using it. The thing is, when you want to use your Cricut Maker, you need to learn how to use Cricut Design Space.

Chapter 2: Cricut Explore Air 2 Vs. Cricut Maker

Cricut Maker

- They have a faster cutting ability.
- They write at a much faster rate compared to other Cricut machines
- They are made up of the rotary blade, which is used for fabric.
- They can cut many more materials than the other Cricut machines available.

Cricut Explore Air 2

- They also get to cut more materials.
- They are made up of fast mode, which aids them in cutting fast.
- The writing speed is also fast.
- They are made up of two holders used for keeping tools.

Cricut Explore Air

- Just like the Air 2, they also contain two holders for holding tools.
- They are Bluetooth enabled.
- They are made up of a dual carriage used for wiring and cutting.

Cricut Explore One

- They are a very useful electronic cutting machine for DIY crafts and projects.
- They are handy for the cutting of different materials ranging from paper and iron-on to adhesive vinyl as well as leathers.

The Cricut maker is the latest Cricut machine and is the very best of all the Cricut machines available, although this might vary according to the purpose of the user. It has about ten times cutting force compared to Air 2, which shows that it has the highest cutting capacity.

The Difference between the Cricut Maker and Cricut Explore Air 2

The following features are those of the Cricut maker that distinguishes it from the Explore Air 2:

- It is made up of the Rotary blade, which is mostly used for cutting fabrics. It is also used in cutting leather, silk, and other materials.
- In the Maker, the scoring pen is replaced by the scoring wheel, which has more delicate scored lines and sharper.
- The Maker is made up of the knife blade used for thick and heavy materials such as balsa wood and heavy chipboard.
- It can use the Digital sewing pattern library, which provides access to hundreds of fabric plans for an instant cut.
- It can cut hundreds of materials ranging from the finest paper to heavy fabrics.
- Unlike the Explore Air 2, the Maker comes without the dial.
- The Maker is also made up of a ridge that is used for placing your tablet devices as well as redesigned storage areas.

Cricut Explore Air 2

- In terms of cost, the Cricut Explore Air 2 offers the best value for money. It has lots of great features despite costing up to half of the price of the Maker.
- It can be used for a variety of projects such as the patterned vinyl t-shirt, reverse canvas project, vinyl on glass water bottles, craft cutting, etc.

The Difference between the Explore Air 2 and the Explore Air

- Both the Explore Air 2, as well as the Maker, can cut, score, and write twice faster than the Explore Air can.

- Unlike the Explore Air that comes in the blue color, the Explore Air 2 does come in pastel colors.

Irrespective of their differences, they are similar in some areas:

- Air and Air 2 are both made up of a dual carriage that allows cutting and writing without having to change any tools.
- Another notable similarity between these machines is that they both work with the deep cut blades and fine point.

Chapter 3: Insights Of Explore Air 2 Machine

The Cricut Explore Air 2 is the latest model in the Cricut Explore family. It is the mid-range machine and is the best one for anyone starting out with crafting and cutting machines.

It comes in a few different colors such as rose, mint, blue, and black. It is a versatile machine that is easy to pack away and store, but big enough to do large designs with. It comes with a few different cutting blades, which give the user a lot of cutting material choices.

The Cricut Explore Air 2 is a fast, accurate machine that makes precision cuts. It comes with dual accessory housing. The housing houses both a drawing pen or a scoring pen and a blade, without having to swap out accessories during a cut.

The Cricut Explore Air 2 Features:

- DIY hobbyists, beginners to crafting, scrapbookers, and gift card designers.
- The machine is capable of writing, scoring, and cutting.
- The Explore Air 2 is easy to set up.
- It is easy to use.
- The machine has a Smart Dial for manual selection at the machine level for certain materials.
- The Smart Dial can also be used to set up the material cutting depth selection.
- Both the material and depth selection can also be set up within Design Space, the design software available to Cricut users.
- The weight and dimensions of the Cricut Explore Air 2 are:
  - Weight = 16 lbs.
  - Dimensions = 24" x 9.5" x 9.5"

- It comes in the following colors:
  - Rose
  - Blue
  - Black
  - Mint
- Bluetooth connectivity comes standard with the machine.
- The machine has USB connectivity.
- The Cricut Explore Air 2 is compatible with over 100 different types of materials.
- It does NOT work with the Card Mat or any of the Smart Materials.
- The maximum material width of the Cricut Explore Air 2 is 12 inches.
- The commercial-grade cutting technology available for the Cricut Maker is NOT available for the Explore Air 2.
- Design Space is the design software of choice for Cricut machines and comes free with each device.

What Comes in the Box?

The following items come packed in the box of a new Cricut Explore Air 2:

- The Cricut Explore Air 2, in the color it was purchased in
- A welcome booklet for the Cricut Explore Air 2
- A power cable for the machine
- A USB cable for the machine
- 1 Cardstock material sample to practice with
- 1 Cricut Premium Fine-Point blade
- 1 Cricut Premium Fine-Point blade housing
- 1 Cricut 12" x 12" StandardGrip machine mat (green)
- 1 Black Cricut Fine-Point Pen

Added extras that come with the Cricut Explore Air 2 are:

- Cricut Access 30-day trial membership

- Access to free Cricut Design Space sewing patterns
- Access to free Cricut Design Space projects

Setting Up the Cricut Explore Air 2

Setting up the Cricut Explore Air 2 is a quick and easy process.

- Unbox the Cricut Explore Air 2.
- Find a place to set the machine up. Ensure there is enough space, at least 10 inches behind and in front of the machine.
- The surface you use must be flat and non-slip.
- Make sure there is a power source close by to connect the machine to.
- There must be enough space for your connected device (PC, Laptop, etc.) as well.
- Take off any packaging tape or protective coverings on the device.

Connecting the Cricut Explore Air 2

First Steps to Connect the Cricut Explore Air 2:

- Once you have your Cricut Explore Air 2 positioned, you can plug the power cable into the round port at the back of the cutting machine.
- Plug the other end of the power cable into the wall socket.
- Place the small, square side of the USB cable that came with the machine in the port to the left of the power socket on the back of the cutting machine.
- Place the other end of the USB cable into the device you will be using with the Cricut Explore Air 2 to run Design Space.
- On the PC, laptop, or mobile device you're using, open your web browser.
- Go to the Cricut setup page
- Switch on the Cricut Explore Air 2 by pressing the "Power" button on the machine, located at the top of the Smart Dial.
- Open the machine by pressing the "Open" button located on the left-hand side of the machine.

- If you are a first-time user on the Cricut Design Space site, you will need to fill out the form to create a user ID.
- Once you have created the user ID, you will be prompted to "Get Design Space plugin". Download the plugin by following the easy and concise on-screen instructions.

Connecting a Device to the Cricut Explore Air 2 Using Bluetooth:

- You must first follow the above steps to connect the machine and create a user ID.
- Go to the Bluetooth settings on the device you want to attach to the Cricut.
- Select the Cricut Explore Air 2 device from the available Bluetooth devices.
- It will ask you for a code. Type in 0000 to pair the Cricut Explore Air 2 with your device.
- The "Power" button on the Cricut Explore Air 2 will turn blue when it is connected to a Bluetooth device.
- If you have created your Cricut user, open the browser on your Bluetooth device.
- Go to the Cricut Design Space website
- When you go to download Design Space, it automatically detects the operating system of the device from which you logged into the software.

Your login details, unless you opt not to have them do so, will be remembered from your last login on Design Space.

Setting Up the Cricut Explore Air 2 and Installing Design Space on a PC

All the Design Space downloads below will require an internet connection for laptops and desktops running Windows or Mac operating systems.

Using Design Space on a Mac

These instructions are for desktop and laptop devices running the Mac operating system.

The minimum requirements to install Design Space on a Mac device are:

- Mac OS 10.12 or later versions are compatible with Design Space.

- The device must support either USB or Bluetooth.
- 1.83 GHz is the minimum CPU requirement.
- 4GB is the minimum RAM requirement.
- 2GB is the minimum amount of free hard drive space required.
- 1024px x 768px is the minimum screen resolution required.

Downloading and Installing Design Space for Windows:

- Open the internet browser on your device to the web page
- Select "Download".
- The download will begin and will indicate its progress. This can take a few minutes, depending on the speed of your internet connection.
- In the "Downloads" folder on your Mac, you will find the following dmg file:
- Cricut Design Space Install v5.11.57.dmg (the version number may differ depending on the updated version.)
- You will need to drag the Cricut Design Space Install v5.11.57.dmg file into the "Applications" folder.
- Double-click on the Cricut Design Space Install v5.11.57.dmg to launch the application.
- If at any time the operating system on your device prompts you to download the application from the internet, click "Open." Otherwise, Design Space will not install.
- It is a good idea to create a desktop icon for the Cricut application to make it easier to find. To create a desktop icon, drag the Cricut Design Space Install v5.11.57.dmg into the "Dock" folder.
- You will need to "Sign in with your Cricut ID" once the installation is finished.

Using Design Space on Windows

These instructions are for desktop and laptop devices running a Windows operating system.

The minimum requirements to install Design Space on a Windows device are:

- Microsoft Windows version 8 or later versions are compatible with Design Space.
- The device must support either USB or Bluetooth.
- 1.83 GHz is the minimum CPU requirement.
- 4GB is the minimum RAM requirement.
- 2GB is the minimum amount of free hard drive space required.
- 1024px x 768px is the minimum screen resolution required.

Downloading and Installing Design Space for Windows:

- Open the internet browser on your device to the following web page
- Select "Download".
- The download will begin and will indicate its progress. This can take a few minutes, depending on the speed of your internet connection.
- In the "Downloads" folder on the PC, you will find the following file: Cricut Design Space Install v5.11.57.exe (the version number may differ depending on the updated version.)
- If at any time the operating system on your device prompts you about trusting the application, you must select to trust the application. If you do not trust the application, it will not install.
- You must follow all the on-screen install prompts.
- It is a good idea to create a desktop icon for the Cricut application to make it easier to find. It usually automatically creates a desktop icon. If not, the application can be found in the "All Programs" taskbar.
- You will need to "Sign in with your Cricut ID" once the installation is finished.

Setting Up the Cricut Explore Air 2 and Installing Design Space on a Mobile Device

You will need an internet connection or data to download Design Space on a mobile device.

Using Design Space on Android

These instructions are for mobile phones and tablet devices running an Android operating system.

The minimum requirements to install Design Space on an Android device are:

- Android 6.0 or later versions are compatible with Design Space.
- Most of the later versions of Android mobile phone devices are compatible with Design Space.
- Most of the later versions of Android tablet devices are compatible with Design Space.
- It should be noted that Chrome books are not compatible with Design Space.

Downloading and Installing Design Space for Android:

- Go to the Google Play Store on your Android device.
- Search for the Cricut Design Space app.
- Install the app on your Android device.
- You can either set up the machine right away or skip over the machine setup step to go to the design section.

Using Design Space on iOS

These instructions are for mobile phones and tablet devices running an iOS operating system.

The minimum requirements to install Design Space on an iOS device are:

- iOS 11 or later versions are compatible with Design Space.
- iPhone 5s and later models are compatible with Design Space.
- iPad Air and later models are compatible with Design Space.
- iPad, iPad mini 2, and later models are compatible with Design Space.

Downloading and Installing Design Space for iOS:

- Go to the App Store on your iOS compatible device.
- Search for the Cricut Design Space app.

- Install the Cricut Design Space app as you would any other iOS app.
- You can either set up the machine right away or skip over the machine setup step to go to the design section.

Chapter 4: Tools And Accessories Needed To Work With Explore Air 2 Machine

Cricut has different models of die-cutting machines and for a beginner; you may be confused about the type that is best for you in the course of crafting. Look no further as I have you covered. I have four machines (Cricut Maker, Cricut Explore Air 2, Cricut Explore Air, and Cricut Explore One) to give insight into their strength and weaknesses while making up your mind to which one of them you will work with.

The type of Cricut machine you may wish to get depends on the type of the project you want to use it for. All Cricut machines have certain things in common including cut, right, and score, a 12" wide cutting area size, can cut a variety of materials, use Design Space software, and "Print Then Cut" feature. What stands them out are the differences between them as will be discussed:

- Double /Single Tool Holder: the main tool holder is what you see when you open the lid of the Cricut machine, designed to move back and forth on the carriage. Double tool holder allows you to write and cut in one step while the single tool holder will do the same function in separate steps. Among the four mentioned Cricut machines, only Cricut Explore One has a single tool holder while the rest has a double tool holder.
- Adaptive Tool System: this is a recent addition to the Cricut machine and available only to Cricut Maker. The adaptive tool system delivers more power to the cutting force (4 kg) which is ten times more than the nearest versions to it; uses a steering system to control the direction of the blade, adjust the pressure of the blade

automatically with each cut pass, and uses a new set of tools and accessories for diverse cuts.

- Fast Cutting Mode: this mode is used to write and cut materials twice as fast, especially when producing large quantities of materials. This feature is common to Cricut Maker and Explore Air 2.
- Cutting with Bluetooth: this feature is common to the Cricut Maker, Explore Air 2, and Explore Air. You can use it to cut your material without using a cable.
- All models of Cricut machines have a slot for cartridge and can be linked to your Design Space account to have access to your cartridge graphics. Newer models like the Cricut Maker come with a digital Design Space library instead of the physical cartridge and if you need to connect a physical cartridge with it, you will need to buy a separate cartridge adapter.
- Tips on How to Use the Cricut Explore Air Effectively
- Test the material you wish to cut first before starting the real project. This will ensure the smooth delivery of the project without encountering any problem. Look out for materials such as fabric, wood, or felt because they can pose all sorts of trouble during the cutting process.
- Roll the Cricut mat backwards away from the material you have finished cutting instead of peeling the material away from the Cricut mat. This will give you a project cut with precision.
- Always clean your Cricut mat after you finish a project. Use a lint roller over the Cricut mat to remove leftovers of dirt and lint from the surface of the mat.
- Organize your blades and knives separately. This will help you apply the correct blade or knife for a particular project. Mixing them up may cause you to use an inappropriate blade for a project which might lead to damage or blunting the blade.

Best Tools and Software for Cricut Explore Air Machine

- Extra mat: make sure that you have an extra mat handy while doing your project. It could be difficult while doing your project if you discover that your Cricut mat is no longer sticky or messing up your work.
- Weeder tool: this tool is particularly useful when lifting vinyl material. There are varieties of weeder tools including Cricut Weeder Tool, Weeder Toolset, Dental Picks, and Pin Pen, and Exacto Knife. They all do the same function and I encourage you to experiment with all to discover which one works for you.
- Tweezers: this tool is a weeding tool that can help you lift materials on the mat, especially vinyl from the middle and not necessarily from the edge. It can also be used to pick up tiny little scraps from the surface of the mat.
- Scrapper Tool: this tool is used to get bubbles out of vinyl materials on the mat. This will help you to get clean cuts and ensure that your materials are not distorted while cutting the fine details.
- Brightpad: this tool is useful for tracing and adapting patterns to your material. It also makes the cut lines visible.
- Trimmers/Cutters: when you need to cut your material in a straight line, then this tool comes in handy especially when the need to size your material on the mat arises.
- Spatula: This tool is useful when lifting a material that can be torn easily from the Cricut mat. This tool is also used to clean the mat from dirt and debris.
- Scissors: this tool is well-known for cutting fine details in small areas when the need arises.
- Brayer: this tool is useful for stabilizing materials before you begin the cutting process. It helps the material to stick to the Cricut mat without damage.
- Cricut EasyPress: this tool is essential for heat transfer of vinyl materials. It saves you a lot of peels after one or two wears.
- 'Sure, Cuts A Lot' is third-party software that allows you to cut any shape you can imagine with ease. It is easy to use with many electronic cutting machines including Cricut Explore/Maker machine, CraftRobo/Graphtec, Vinyl Express, and more. To

work with your Cricut Explore machine, use 'Sure Cuts A Lot' to design your shape then export it to your Cricut machine Design Space using a compatible file format. It is a wonderful software for craftsmen. Give it a try, you will not regret it.

Note that this software requires a firmware update to your Cricut Explore machine; includes freestyle drawing tools, uses auto trace features, and with more than 200 shapes built-in.

Chapter 5: Insights Of Cricut Maker Machine

Cricut Explore Air 2 is an equipment that helps a lot in some or all stages of creative work such as Sewing, Scrapbook, Party Scrap, Home Decor, Stamping, Custom Stationery, Making Stickers, Making EVA pieces and also helps who works with Painting because with it you can make stencil your way, very personalized.

In this manual, we'll not only stay on theories, but we will teach how to use Cricut Explore Air 2! That's right! So, let's get your hands dirty, installing your machine so you can make the first cut, as well as showing you some creative techniques that can be done with it!

How to Install Cricut Explore Air 2

First step: Take your Cricut Explore Air 2 out of the box and check out all its components:

- Power cable
- USB cable
- 01 Premium Blade and Thin Tip Blade Holder already pre-installed
- 01 Standard cutting base (StandardGrip) or Light Fixation (LightGrip) 30.5 cm x 30.5 cm (12 in x 12 in)
- Welcome Book
- Materials for the first project
- 01 Fine tip pen in black color
- The software provides you with 50 ready-to-use projects

Items checked successfully; now it's time to choose where your machine will be.

Here's a tip: to use it, remember to place it in space enough to leave 25cm in front and 25cm behind.

So now press the "OPEN" button…

Wow!

Like magic, an automatic opening is present in front of you! You can take the bucket because you drooled too much!

Now with great care, remove the seals and protections from all the parts you find.

Now, to get to know a little more about your Cricut Explore Air 2, notice that it has an Intelligent Panel on the right side, which already contains the cutting settings for the most used materials in everyday life. However, it cuts out more than 100 materials, but we will talk about that later.

In the central part, there are two "drawers" to store blades and tools. Also, on the left side, there is a compartment for tools and pens. Finally, there is an entrance to connect physical cartridges that are still used by people who bought files in this mode in older versions of Cricut machines.

Now that they are appropriately presented let's start by installing the Design Space, following the steps below.

How to Install Cricut Design Space

Access Design Space in your browser.

Select the Product you want to Configure/Register. Here, we'll go with Cricut Explore Product Family" option.

Design Space is available for Android and iOS, in addition to Windows and iMac. For cellular systems, there is an offline version of the program. However, on the computer, the offline version is still beta, so it is not available to all users.

TIP:

If your screen is in other languages, remember that you can download and install the Google Translate extension on your computer, this way almost the entire process will be in English.

The next screen prompts you to log in with your Cricut account. If you don't already have a Cricut ID, create it on this screen. However, if you already have a Cricut ID, click on the "Login" button and enter your login and password.

After logging in, click on "Download".

Wait for the download to complete.

When the download is complete, the Cricut icon will appear in the file name.

Click on the ".exe" file to install.

Finally, follow the instructions on the screen.

Click "Finish". However, it is important to know that your machine is automatically registered during its configuration.

Click "Continue".

How to Connect Your Cricut Explore Air 2 Machine

It's time to plug in your Explore Air 2 and turn it on.

If you prefer, you can also connect it via Bluetooth, since it is already integrated with Cricut Explore Air 2.

However, if you need help pairing your computer to Cricut Explore Air 2 via Bluetooth, you'll get to see a more detailed explanation before the end of this portion. It can be done at any time so that we can proceed with the connection via USB cable.

With the machine turned on, the installation process itself checks whether the firmware is up to date or not.

After verification, the next screen shows you the option to subscribe to Cricut Access or not. This is the Cricut store, where you can find thousands of image files, projects, fonts, and many beautiful creations.

You can have a free month to try and then cancel your subscription at any time, or you can choose to subscribe later. However, if you decide not to sign at this time, don't worry! There are many free designs available for you to use.

Well, going back to the subject, the next screen is where it all starts, and you can follow step by step all the commands in detail. Therefore, use the materials and tools that come with the machine: papers, Cricut black pen, and the blade.

Above all, you must follow each step of the guidance and add a little more so that you begin to understand the process of creating a piece. Pretty cool. Practical and gradual learning!

Well then, let's proceed to learn about the accessories and the creative possibilities of your Cricut Explore Air 2.

Cutting Base, Cutting Blades and Accessories

Now let's talk a little bit about cutting bases, blades, and other accessories that you can use on your Cricut Explore Air 2, in addition to showing some creative possibilities.

- Cutting bases

There are four types of cutting bases, and all of them can be used in Cricut Explore Air 2. Therefore, for purging, each floor has a color to differentiate the glue's adhesion from each one.

They are:

- Blue base = light fixation
- Green base = standard fixation
- Pink base = specific for fabrics
- Purple base = for heavier materials.

Important:

The Purple Base is not required for use with Cricut Explore Air 2 because it is more targeted at materials of greater thickness that are cut in the Cricut Maker, but if you want to use it, no problem.

- Cricut Cutting Blades

With four types to choose from, the blades that can be used on the Cricut Explore Air 2 are:

For materials up to 1.1mm:

- Fine Point Blade (silver) is ideal for cutting materials such as paper, thinner acetate, vinyl, transfer, tracing paper, and other materials.
- Premium blade (slightly golden) - has more extended durability than the traditional Ponta Fina.
- Fabric Blade (light pink) - for thinner fabrics. It is the same as the Ponta Fina blade, but the holder's color is different so that you can identify each one's function. In this way, you preserve the cutting edge and help to prolong the durability of your blades.
- Deep Cut Blade - For materials up to 1.7mm, it cuts EVA, thin cork, among other thicker materials precisely.

Changing the blades is very simple and cost-effective, even better because once you have the support, you only need to purchase the tip, that is, the blade, in fact!

Other tools and accessories will also give your pieces a special touch.

You know that perfect continuous crease, beautiful to live in?

Well, the Crease pen is responsible for all of these. Therefore, its role is essential to make folds in boxes, invitations, or even give an extraordinary detail to part of the project. It supports "A" on the cart's left side while the blade supports "B."

These pens can also be great allies to your creativity. Like the crease pen, Cricut pens are used in the "A" support of the cart.

Cricut has several types: Fine point, medium point, with sublimation ink, and even washable pen for fabrics. Yes! You draw, sew your piece, wash it, and the paint comes out, and the finish of your work is perfect!

Cut with EVA?

Yes! The Deep Cutting Blade makes it easy to work with more material options. There are lots of these practical and straightforward bookmarks, but you can create much more!

Working with Stamping

T-shirts, stuffed animals, bags, caps, shoes, backpacks, and whatever else your imagination sends! Cricut has so many types of heat transfers that we don't even know where to start! The desire is to use them all at once!

Another type of printing material that Cricut supplies are Infusible Ink. The materials in this line have sublimation technology that you can wash without worrying about whether it will come out or fade after washing.

Therefore, when using Infusible Ink materials, you can make 100% polyester fabrics and many other materials that come with stunning and vibrant colors!

Here we only put a little bit of what your Cricut Explore Air 2 is capable of!

There is a lot more!

So, let's work that Cricut Explore Air 2 is waiting for you to make incredible creations!

Below you learn how to configure the Cricut Explore Air 2 to use via Bluetooth.

How to Use Cricut Explore Via Bluetooth

However, remember that this form of connection is optional but very useful for those who do not have much space to leave many wires on the table or bench where they work. Therefore, you can even work with the device away from Cricut, considering a maximum distance between 3m to 4.5m.

First, to use Bluetooth, your computer must also have this device. Most of them already come with Bluetooth.

To check if your computer already has Bluetooth, right-click on the "Start" button and click on the "Device Manager" option.

Therefore, if Bluetooth is listed among the options, it means that your computer already has it.

However, if Bluetooth does not appear on the list and you want to use it, you can buy a Bluetooth Dongle device to allow the configuration of your computer with other equipment via Bluetooth.

Remember: if you don't have Bluetooth installed on your computer, that doesn't stop you from using your Cricut Explore Air 2. Just connect it via USB cable and be happy!!

Now that we know if your computer has Bluetooth or not close the Device Manager.

If your computer already has Bluetooth installed, it's time to set it up!

Chapter 6: Tools And Accessories Needed To Work With Cricut Maker Machine

Right now, there are five unique edges and various accessories to either score or draw with your Cricut. Look at an outline of the entirety of the tools you can use with any of the Cricut family machines.

Cricut Maker and the entirety of the tools inside it:

Fine Point Blade

The fine point cutting blade is the most well-known sharp edge, and it accompanies the entirety of the Cricut Machines. It is made of the German Carbide, which is an incredibly solid and great material most ordinarily utilized for cutting tools materials.

This sharp edge is ideal for making mind-boggling cuts, and it's intended to cut medium-weight materials. It used to be silver; however, it presently arrives in a lovely brilliant shading.

Profound Point Blade

In the event that you have to cut thicker materials, the Deep Point Blade will be your closest companion. You can utilize it with any of the Cricut Explore Family machines or potentially Cricut Maker! The edge of this cutting blade is such a lot more extreme–60° contrasted with 45° for the fine point sharp edge–This truly permits the edge to infiltrate and cut mind-boggling cuts in thick materials.

Reinforced Fabric Blade

The Bonded Fabric Blade was explicitly intended to cut texture. Try not to utilize this sharp edge for some other sort of material. You will demolish your cutting edge! There's a major admonition with this cutting edge, however. The texture you are going to cut should be clung to a sponsorship material. In the event that you are a sewer, you may comprehend what reinforced texture; yet on the off chance that resembles me and have no related knowledge with textures, let me disclose to you genuine speedy.

Cutting Edges, Black Pen and Scoring Stylus

Fundamentally, the support is a kind of material–like heat and security–that you have to follow–security–to your textures so as to be cut with this sharp edge. Consequently, the name of Bonded Fabric Blade.

Scoring Stylus

The Scoring Stylus is a tool that permits you to make an overlap on your materials. It's ideal for making boxes and card making.

Cricut Pens

The Cricut Pens are stunning, in light of the fact that you can cut and score. However, you can likewise compose on your materials. The Pens permit you to make a progressively customized project.

Print Then Cut

This isn't simply a tool; however, it is an element that permits you to print–on white shading paper–your plans and afterward cut them. This is extraordinary if you are into organizer stickers, designs, card making, and so on.

The Cricut Maker bolsters everything! Look at all of the subtleties, so you can see the capability of this machine. The Cricut Maker permits you to utilize the entirety of the accessible tools and highlights of the Explore, and this is the reason I get increasingly slanted to prescribe the Maker. I know it's increasingly costly; however, you find a workable pace with your machine since gossip has it that there are more tools coming up soon.

Note: The Print Then Cut alternative permits you to print on hued paper!

Blade, Scoring Wheel and Rotary Blade

- Rotating Blade

The Rotary Blade cuts through, essentially, any kind of texture. What's more, the best part is that you needn't bother with any sponsorship material to balance out the texture on the tangle. That by itself ought to get you too cheerful!

This sharp edge likewise accompanies the Cricut Maker (this is a serious deal since you regularly need to purchase these sorts of tools independently or in a pack) and must be utilized with the "Fabric Grip Mat".

- Blade

This cutting edge is the thing that makes the Cricut Maker an absolute making machine. The blade edge is the most grounded of all, and with it, you can cut extremely solid materials, for example, thick calfskin, balsa, and basswood.

The projects you can do with this child are simply stunning. You can make wood signs for your home, boxes, amazingly strong cake toppers, and that's just the beginning.

Fast Swap Tools

Not at all like the remainder of the cutting edges that have an alternate lodging, The Quick-Swap framework permits you to utilize five unique tools (2 sharp edges, and 3 hints).

- Perforation Blade
- Scoring Tip
- Wavy Blade
- Engraving Tip
- Debossing Tip

Something cool, and that I am very appreciative of, is that you can utilize these tools with a similar lodging and that, my companion, rises to reserve funds! We should see, somewhat progressively, pretty much these tools.

The Scoring Wheel is a device that permits you to make lovely, tense, and firm overlap on your resources. To supply you with the finest outcomes, Cricut has structured this tool with two distinct tips, 01 and 02. Contingent upon the resources you hand-picked, Design Space will propose to you the tip that's required.

The Engraving Tip is something that numerous crafters have been hanging tight for! With this tool, you'll have the option to etch a wide assortment of materials.

The Debossing Tip will shove the resource in, and it will make wonderful and point by point structures. The debossing will carry your projects to an unheard-of level due to the detail you would now be able to add to your structures.

With the Wavy Blade as opposed to cutting on straight lines like the turning or fine point edge, this tool will make wavy impacts on your polished products.

The Perforation Blade permits you to do projects with a tear finish. With this tool, another universe of conceivable outcomes has open. You can make coupons, wager tickets, and so forth!

Weight and Color:

The Cricut Explore Air 2 comes in such huge numbers of hues, yet the maker just accompanies three which are Champagne, Blue, and green.

Extra room:

The two machines have great stockpiling for the tools and edges that they are equipped for utilizing. The Maker has much more stockpiling than the Explore. I like this since I am ready to store more treats in it.

Cartridge Slot: B

Before, you could purchase physical Cartridges and associate them with your machine. A Cartridge has a lot of pictures or potentially prepared-to-cut projects; presently, these Cartridges can be purchased inside the product itself, with that goal, that's the reason the Maker doesn't have space for them.

Smart Set Dial:

It permits you to choose from a scope of supplies earlier when you cut. I LOVE this since it has the most well-known materials for you to look over. A few people like to choose them on the product. I PREFER the dial.

Adaptive Tool System:

This framework is the thing that makes the Maker 10X more grounded than any of the Explore Family Machines. This innovation controls the heading and of the cutting edge steadily. Reality be said, this tool is astounding to such an amount that it can change the pressure of the sharp edge to coordinate the materials you are working with!

Docking Station:

The Maker permits you to dock your telephone or iPad over the machine. On the off chance that you plan on utilizing your iPad or Phone, this is a cool component. There's additionally a USB port that permits you to charge your gadget also.

Chapter 7: How To Use Design Space

Purchasing a Cricut is futile if you don't learn exactly how to master Style Room since you will always require this software to cut any kind of job. In my opinion, Cricut Style Room is an exceptional device for newbies, and also if you have no experience with any other Layout programs like Photoshop or Illustrator, you will certainly discover that, although it looks overwhelming, it's quite simple.

Layout Space, it's mainly to touch up your projects and create marginal designs with Forms and Fonts.

If you desire something a lot more innovative, you are most likely to need your own designs or Cricut Accessibility. There's a subscription where you obtain access to their supergiant library. Find out more about it in this write-up and also the guide I create.

When you log into your Cricut Design Area account and also intend to start or modify a new project, you will certainly do every little thing from a window called canvas. The Canvas Location in Cricut Style Space is where you do all of your modifications prior to you cut your tasks.

There are numerous switches, options, and points to do that you might feel shed. Do not worry, I am below along the way, applauding you up and motivating you to keep going. In this publication, you are about to learn what each and every single symbol on the Canvas area is for. To keep every little thing in order as well as easy to understand, we are going to divide the canvas into 4 areas and also 4 colors:

- Top Panel Yellow-- Modifying Area
- Left Panel Blue-- Insert Location
- Right Panel Purple-- Layers Panel
- Canvas Location Green

Pointer: This is not a short message, so I encourage you to get a cup of coffee with some donuts or cookies if possible.

Top Panel Cricut Design Space

The top panel in the Style Space Canvas area is for editing, enhancing, and preparing aspects on the canvas area. From this panel, you can pick what type of font style you'd like to use; you can transform dimensions, straighten styles, as well as other features! This panel is divided into two sub-panels. The very first one permits you to save, name, and finally reduce your jobs. And also, the second one will enable you to regulate and also modify points on the canvas area.

Sub-panel # 1 Name Your Project and Cut it

This sub-panel enables you to navigate from the Canvas to your account, projects, as well as it additionally sends your completed projects to cut.

Toggle Menu

When you click on this button, one more entire menu will move openly. This menu is a useful one. However, it's not part of the Canvas, and that's why I won't be entering into a lot of detail. Primarily, from here you can most likely enter your profile and also transform your photo.

There are various other useful and technological points you can do from this Menu like calibrating your maker, blades; additionally, updating the Firmware-- Software-- of your tool. You can as well manage your memberships from Cricut Accessibility, your account details, and more. I suggest you to click on every web link to make sure that you discover every little thing that Cricut Style Room has for you.

Note: On the settings 'choice', you can transform the visibility as well as measurements of the Canvas; this is explained much better at the end of this article when I describe everything about the canvas area.

My Projects

When you click "My Projects", you will certainly be rerouted to your collection of points you have currently developed; this is excellent because often you may wish to re-cut a previously developed job. So, there's no need for you to recreate the same job over and over.

Save

This option will certainly turn on after you've placed one component on your canvas area. I suggest you save your project as you go. Although the software program is on the cloud, if your browser accidents, there goes your hard work with it!

Maker-Explore (Machine).

Depending upon the sort of maker you have, you will certainly require selecting either the Cricut Maker or the Cricut Explore Machine; this is really crucial because on the Cricut Manufacturer you will discover choices that are only readily available to that specific maker. So, if you have a Maker and you are making with the Explore alternative ON you won't be able to turn on the tools that are for the maker.

Make It.

When you are done posting your files, and also ready to cut click on "Make it"! Your tasks are separated by mats according to the colors of your task. From this home window, you can likewise boost the variety of projects to cut; this is excellent if you are planning on developing greater than one cut.

Subpanel # 2-- Modifying Food selections.

It's incredibly useful, and also it will certainly help you to modify, prepare, and also organize font styles as well as pictures on the Canvas Location.

Undo & Redo.

Occasionally while we work, we make blunders. These little buttons are a great means to correct them. Click Undo when you develop something you do not want such as or make a mistake. Click Redo when you inadvertently remove something you didn't wish to erase or modify. (If only there was something comparable forever itself lol).

Line Type and Fill

This option will inform your equipment what tools, as well as blades you are going to utilize. Bear in mind that relying on the Maker you have actually picked on the top of the home window (Manufacturer or Discover), you will have different choices.

Line type

This alternative will inform your device when you are cutting your job, what device you will certainly be using. Right here and now, here are seven choices (Draw, Cut, Engrave, Wave, Deboss, and Perf). If you take a Cricut Maker, all choices will certainly be readily available, however, if you own an Explore you will solitarily have the Cut, Draw, and the Score choice.

Right at this point is a much more comprehensive description of a piece tool.

Cut

Lest you published a JPEG, otherwise PNG photo to the Canvas. 'Cut' is the defaulting line type that every one of your basics on your canvas will certainly have; this means that when you press 'make it', your maker will certainly cut those designs.

With the Cut choice chosen, you can transform the fill of your components. At the end of the day, this converts in the different shades of materials you will certainly utilize when you cut your jobs.

Draw

If you intend to create on your layouts, you can do it with your Cricut! When you appoint this line type, you will certainly be prompted to choose any one of the Cricut Pens you have (You require detailed pens, unless you have a 3rd event adapter). When you select a specific layout, the layers on your canvas area will certainly be outlined with the shade of the pen you picked.

With this tool, when you click on "Make it"; rather than reducing, your Cricut will certainly create or draw. Keep in mind: This option doesn't tint your styles.

Score

Score is an extra powerful version of the Rating line situated on the left panel. When you appoint this attribute to a layer, every one of the designs will certainly show up scored or rushed. This time, when you click on 'make it', your Cricut won't cut, yet it will score your products. However, keep in mind the wheel just collaborates with the Cricut Manufacturer.

Engrave, Deboss, Wave, as well as Perf

These are the newest tools that Cricut has released for the Cricut Maker, and with them, you will have the ability to create incredible results on various sorts of products. I do not have these tools yet due to the fact that they will certainly be coming out in a number of weeks, once I have them on my hands, I will certainly offer you a quick upgrade.

Fill

The fill option is primarily to be used for printing as well as patterns. It will only be triggered when you have cut as a "line type." Do not fill in forms that will not print anything. Print is by far, one of the best functions Cricut has due to the fact that it enables you to print your styles and then cut them; this is remarkable, and truthfully, it's what motivated me to obtain a Cricut in the first place. When this Load alternative is active, after you click "Make it"; first, you'll send your data to your home printer and afterwards, have your Cricut do all the hefty training. (Cutting) One more excellent choice for the Print Kind is Patterns!!! You individuals, this is so trendy. Usage Cricut's options, or publish your own; you can include a pattern to practically any kind of layer. Let's claim it's Valentine's Day. You can make a stunning card with a currently developed pattern from Cricut Access (Subscription, not totally free), or your own. After all, it prints as well as cut at the same time.

Select All.

When you need to relocate all of your components inside the canvas area, you may have a hard time to select them individually. Click "Select all" to pick all of the elements from the canvas.

Edit

The cut and also copy option will certainly be turned on when you have a choice of several elements from the canvas area. The Paste choice will certainly be made it possible when you duplicate or cut something.

Align

If you have experience with various other visuals style programs, more than likely you'll recognize just how to utilize this food selection. If you aren't aware of the Align Equipment, let me tell you something; the Align Food selection is something that you intend to understand perfection.

Here's what every align feature means:

- Align: This function permits you to align all of your layouts, and also, it's turned on when picking two or more elements.
- Line up Left: When utilizing this setting, all of the aspects will certainly be lined up to the left. The furthest aspect to the left will certainly determine where all of the various other components will certainly move towards.
- Align Right: When using this setting, all of your components will certainly be straightened to the right. The outermost aspect to the right will certainly dictate where all of the various other elements will certainly relocate.

Chapter 8: Design Space Software Secrets And The Design Space App

What Is Cricut Design Space?

Cricut Design Space is a software created by Cricut which permits smooth communication with your machine by telling it what to do.

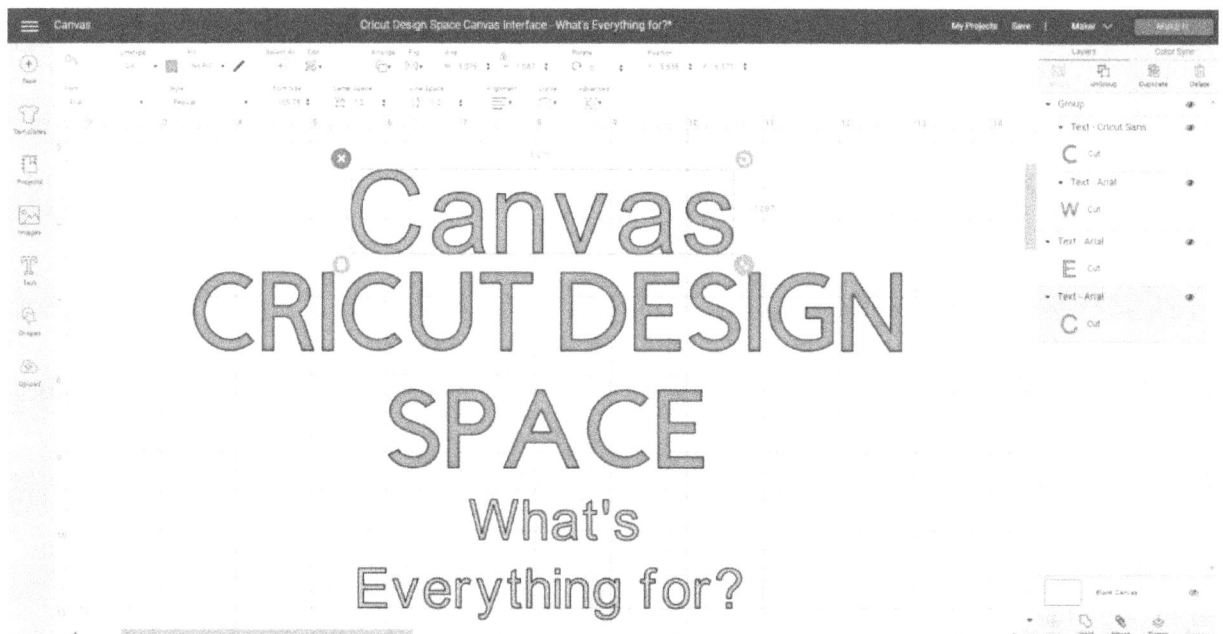

With the software called Cricut Design Space, you can upload your own images and fonts in various file formats (JPG, PNG, SVG, etc.) and control them to match your various designs.

As of January 2020, the design program can only be accessed through the desktop app version. When I downloaded my app, I just clicked the link and was directed to download it. I then followed the on-screen guides to install it on my PC, but you can as well install it through your Mac.

Features of Cricut Design Space

The following are various Design Space features that are available across Design Space platforms: Attach, Bluetooth Connection, Contour, Cut & Write in one Step, Flatten to Print, Writing Style Fonts, Machine Setup, Print then Cut, Slice, and Weld, System Fonts, Offline, Photo Canvas, 3D layer Visualization, Smart Guide, Snapmat, Pattern Fills, Templates, Image Upload, Link to Physical Cartridges, Curve Text, Knife Blade Cutting.

Using Cricut Design Space

Cricut Design Space is an amazing tool in making your <projects idea; at the beginning, the learning may seem very difficult but never you worry as time goes on you will get over them soon. When I started using the Design Space, everything looks new to me not until I sat down last summer; gave more time, patients, and concentration and finally I figured it out. You too can achieve it, if you are really determined to.

About some weeks ago I went to a friend's house only to see a brand-new machine based on my recommendation, but guess what, the challenge he had was how to use the Design Space. All I did was to take him through the basics, as soon as I was done, he was very grateful I came. Right now, he can use the Design Space all by himself. One of the ways of successfully going through the Design Space is to start from the known to the unknown by understanding how things work when you make simple use of predesigned projects.

As we go through the step-by-step guide on using the Design Space, bear in mind that you will start simply by selecting a design that is already created for you in Cricut Design Space.

1. Open your Cricut Design Space on your computer but, as for me, I like using the app.
2. Click on the square showing "Create New Project". You will be taken to the design area where the whole miracle is done.
3. Click on the image of your choice at the bottom of the screen.
4. Click on the square at the top and type in what you would want to make. If what you needed to do is to appreciate those who attended your wedding last weekend. Just type in, "Appreciation Card". You can think of other words and find out for yourself.

5. After you have selected your project, click the "Insert" button at the bottom of the screen.
6. Now your project is in the workspace. Click on the arrow pointing to the right and scroll through to see each mat that you will be using. I always like looking through them and get my paper ready in the manner they will be cut.
7. Then scroll back to the beginning and click on the "Continue" green circle. The Design Space will guide you through, so just follow the instructions as they pop up. Whenever you are working in the design space it will ask you to connect with a nearby device. Don't worry, this is actually okay.
8. The project I chose during my Appreciation Card design uses the scoring stylus. I think you would love that because it will be so helpful.
9. Ensure the style is all in the way. You must click as soon as it is down. Then shut the latch and it's all complete.
10. The flash keys on the machine are next to the press. The essence of the initial one is aimed at loading, while the second starts scoring and cutting. As soon as you are at it, be sure the dial is set on the material you are using.
11. The prompts will continue to pop up following the steps. This will tell you when and how to load and unload.

I enjoy seeing the Machine cut my design. It is so amazing for me every moment. In making my Card, it all took me about half an hour and I had Cards and envelopes ready to send gratitude to all my wedding guests. Now is over to you. You can achieve this! If I did, all you need to do is to start with something simple so you can get used to the design space and its workability.

Tips and Tricks to Make Projects

- Starting New Project:

Generally, there are 2 ways to start a new project which are: from the design tab or from the project tab.

Tip: Ensure your project is saved as you continue working to enable been saved up in the cloud for later use during cutting and design. As soon as your project is saved, it can easily be accessed through a desktop computer, laptop, iPad, or phone.

Let's go all the way to starting a new project from the Design tab.

Step I: You will open the Cricut Design Space app to the Design tab.

Step II: You have to sign in to your Cricut ID by tapping the Account menu. To show that you have successfully signed in, the Account menu sign will showcase a checkmark in it.

Step III: Click on the "New Project" button.

Now let's look at starting a new project from the Project tab.

Step I: You will open the Cricut Design Space app to the Projects tab.

Step II: You have to sign in to your Cricut ID by tapping the Account menu. As soon as you have successfully signed in, the Account menu icon will showcase a checkmark in it.

Step III: You have to tap the project tile labeled "Start a new project from scratch".

- Saving A Project:

Tips: As you continue with your project Design, ensure you save it to be available in "My Projects" on your Desktop computer, iPad, or any other device you are using for future use. Starting a new project on your iPad or PC will prompt you to save or discard it. As soon as you click discard, you will never see it again in your system. However, ongoing projects on your iPad are saved automatically in your iPad. Even if you decide to leave the app suddenly and later return back to it again, it will remain the way you left it. But bear in mind that it is not saved to the cloud unless you push the save button.

Step I: You will open the Cricut Design Space app on the Design tab.

Step II: Tapping the Account menu will prompt you to sign in using your Cricut ID.

Step III: Immediately you are signed in, the Account menu icon will appear with a checkmark in it.

Step IV: Then save the project, the menu should be tapped while you select "to save."

Step V: In the case of the project tab, the saved project will display as a project tile in the project tab.

- Accessing Saved Project:

Tips: You can access your projects via your Mac, PC, or iPad using the Cricut Design Space app. As soon as you tap outside the project preview pane, it will dismiss and you will be returned back to "My Projects". You can bypass the project preview pane by double-tapping on a project tile directly in the Design tab.

Step I: You will open the Cricut Design Space app on the Project tab.

Step II: You will sign in to your Cricut ID by tapping the Account menu.

Step III: Immediately you are signed in, the Account men icon will appear with a checkmark.

Step IV: You will have to select "My Projects", by tapping the Project menu.

Step V: Projects that are saved using the Cricut Design Space app will show you a preview image in the project tile. If you want to continue, tap the project tile.

Step VI: The project preview pane is like this:

Customize: It opens on the design screen for you to make changes to the project.

Date Modified: If there were any Modifications done previously it will display here.

Delete: Once this choice is selected, your project will be completely deleted from the list of Projects saved.

Duplicate: This option enables you to duplicate your project. Meanwhile, your duplicate project will be assigned a fresh name.

Make It Now: opens the project director in the mat preview, to enable you to make your project without any alterations.

Preview: It displays the project as positioned on the design screen.

Price: Discounts on the project price is made based on your images price or your subscription.

Project Name: This has to do with the particular name you wish to give your project.

Project Resources: This represents your larger images in the project on a small scale. If you want to view it on a larger scale, scroll down.

Step VII: Close to the Picture, you will see images that are required to complete your project. Below each image is a display of whether you own it, the image available on subscription, free image, or the price of each.

- Sharing Your Projects:

The very essence of Design Space is to derive inspiration so you can inspire others too, that is why any project I make I love sharing it with the Cricut Community. Below are the steps I took in sharing my Projects.

Tip: Sharing of Project is possible now on Windows/Mac and iOS platforms but not yet ready on Android.

Step I: Sharing a project on Pinterest or Facebook, you have to open a design Cricut website in your browser, preferably Chrome.

Step II: Insert your Cricut ID and password, and then sign in.

Step III: If the login is successful, click on the "View All" link at the top of the 'My Projects' toolbar.

Step IV: Go through your list of already made projects and choose the one you would love to share with the Cricut Community.

Step V: You can now click on the share link at the down part of the tile. Design Space will ask you to add more information.

Step VI: By clicking on Add Details, your project will open in edit mode.

Step VII: For uploading a photo of your project, you should click on the addition button below the photo's header. You will select a photo from your desktop.

Step VIII: In case you wish to turn your image, use the rotate control.

Step IX: You will use the Zoom control to size your image up to a limit of 300% larger than the normal size. You will use your mouse to do navigation.

Step X: Ensure the project toggle is visible to others by moving the toggle to the right.

Step XI: To edit your project name, just change the title of your project so that other users of Cricut will be able to comprehend.

Chapter 9: Best Projects You Can Do With Cricut Maker

Vinyl Decals and Stickers

One of the projects you can carry out with the Cricut Maker is the cutting of vinyl and stickers.

You just have to create your design in Cricut Design Space, instruct the Maker to cut, then weed and transfer the design to whatever surface you choose.

Fabric Cuts

The presence of the Rotary Blade in the Cricut Maker makes it a well-respected machine. The Maker can cut any type of fabric including; chiffon, denim, silk, and even heavy canvas. With this machine, you can definitely cut huge amounts of fabrics without using any backup, and this is because it comes equipped with a fabric cutting mat. Awesome machine!

Sewing Patterns

One major benefit of owning the Cricut Maker machine is the extensive library of sewing patterns that you'll have access to.

The library has hundreds of patterns, including some from Riley Blake Designs and Simplicity; all you need to do is select the pattern you want and the machine will do the cutting.

Balsa Wood Cuts

The Knife Blade coupled with the 4kg force of the machine means that the Cricut Maker can easily cut through thick materials (up to 2.4mm thick).

With these features, thick materials that were off-limits for earlier Cricut Machines are now being done.

Thick Leather Cuts

Just like Balsa wood, the Cricut Maker is also used for thick leather cuts.

Homemade Cards

Paper crafters use the Cricut Maker because the power and precision of the machine make the cutting of cards and paper far quicker and easier. With the machine, homemade cards just got better.

Jigsaw Puzzles

With the Cricut Maker, crafters can make jigsaw puzzles because the Knife Blade cuts through much thicker materials than ever before.

Christmas Tree Ornaments

Cricut machine owners can easily make Christmas tree ornaments. All you have to do is to go through the sewing library for Christmas patterns, use any fabric of your choice to cut out the pattern, and sew them together. Remember the Rotary blade cuts through all sorts of fabric.

Quilts

Thanks to the partnership between Cricut and Riley Blake Designs, Cricut Design Space now has a number of quilting patterns in the sewing pattern gallery.

The Cricut Maker is now used to cut quilting pieces with high precision before they are sewn together.

Felt Dolls and Soft Toys

The "felt doll and clothes" pattern is one of the simplest designs in the sewing pattern library. Thus, it is used for homemade dolls and toys.

The process is easy; just select the pattern you want, cut, and then sew.

T-Shirt Transfers

The Cricut Maker is used for cutting out heat transfer vinyl for crafters to transfer their designs to fabric. To achieve this, you have to make your design in Design Space, load the machine with your heat transfer vinyl, cut the material, and then iron the transfer onto the t-shirt. Alternatively, you can use the Cricut EasyPress to transfer the vinyl.

Baby Clothes

The Cricut Maker cannot cut adult clothing patterns because the mat size is only 12'x24. However, you can easily make baby clothing patterns with the machine.

Doll Clothes

Just like baby clothes, the Cricut Maker can easily make doll clothing patterns because the mat size is big enough.

Fabric Appliques

The bonded fabric blade doesn't come with the Cricut Maker, but if you buy it, you will be able to use your machine to cut complex fabric designs like appliqué. For the bonded fabric blade to cut effectively, there has to be bonded backing on the material.

Calligraphy Signs

The stand out feature of the Cricut Maker is the Adaptive Tool System. With this feature, the machine will remain relevant in the foreseeable future because it fits with all the blades and tools of the explore series, as well as all future blades and tools made by Cricut.

The Calligraphy pen is one of such tools, and it is ideal for signing and card making.

Jewelry Making

For crafters that like to explore jewelry making, the power of the Cricut Maker means that you can cut thicker materials, and while you can't cut things like diamond, silver or gold, you can definitely try to make a beautiful pair of leather earrings.

Wedding Invitations and Save the Dates

Weddings are capital intensive and we all know how the so-called 'little' expenses like STDs and invitation can add up to the huge cost. However, if you have the Cricut Maker machine, then you can make your invitation and STDs yourself.

The Maker is capable of making invitations of the highest quality. It cuts out intricate paper designs and the calligraphy pen is very useful too.

Wedding Menus, Place Cards, and Favor Tags

The Cricut Maker is not restricted to the production of pre-wedding Invitations and STDs. With the machine, you can also produce other items such as place cards, wedding menus, favor tags, etc.

In order to keep the theme front and center, the crafter is advised to use a similar design for all their stationery.

Coloring Book

With the Cricut Maker, you can make 'mindful coloring' books from scratch. To achieve this goal, you need a card, paper, and a beautiful design. Then you command the Cricut Maker to create your personal and completely unique coloring book with the aid of the Fine-Point Pen tool.

Coasters

In the sewing library, there are a number of beautiful coaster patterns and as such, the Maker is used to coasters.

With the Cricut Machine, you can work with materials such as metallic sheets, quit, leather and everything in between.

Fabric Keyrings

The Cricut Maker makes fabric keyrings and the process is simple – It cuts out the pattern and then sews it together. Besides, there are a number of designs for fabric keyrings in the sewing pattern library.

Headbands and Hair Decorations

The Cricut Maker is known to cut through materials like thick leather and this has gone on to inspire the production of intricate headbands and hair decorations. The machine is so inspiring; crafters in the fashion world use it for creative designs and projects.

Cut-Out Christmas Tree

It is a normal tradition for people to buy Christmas trees during the holiday season. However, if you don't have enough space for a big tree in your living room, or maybe you're allergic to pine, then you can definitely create your own Christmas tree.

The production of an interlocking wooden tree is something the Cricut Maker does easily because the blade is capable of cutting through thick materials like wood. With the Cricut Maker, you don't need a laser.

Cake Toppers

When Cricut bought over the Cake cutter machine, the idea was to create shapes made of gum paste, fondant, and others.

It is obvious that the Cricut Maker can't cut as good as the Cake machine; however, it can be used to produce tiny and intricate paper designs that can be used to decorate cakes.

Fridge Magnets

Cricut machines like the Maker and Explore air are capable of cutting out magnetic materials. Thus, crafters can use the Maker to make those fancy magnetic designs placed on refrigerators.

Window Decals

If you're one of those that love to display inspiring quotes on your window or even fancy little patterns on your car, then the Maker got you covered. You just have to load the Maker with window cling and get your design created.

Scrapbooking Embellishments

The Cricut Maker is used for embellishments when scrapbooking. It is public knowledge that Cricut machines are super when it comes to cutting intricate designs. However, the Cricut Maker takes it to a whole new level, and the responsive new blades take away all forms of complexity.

Craft Foam Cuts

In the past, Cricut machines found it difficult to cut craft foam (especially the Explore Machines), however, the Cricut Maker, with the 4kg of force cuts through craft foam very easily.

Boxes and 3D Shapes

The Cricut Machines comes with a Scoring Stylus and this tool can create items with the sharpest edges imaginable.

We all know that the Cricut Maker can execute all kinds of sewing patterns thrown at it. It can also cut paper crafts including 3D shapes and boxes.

Stencils

The Maker comes in handy for people that create things that are used to create other items. The machine is incredible for making stencils, bearing in mind that you can utilize thicker materials to create the stencils.

Temporary Tattoos

If you're one of those people that want to have tattoos, but don't want them permanent for life, then the Cricut Maker is your go-to machine.

With the Cricut Maker, you can etch your design on tattoo paper (mostly coated with transfer film) and use it on your skin.

Washi Tape

Crafters that use Washi tape for scrapbooking can testify to how expensive it can be, especially when buying in bulk from craft stores. However, those that own the Cricut Machine can use it to cut out Washi sheets – they can print and cut their personal designs on it.

Addressed Envelopes

The Cricut Maker is an astounding machine that can save you from spending on certain items. Remember we talked about making handmade wedding invitations; with the Cricut Machine, you can also make envelopes to go with the cards. Another good feature about the machine is that it is equipped with a Calligraphy pen and a Fine-point pen, meaning that it is capable of addressing your envelopes automatically. All you need to do is to make sure that the words are clear enough for the postman to read.

Glassware Decals

With a Cricut Maker, you can cut vinyl to make glassware designs. People that host themed parties will love this one; e.g. if you're hosting a summer house party and you're serving mojitos, then you can decorate your drinking glasses with coconuts and palm tree decals. Also, people holding Xmas parties can design and cut themed stickers to use on their cups.

Decorations

There are a couple of other desktop craft machines that are used to create general household decorations, but the Cricut Maker is one of the best – If not the very best.

With the Cricut Maker, you'll be empowered to create 3D wall hangings, beautiful cut-outs in the living room and even things like signage in your closets, etc.

Cushion Transfers

With your Cricut Maker, you can brighten up your cushion and pillows by adding your homemade designs. With the flocked iron-on vinyl, you can create a lovely textured cushion by using heat transfer vinyl on the Cricut Machine.

3D Bouquet

The machine takes us back to the wedding theme once more.

Remember, with intuitive tools like the scoring stylus and the Fine-Point, the Cricut Maker is superbly equipped to carry out intricate papercrafts. Thus, you can introduce a touch of homemade crafts to your wedding, or even create flowers to design your home, knowing that you don't have to water them.

With the Cricut Maker, you can have yourself a lovely, beautiful and immortal bouquet.

Chapter 10: Best Projects You Can Do With Explore Air 2

Cutting Letters and Shapes for Scrapbooking

Shapes are one of the most vital features in Cricut Design Space. They are used for creating some of the best designs. In this tutorial, you will learn how to cut letters or texts, how to add shapes and how to adjust the size, colors and rotate shapes.

To add a shape;

1. Log into your Design Space.
2. From the drop-down menu, click "Canvas". You will be taken to the canvas or work area.
3. Click "Shapes" on the left panel of the canvas.
4. A window will pop-up with all the shapes available in Cricut Design Space.
5. Click to add shape.

We have explained the process of adding a shape. Now, to cut a shape;

1. Click "Line type". Line type lets your machine know whether you plan on cutting, drawing or scoring a shape.
2. Select "Cut" as Line type and proceed with cutting the shape.

Cutting Letters

1. First of all, you need to add the text you want to cut. Click "Add Text" on the left panel of the canvas.

2. Place text in the area where you want to cut it. Highlight the text and click on the slice tool. If you have multiple lines of texts, weld them and create a single layer. Then, use the slice tool.
3. Move the sliced letters from the circle and delete the ones you don't need.

How to Make Simple Handmade Cards

If you want to test your crafting skills, the Cricut Explore Air 2 has made it possible for you to be creative with designing whatever you want to create on the Design Space. We will be teaching you how to use your Cricut Explore Air 2 to make simple cards.

1. Log into Design Space with your details. Do this on your Mac/Windows PC.
2. On the left-hand side of the screen, select "Shapes". Add the square shape.
3. By default, there is no rectangular shape, so you have to make do with the square shape. However, you can adjust the length and width. You can change the shape by clicking on the padlock icon at the bottom left of the screen. Change the size and click on the padlock icon to relock it.
4. Click "Score Line" and align.
5. Create your first line. It's advisable you make it long. Use the "zoom in" option for better seeing if you are having difficulties with sight.
6. Select the first line you have created and duplicate. It's easier that way than creating another long line. You will see the duplicate option when you right-click on your first line.
7. Follow the same duplication process and create a third line.
8. Rotate the third line to the bottom so that it connects the other two parallel lines you earlier created. Remember to zoom in to actually confirm the lines are touching.
9. Duplicate another line, just like you did the other. Rotate it to the top so that it touches the two vertical parallel lines. You should have created a big rectangular shape.
10. Highlight your rectangular shape (card). Select "Group" at the upper right corner.

11. Now, change the "Score" option "cut". You can do this by clicking on the little pen icon.
12. Your lines will change from dotted to thick straight lines.
13. Select the "Attach" option at the bottom right-hand side of the screen. The four lines will be attached and will get the card ready to be cut on the mat correctly.
14. You can adjust the size of the card as you like. At this point, you can add images or texts; beautify your card anyhow you want it.
15. After you are done, select the "Make it" button and then "Continue" to cut your card out.

If you don't know how to create a style on your cards with shapes, follow these simple steps to create one.

1. Select your choice of shape. Let's choose stars for example. Select the "Shape" option and click on the star.
2. Add two stars.
3. Select the first star and click "Flip" and then select "Flip Vertical".
4. Align both stars to overlap them at the center.
5. Select "Weld" to make a new shape and add a scoreline.
6. Align them at the center and attach them.
7. Select the "Make it" button and then "Continue" to cut your card out.

If you don't know how to add text or write on a card, follow the processes below.

1. Select your choice of shape. Let's choose a hexagon for example. Select the "Shape" option and click on the hexagon shape.
2. Use your favorite pattern.
3. Add a scoring line and rotate it.
4. Click "Add Text". A box will appear on the canvas or work area of your project. Write your desired text. Let's say you choose to write "A Star Is Born Strong" and "And Rugged" on the two hexagonal shapes. Choose the fonts and style of writing.
5. Select the first text and flip vertically or horizontally.

6. Select the second text and flip vertically. Click, "Flip" and select flip vertically. Doing this will make the text not look upside down.
7. Select the "Make it" button and then "Continue" to cut your card out. Follow the cutting process on the screen to full effect.

How to Make a Simple T-Shirt?

You can use your Cricut Explore Air 2 to make nice T-shirt designs and it's quite easy to do. Cricut cuts out an iron-on vinyl design in an easy and simple way. I will teach you how to make a simple t-shirt with the Cricut Explore Air 2.

In this tutorial, we will be using iron-on vinyl. Iron-on vinyl is a type of vinyl, like an adhesive that will stick to any fabric when applied using an iron.

1. Log into your Design Space.
2. Select "New Project" and then, click on "Templates" in the top left corner. Choosing a template makes it easier to visualize your design to know how good or bad it will be on your T-shirt.
3. Choose "Classic T-Shirt" and pick your preferred style, size, and color.
4. You will see tons of beautiful designs for iron-on T-shirts. Browse through the images before you make your choice.
5. Remember, if your preferred design isn't available, you can upload your pictures to the Cricut Design Space. We have created a tutorial on how to upload your own images to Cricut Design Space.
6. After you have selected the image, resize the image to fit the T-shirt. You can do this by clicking the resize handle in the bottom part of your design and dragging the mouse to enlarge or reduce.
7. When you are done, click the "Make it" button in the top right corner. You will be told to connect your Cricut machine.
8. Toggle the green "Mirror" button on. Toggling it on will make sure your design is not cut backward.

9. Face the shiny part of your vinyl design down on your cutting mat. Remember to move the smart set dial to the iron-on option.
10. Remove all the vinyl designs you don't want to be transferred to your project when it's ironed. Use your weeding tool to remove those little bits that will jeopardize your beautiful design. This process is called weeding.
11. Transfer your design to your T-shirt when you are done weeding. You can either use an iron or an EasyPress. Preheat your EasyPress before use.

How to Make a Leather Bracelet

The Cricut Explore Air 2 can be pretty amazing in doing a variety of things. One of those things is being able to make a leather bracelet with your Cricut. You can make pretty cool designs that you can turn into wearable pieces of jewelry.

To make a leather bracelet, you need your Cricut Explore Air 2, a deep point blade, faux leather, marker, ruler, craft knife, bracelet cut file, transfer tape, and a grip mat. You will also need glue, an EasyPress or iron and an SVG design to crown it up.

Follow these steps to create your leather bracelets.

1. Log into your Design Space account menu.
2. Select "Canvas".
3. Upload an art set from Jen Goode into the Design Space. The Jen Goode is a set of designs with 4 different image layouts.
4. Ungroup the designs and hide the layers you don't require after selecting your design.
5. Create a base cut of the shape you want to use. Use a cut file and create the shape you want. For example, you can use a shape tool to create a circular design.
6. Add circle cutouts with basic shapes. Duplicate the layer so that you will use it for the back of the bracelet.
7. Set your iron or EasyPress ready and apply the vinyl to the uppermost layer of your leather.
8. Spread a thin coat of glue on the back of the duplicated layer and press it with the other layer together.

9. Add your bracelet strap or chain together with some other ornaments.
10. Congratulations! You have just made your first leather bracelet.

Making a Stencil for Painting with the Cricut Explore Air 2

To make a stencil, you can either use the ready-made designs or make your own design. This tutorial will be based on how to create a stencil for painting.

1. Log in to your Design Space.
2. Click "Canvas" from the drop-down menu.
3. Click "Add Text".
4. Highlight text and change to your preferred font.
5. All your letters must be separated. If they aren't, click the ungroup button to separate. The letters must overlap. This will allow you to drag each letter as you please.
6. Arrange your text line as you want it. If you notice each letter is still showing individually, highlight the text box and click "Weld" at the bottom right of the panel.
7. Click "Attach". Make sure the text is highlighted. This will make the letters arranged properly when it goes to the cut mat.
8. Your stencil design is ready!

Making a Vinyl Sticker

First of all, you need to have an idea of the vinyl sticker that you want. Get ideas online or from forums. Once you have gotten the picture, make a sketch of it to see how the sticker would look. After you have done this, follow the steps below;

1. Use an image editing software like Photoshop or Illustrator. Design to your taste and save. Make sure you know the folder it is saved too.
2. Now, open your Design Space.
3. Click "New Project".
4. Scroll to the bottom left-hand side and click "Upload".
5. Drag and drop the design you created with your photo editing app.
6. Select your image type. If you want to keep your design simple, select simple.

7. Select which area of the image is not part of it.
8. Before you forge ahead, select the image as cut to have a preview. You can go back if there is a need for adjustments.
9. Select "Cut".
10. Weed excess vinyl.
11. Use a transfer tape on top of the vinyl. This will make the vinyl stay in position.
12. Go over the tape and ensure all the bibles are nowhere to be found.
13. Peel away the transfer tape and you have your vinyl sticker.

Chapter 11: Tips And Tricks To Make Cricut Machines Easier And Efficient

There are a lot of things which you can achieve by making the correct use of your machine. However, it is not just enough to know these; you need to know easier and more improved ways to make use of the machine you have acquired. To make the most out of your newly-acquired machine, here are a few things you should do.

Test Out Your Machine First

This is a no-brainer, and you should do it as soon as the machine arrives. It is always a safe idea to start by testing out the components of your machine and double-checking to ensure that your machine has all the accessories that were promised. If at this stage, you discover that your machine is missing a few things, you may want to reach out to membership support immediately and get the issues rectified.

Keep the Components of Your Machine (Especially the Cutting Mat) Clean

This is one of the parts of the machine that is constantly subjected to wear, tear, attack by dirt, and spoiling. In order to make sure that your machine remains in the best of conditions, take out time to clean your mat frequently. Best practices when you are trying to get this done is to make use of a lint roller to wipe down the mat after every use and to also scan over the mat once you are done with it to make sure that you take out all the little pieces that may remain from the materials you just cut. Also, be sure to frequently replace the plastic protective sheet that came with the mat, and it is not entirely unheard of for you to wash the mat frequently too. However, washing the mat can be a tricky business. Considering the fact that the mat is meant to be in a specific way, you need to make sure that you wash it in such a way that you do not compromise the integrity of the material the mat is made of. For best practices, wash with lukewarm water and mild dish soap. With these, scrub gently in circular patterns, rinse and allow the mat to drip dry.

Cutting Certain Materials Require for Your Mat to Be A Bit Sticky

So that it can hold the material you are looking to cut in place. Due to some factors like prolonged use, and continuous subjection to heavy work, there may be times that you would need to cut something that requires that the mat has a firm grip on the material, but you may not have access to a good mat that has not lost its stickiness at that time. As a way around this, you can resort to using masking tape or painter's tape to hold the material you are looking to cut in place. However, take this as a cue to change mats because this option won't work forever.

Pattern on Storing Blades

In order to prevent the confusion that can come as a result of having to deal with many blades that you will need for your different projects, it can be safe to adopt the pattern of storing up your blades in such a way that you can tell almost instantly what blade is used to cut what material. In essence, it is vital for you to learn to separate your blades. Let there be blades that you use to cut vinyl, then the ones you use to cut paper, and wood, and all the rest of them. This will ensure that your blades last for much longer and that you don't use the wrong blades for the wrong projects, thereby creating trouble for your new machine. You can get started by finding small jars to hold the blades, and then labeling each jar to signify which blades go into it. This way, you do not run the risk of making a mistake with your blade placement.

Color of Vinyl

You do not always have to have the right color of vinyl for you to embark upon your projects. Let's assume that you are about to get started with a project and you need some green vinyl, but all you have is pink-colored vinyl, you must not get dressed and go off to the mall to get the green-colored ones because there is a way around it. Instead of running off to the mall every time you need a different color of vinyl, why not get some Rust-Oleum Metallic Spray paint for the future. With this, you can give your un-cut vinyl some spraying and color-over without having to spend money every time. Just for a few bucks, you can get this over with.

Recommendable Websites

Dafont and **1001freefonts** are amazing websites where you can find tons of fonts that you can make use of to create even more epic designs. If you have searched through the design space and you have not been able to see something that piques your interests, or you just need to try out something new, you may want to visit those platforms and see what they have in store for you. Also, you will find a lot of support groups on Facebook where you can find a lot of helpful information in regards to your creative journey with the machine you have just acquired. Join these groups, and be sure to be an active member of them. You will see that there are some things that may bother you that can be a walkover for another person; all you need to do is reach out. Furthermore, these platforms serve as hosting sites for a ton of helpful tools that can even unclog your creativity even more. Find them as pinned documents, helpful DIY tips, post and comment threads, and in all other formats as they come. The goal is to make sure that you do not try to do this on your own.

Stenciling Tips

Want to do some stenciling, but you are not sure where and how you can get started?

There's no need for you to be confused when you can make use of freezer paper to create custom stencils for your projects. With the Cricut Explore Air 2, you can get to cut the paper and fashion it into some custom-design stencils for your projects.

Make Use of Tin Foils to Sharpen Your Blades.

Notwithstanding how careful you are with the blades, and how you do not mistake them for cutting different materials, it is not possible for your blades not to get to a point where they become blunt and weak. When your blades get blunt, a great way to get them up and running once again is by making use of tin foils to sharpen them. By sharpening with tin foil, you can extend the life of your blade, almost by x3. Sharpening is very simple, all you need to do is to unclamp the blade and run the tip of the blade through the tin foil between 10-15 times.

Using Pens Other Than the Cricut Pens to Write

Next to the Cricut pens, there are a ton of other brands that you can make use of, even with your machine. They include:

- Uni-ball Signo UM-153.
- Tombow Dual brush pens.
- Sakura gelly roll.
- Bic marking and Bic crystal.
- Pilot Precise.

The list is basically endless. The best part is that for all these pens, you can find them online, and with just a few dollars, you can have them added to your bucket list of pens to work with. However, to make use of these pens with your machine, you need a pen adapter. Pen adapters work for the Explore Air 2 or newer models of the Cricut machine. With these, you can connect any brand of Cricut pens and draw/write away.

Increase Your Image Options by Learning How to Make Your Own SVG Files Online.

While the design space and the internet provide you with endless numbers of images, you will agree that there are those times when even the most intricately designed picture does not quite cut it; it does not do justice to what you want to create. Under these circumstances, you need to learn how to bring your inner genius to life.

Using Inkscape, you can create your own SVG files from scratch or convert your boring pictures to two-layered SVG files. Inkscape is a free tool that you can make use of, and making use of it is relatively easy.

Chapter 12: Best Software To Use With Cricut And Create Super Design Templates

Design Space

Design Space is for any Explore machine with a high-speed, broadband Internet connection that is connected to a computer or an iOS device. This more advanced software allows full creative control for users with Cricut machines.

Craft Room

Some machines, such as the Explore and Explore Air, cannot use Craft Room, but many other models can. Craft Room users also have access to a free digital cartridge, which offers images that all Cricut machines can cut.

Moving on to Creating Your Project Template

On the home page, select "New Project", which will be followed by a page with a blank canvas that looks like the grid on your Cricut mats. To any artist, the words "empty canvas" is a nightmare in themselves so please just bear with me since we will fill that bad boy up in a second. But first, let's go through the menu options.

New, Templates, Projects, Images, Text, Shapes, and Upload; these are the things that you will see on your left-hand side when you have the canvas open on the screen.

- New

New means that you will start a new project and clicking the tab will redirect you to a blank canvas. Be sure to save all changes on your current project before you go to the new canvas. Otherwise, you will lose all of the progress you have already made on that design.

- Templates

Clicking on Templates will allow you to set a template to help you visualize and work with sizing. It is very handy for someone who is not familiar with Cricut Design Space and doesn't know what sizes to set. If you are cutting out wearable items on fabric, you can change the size of the template to fit whoever will be wearing it. I'm sure you can agree that this feature is especially beneficial for the seamstresses out there.

- Projects

Projects, meanwhile, will lead you to the ready-to-make projects so that you can start cutting right away. Some of the projects are not customizable, but others are when you open the template, which is pretty cool. Many of these are not free either, which irks me to a new extent. You can choose the "Free for Cricut (whatever machine you have)", and the projects that will turn up won't have to be paid for.

- Images

Images are where you can search for thousands of photos to use for the craft. Those images with the green flag with the "A" on them are the ones that come only with Cricut Access so be aware if you do not have it. It is sort of like a Pinterest image search engine with a lot of pictures in its database.

- Text

The Text basically goes without saying. When you select this option, you can type whatever you want and scale it onto your canvas. You may select any font saved in your computer too; that's why collecting those has never been more useful! There is also an option called "multi-layered font", which gives your text a shadow layer. If you are cutting out the letters and shadow layers, the Cricut will do them separately and combine the two later if you wish to. It can create very cool effects so make sure you try that option out. Furthermore, remember that when you are being paid to do a job, the font you are using might require a license to use.

- Shapes

Shapes lets you add basic forms to your canvas, which you can tweak to fit your own needs. The shapes include circle, square, rectangle, triangle, etc.

- Upload

When you click the Upload tab, you can upload your own images and transform them into cuttable pieces. This, along with the text, is the only reason why I still use Design Space. It is really awesome to be able to use this feature.

Cricut Basic

This is a program or software designed to help the new user get an easy start on designing new crafts and DIY projects. This system will help you with the image-selection for cutting in the least amount of time spent on the design stages. You can locate your image, pre-set projector font, and immediately print, cut, score, and align with tools that are found within the program. You can use this program on the iOS 7.1.2 or later systems as well as iPad and several of the iPhones, from the Mini to the 5th generation iPod touch. Since it is also a cloud-based service, you are able to start on one device and finish from another.

Sure, Cuts a Lot

This is another third-party software that has a funny name that gives you the ability to take control of your designs without some of the limitations that can happen when using cartridges used within the Cricut Design Studio. You will need to install an update to your software to use this program; you can download it for free. It allows for the use of TrueType and OpenType font formats as well as simple drawing and editing tools. You can import any file format and then convert it to the one that you need. There is an option for blackout and shadow.

Cricut Design Studio

This program allows you to connect with your software and provides you with much more functionality as far as shapes and fonts are concerned. There are various options for tools that provide you resources for designing more creative images. You will be able to flip, rotate, weld, or slant the images and fonts. However, you will still be limited in the amounts or types of fonts that you can use based on the ones on the cartridges. There is a higher level of software features that allow for customization.

Cricut Sync

This is a program designed for updating the Cricut Expression 2 as well as the Imagine machine and the Gypsy device. You just connect your system to the computer and run the synced program for an installation of updates on the features that come with your machine. This is also used to troubleshoot any issues that could arise from the hardware.

Play Around and Practice

You can combine your shapes and images, add some text, and create patterns. The possibilities are endless. The best thing to do is familiarize yourself with the software before you attempt on cutting expensive materials. Start small and cheap - printer paper will be an ideal choice - and cut away. See what works well for you and stick with it. There are many options concerning the Cricut Design Space, and the only way to learn all of this is to experiment and click on every tab you see and try different combinations and options when playing around on the software.

Make the Cut

This is a third-party program that works with the Cricut design software. It offers a straightforward look at the design features that Cricut has. This system can convert a raster image into a vector so that you can cut it. There is also a great way to do lattice tools. It uses many file formats and TrueType fonts. There are advanced tools for editing and an interface that is easy to learn and use. This system works with Craft ROBO, Gazelle, Silhouette, Wishblade, and others. It allows you to import any file from a TTF, OTF, PDF, GSD, and so on and convert them to JPG, SVG, PDF, and so on. It is flexible and user-friendly.

Conclusion

If you are a craft blogger, then this machine was built for people like you in mind. Purchasing the Cricut depends entirely on your needs and how often you make crafts. If you love to craft, make personalized projects, you do plenty of scrapbooking—then this machine will save time and money for you in the long run.

How often you use the Cricut will also determine whether this machine is worth the price. Would you use it once every three months? Would you only use it when Christmas is around the corner, and you want to make personalized gifts? Would you use it every week? Do you want to make labels and stickers for your business? Do you want to have a machine that helps you create signage for your events or catering business?

All the answers to these questions will determine if the Cricut is indeed worth its money. One of the ways to use the machine as many times as possible is to consider turning your crafting hobby into a side income.

Focusing on online-selling requires a higher technical knowledge base; yet, as I can confirm, you don't need to be a programmer to make it work. You can generate income with vinyl online by offering top-quality personalized jobs, ending up being a details Centre, or supplying bulk offerings. Again, it's not advisable to try to do it all.

Your time is ideal invested working in among these three alternatives to begin. So, if you decide to give a custom job, don't additionally attempt to become an info hub at the same time. After developing your initial footing, and obtaining profitable sales, you can intend on how to use that cash to turn into the other classifications.

Personalized Job-- This is just how I obtained my beginning. For the best individual, I truly believe this is a fantastic means to kick off your Silhouette or Cricut vinyl business.

Progressively, individuals are resorting to a Google search to find a custom-made job. With existing markets or your website, you can end up being the one they rely on.

Examples:

Existing web sites that permit you to offer custom-made design solutions.

- Etsy
- Amazon Personalized
- Amazon Handmade is the most widely known.

Various other options consist of:

- Artfire
- DaWanda
- Gold Mine
- Depop
- Tictail.

One more option is to release your very own website. A fantastic instance of this can be seen with "A Wonderful Impression". They released an inspirational wall decal website, along with a custom-made layout solution. You can get any kind of sticker, in any type of dimension you desire from them.

If you sell on an existing system, the startup costs are more reduced. The minute you launch, you're competing in the worldwide marketplace. You have access to countless prospective clients.

Additionally, distinct designs will certainly permit you to bill a premium price. However, on the internet, custom costs tend to be lower than the very same work done locally. It's a chance to polish up and increase your design capability as well.

CRICUT DESIGN SPACE

Introduction

Like many machines that are being placed on the shelves, Cricut also comes with its unique software filled with different settings and features to toggle with. All these components ensure that by using this instrument, it ends up with a beautiful, customized, and accurate product. Cricut's proprietary software is called "Cricut Design Space" and all Cricut devices come with this software, whether it's Cricut mini or Cricut Explore Air. Every Cricut owner must have this software installed on their device and ready to use at any moment. The Cricut must be directly connected to the device via cable or by Bluetooth. Either way, the device needs to be close to the machine. The software is free and has a good user interface that makes it clear and easy to work with, even if you don't have any prior experience with working with a similar device. Its user-friendly feature encourages creativity in an individual. The program is based on Cloud, so even if your device is destroyed or has become inaccessible for any reason, the different design files can be safely recovered. It can be opened onto almost every device, and available at any moment. A laptop, tablet, or mobile can be used as well, and starting a project on one device and switching in between to another is possible. It can even be accessed offline. After the program has been installed, you need to create the designs from the beginning or use any one of thousands of templates already stored in its library. Design Space has a large, diverse collection to push a freshman to start constructing and inventing. One can play around with a variety of fonts, images, and new inspiring ideas. For optimum usage, a Cricut Explorer connected to a computer will be sufficient. This way, all of the features are available, and the machine works without lag.

What can I do with it?

Crafting is a hobby that knows no borders, pretty much any shape or design is achieved through this marvelous machine opening to endless uses. For any material needed to be cut, engraved, or etched this machine will fulfill that need. The only boundary would be the lack of one's imagination or capability. From making a few mundane everyday accessories to creating parts for cars, this piece of technology will do the job without fault. Some ideas to use it are as follows:

- For a beginner, it is recommended that they should start working on less complicated projects such as paper crafting. Many people have made a scrapbook in High School, which may or may not be up to the mark, but with this new machine, you can create any papercraft project not only easily but also competently.

- You can use it to make paper pennants to use in a party, or to use it as an accessory to bring to local games and show your support to your team. You can design and shape the flag themselves to give it a hint of uniqueness.

- Cricut can also be used to make greeting cards. Sending your loved ones, a unique and customized card will not only separate you from the crowd but show them that they are special to you. Making greeting cards is very easy even for a beginner by using Cricut.

- The design and uses are not only limited to paper, but you can also make a leather bracelet by using different features in the software provided. Even thick materials and complicated structures cannot hold the Cricut machine back.

- You can make iron-on vinyl T-shirts. Customize T-shirts are usually expensive to order, but you can make them through Cricut easily.

- It can also be used to make new utensils such as customize jars, mugs, plates, etc. You can even make a doormat using this device.

- It can also be used to make home decorations. On holidays you can simply sit at home rather than go out shopping for different decorating items.

- You can make your customized pillows blankets and bed sheets.

- It can also be used for making models of things such as an airplane.

- You can even design beautiful and artful pieces of jewelry.

- Some people use it to make different parts for their cars, motorcycles, etc. if they can't find the right parts anywhere else.

- It can also be used to make banners and signs to attract customers.

The History of Design Space

The first Cricut machine was called the Cricut Personal and was quite a clunky machine. It was heavy, and yet it was smaller than the latest models with a limited cutting space of only 5.5" x 11". It also did not need a computer connected to it to cut, instead, it used cartridges with preloaded images and designs.

The Cricut Personal had a little screen and a lot of buttons. The Cricut Expression 1 was one of the first Cricut cutting machines that could be used both, stand-alone or attached to a computer. It was also the first Cricut machine to have a 12" x 24" cutting ability.

This machine worked with the first version of Cricut software, the predecessor of Design Space, which was known as Cricut Craft Room. As the machines developed so did the Cricut software, with the latest cloud-based system inline according to the newer online trends.

The Cricut Mini was one of the first Cricut cutting machines to rely on a computer to make designs. Up until the introduction of this little crafting machine, the large Cricut cutting machines could use both stand-alone cartridges and Cricut Craft Room. By this time, there was also the Cricut Image Library where Cricut users could download images.

With the launch of the Cricut Explore machine models came Design Space, which eventually took over the roles of both the Cricut Craft Room and Cricut Image Library. The official shutdown of the Cricut Craft Room and Cricut Design Library was announced in 2018.

Since 2018, Cricut Design Space has been greatly improved upon. It is easy to use, and users can upload their images as well as designs. The software is still compatible with the Cricut Cartridges, and Cricut has rolled out a USB cartridge plug for use with machines that no longer have the cartridge slot.

Chapter 1: The Platform Design Space: Getting Started

Setting up your machine could look somehow complicated or tedious. However, this chapter is majorly written to guide you through it, the unboxing process, and the setting up. So, relax and bring that Cricut machine out wherever you've stashed it. It takes approximately 1 hour to finish setting up a Cricut machine. With this guide, you should be done in less than an hour. Let's get right on it, shall we?

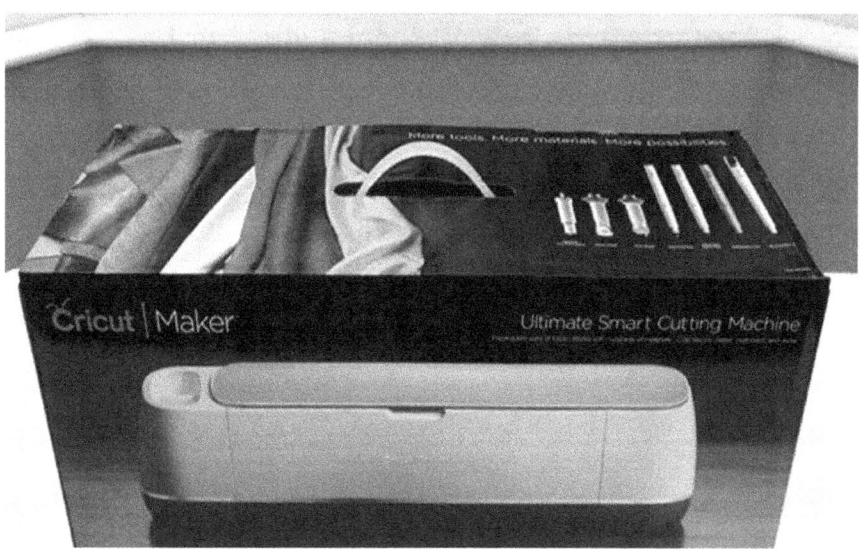

Step 1: Opening the box

To make sure that we are together all the way through, we will go through even the most trivial step; opening the box.

You should have several boxes right now in front of you if you went for the whole Cricut bundle. And there should be a big box among those boxes which contains the Cricut machine itself. If you open that big box, the first thing you should find is a Welcome packet; most of the tools will be in that packet. You should find a welcome manuscript, rotary blade and cover, a USB cable, a fine-point pen, and a packet that contains your first die-cutting project. The USB cable is sometimes the last thing you'll see in this packet, it's probably hidden under every other stuff. Underneath this welcome packet is your Cricut machine.

To find the power cable, you first need to bring out the machine from its box. You will then discover the power cable underneath the box with two cutting mats of standard sizes. That looked easy, right? Let's proceed to the following step.

Step 2: Unwrapping your Cricut machine and supplies

We are getting to the exciting part. Let's unwrap your machine and find out what's inside.

When trying to unwrap your machine, you'll find it covered in a protective wrapper that looks filmy and also with a cellophane layer. Try to carefully unwrap the top foam layer so you can see the machine clearly. After that, go on to remove the remaining part of the Styrofoam that protects the inner machine housing.

When you unbox the whole casing, you should expect to find the following tools:

1. Cricut Machine.

2. USB and Power Cables.

3. Rotatory blade with housing.

4. Fine point blade with housing.

5. Fine point pen.

6. Light-Grip and Fabric-Grip Mats (12 x 12).

Step 3: Setting up your machine

Finally, we can move on to getting your machine up and running. Most of what you'll be doing will be technically inclined. You basically need electricity, a mobile phone or computer with internet access. Once you have access to all these, plug your power cord into an electronic outlet, and then switch on your machine.

I'll assume your Cricut machine has Bluetooth function. If it does not have this function, either make use of the USB cable to connect your computer and the Cricut machine or purchase a Bluetooth adapter as soon as you can.

Once they are all connected, open your computer browser to continue the setup. Visit the Cricut Sign-in Page and click on the Sign-in icon. You will have to either sign in with your account details or create a new account for yourself if you don't already have one. This is necessary to access the Cricut Design Space.

If you do not have an active account yet, don't bother to fill in any information on the sign-in fields. Click on the Create Cricut ID in the green box, fill out every field with the required information, and then click on Submit.

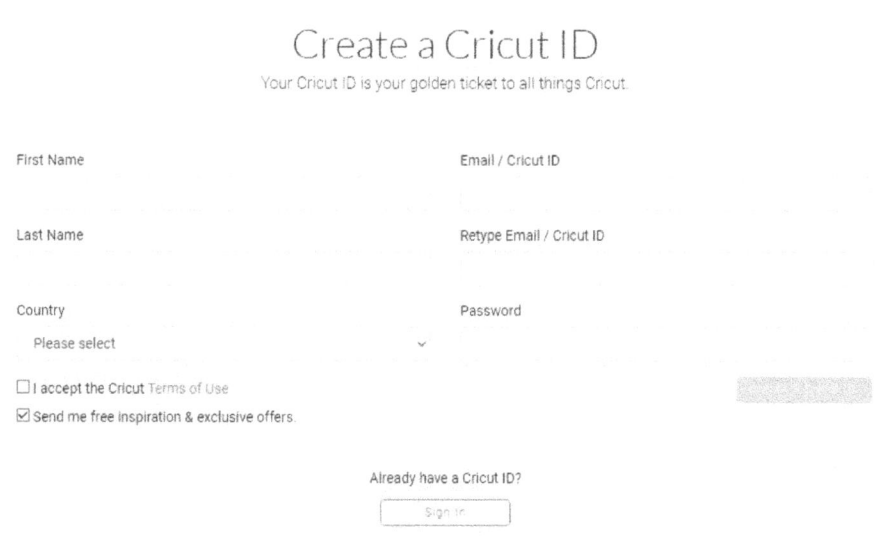

Now, it's time to link your machine to your account. It takes some people a lot of time to finish this part successfully. To make it easier, follow the procedures below:

1. After signing in, go to the upper left corner of the page and click on the drop-down menu icon (with three lines) beside Home.

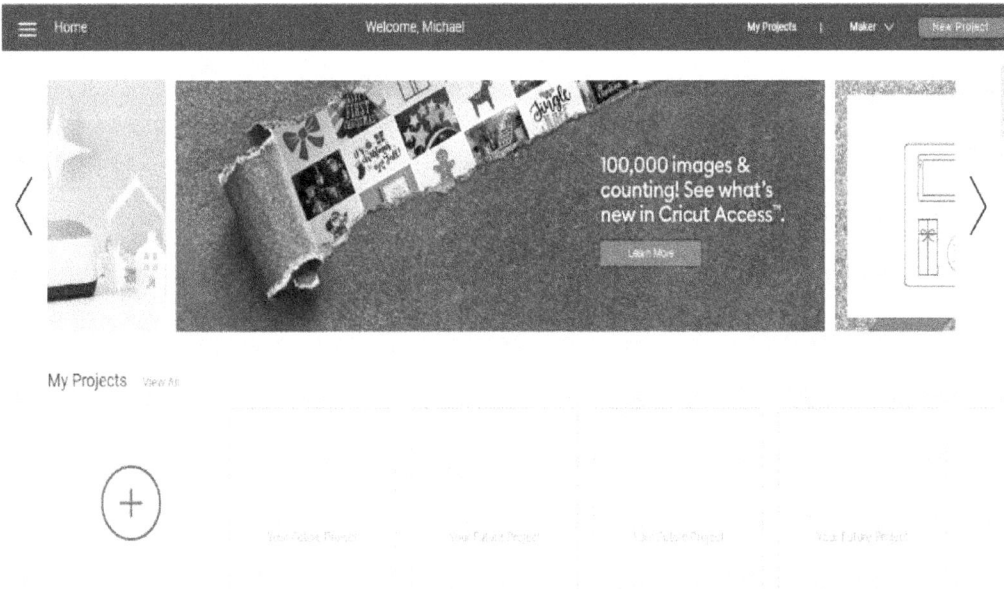

2. When the drop-down menu appears, select the New Machine Setup.

3. On the following screen that pops up, click on your Cricut machine model.

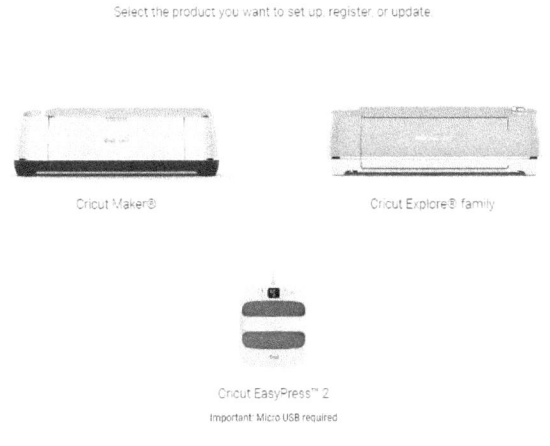

4. Another webpage will appear with instructions on how to connect your machine. Follow the instructions accordingly.

When you follow the instructions, it automatically detects your machine and prompts you to download and install the software.

The site is user-friendly, so you'll be directed on how to go about the installation. And if you already have an account, you may still need to download it again. Cricut updates their design space often, there could be some new tools in the latest version that you don't have access to. It only takes about five minutes to get the installation done.

And there we go; we have concluded the setup procedure on your PC. That wasn't too hard, was it?

You might find the software a little bit complex for you when you first start to explore it. But with constant usage, you'll master it.

Step 4: Claiming your bonus

When you have successfully created an active account on Cricut, you can claim access to Cricut for a whole month for free! It's a welcome bonus from Cricut. You'll have access to different projects, fonts, as well as Cut files. You can exploit this opportunity by making use of the accessible library to work on several fun projects.

Step 5: Commencing your first project

You may want to start practicing with some old projects done by other people or study how they are done before initiate a personal project. Every Cricut machine comes with a trivial project. You'll find it in the welcome pack. You can use this to get familiar with the tools the machine came with.

It may be challenging to make use of the Cricut Design Space without fully knowing its environment. So, stick with small projects till you get better, or ask someone who has more knowledge and experience with Cricut tools to guide you through.

Chapter 2: Tools And Functions

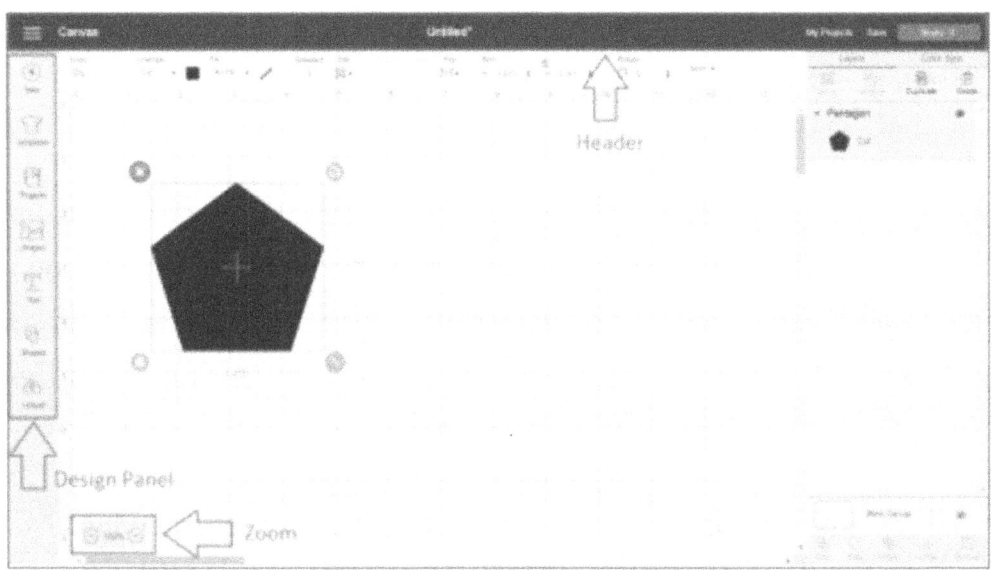

Design Panel

- **New**: To start building a new project you must always click on the 'New' tab.

- **Templates:** To view your final design in the real-life background, you can use any of the relevant templates by clicking on the Template tab.

- **Projects:** To search, select, and cut designs from an already existing project, you can use the Projects tab, which will contain a variety of other projects along with your projects.

- **Images:** The Cricut Image Library contains a wide variety of pictures available at your fingertips for free and to buy. The Images tab will also contain any image that you may upload. So, you can click on the images icon to search, select, and insert any desired image into the Canvas.

- **Text:** You can use the Text tab to add desired phrases or words directly to the Canvas.

- **Shape**: You can use the Shape tab to insert simple shapes square, rectangle, triangle, circle, and score lines into your Canvas.

- **Upload:** You can use the Upload tab to use your image files including jpg, gif, png, bmp, svg, and dxf at no charge.

Header

- **Menu:** The "hamburger" icon on the top left of the screen will allow you to navigate through Cricut Design Space. You can directly access Home, Canvas, and several other Design Space features, such as New Machine Setup, Settings, Link Cartridges, Help and Sign Out.

- **Page Title:** This will help you remember whether you are on the Home or Canvas page of Design Space. By clicking on the Page Title, you will be able to close an open tab.

- **Project Name:** This will show you the name of your project. If you've not already saved your project, then Untitled will be displayed as the name of the project.

- **My Projects:** You can open your saved projects by clicking on My Projects.

- **Save:** To access your projects across your devices and multiple platforms, you must save your projects to your account by clicking on the Save icon, and providing a name for your projects. Note, if you would like to keep your project private and all to yourself then make sure you uncheck the Public option while saving your project. If you would like to rename your project once has been saved, just click on Save As, and enter a new name for your project.

- **Make it:** Click on the Make it icon when you have prepped your mats and are ready to transfer your project to your Cricut machine.

Zoom

You can Zoom In to look at the finer details of your project, and Zoom Out to see an overview of the same.

The editing panel

The editing panel is at the top of your Canvas Area. It harbors the controls that make it easier for you to work around a project.

The editing panel is divided into two subpanels:

- **Subpanel one:** To allow you to create, name, save, and cut a project.

- **Subpanel two:** To give you all the editing tools.

Subpanel one

The Subpanel one has few icons on it. Let's get the icons explained:

a. **Canvas:** I refer to this as the main button on the design space area. A click on the icon/button and a drop-down menu will appear with a range of options. From the drop-down menu, you can do a lot of settings.

Home

Canvas

New Machine Setup
Calibration
Manage Custom Materials
Update Firmware
Account Details
Link Cartridges
Cricut Access
Settings
Legal
New Features
United States ▼
Help
Sign Out

From this drop-down menu, you can manage your profile. Also, you can calibrate your machine, update firmware, link cartridges, etc. If you have premium access to Cricut Design Space, you can manage your subscription from the drop-down menu. I always advise beginners to take their time and click on all the options on the drop-down menu to understand their functionalities.

b. ***Project name:*** In Cricut Design Space, all new projects are by default Untitled. You can only give a project a name when you have started working on it either by placing an element or a text on it.

c. ***My projects:*** A click on this icon will lead you to all your prior designs if you have any.

d. ***Save:*** This icon becomes functional when you have started working on a project. It is always advisable that you save your project as you design in case of anything going wrong. I learned this the hard way. During my early days with Cricut, I'd only save when I was done with a project until one day, I was about done with a particular project when my browser crashed and that was it with my project. I couldn't recover it because I never save it.

e. **Maker (Machine):** This icon has two sub-options when you click on it. The two sub-options include Cricut Maker and Cricut Explore Family. Depending on the machine you are using, you will need to select either of the sub-options while working. These two options have different tools.

f. **Make it:** When you are done designing and uploading your projects, this is the final icon you click on to have your project cut.

When you click on Make It, there will be a display on your screen which shows the different colors of your project. From the displayed window you can perform other functions like increasing the number of projects to cut, etc. When you are done with your selection, you can click on Continue to proceed.

Subpanel two (Editing menu)

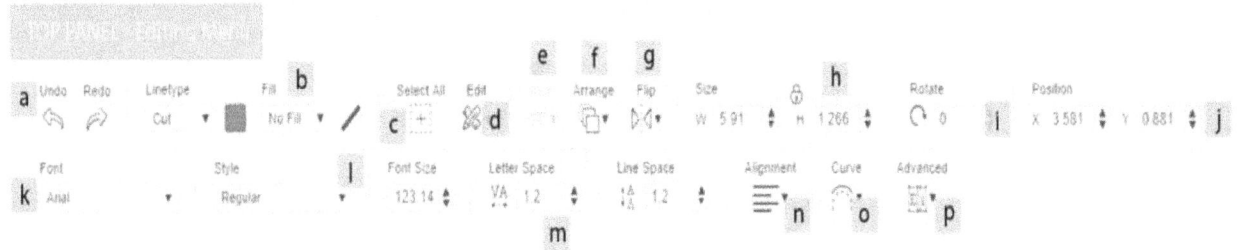

The image above represents the editing panel of the Cricut design space. I will take the icons one after another and explain their functions and usefulness. I lettered the different icons to make it easier for better understanding.

a. **The Undo and Redo:** This is a very important icon in your design Canvas. This icon helps you make corrections either by taking you back or forward a bit.

Whenever you are designing, there is possible that you will make mistakes. With the undo and redo option, when you delete something by mistake, clicking redo will bring it back. When you make a mistake in your design space, clicking undo will get out.

b. **Linetype and Fill:** The Linetype and Fill icon tells your machine the tools and blades you are going to use for cutting your project.

There are seven options on the Maker Linetype, these include Cut, Draw, Score, Engrave, Deboss, Wave, and Perf.

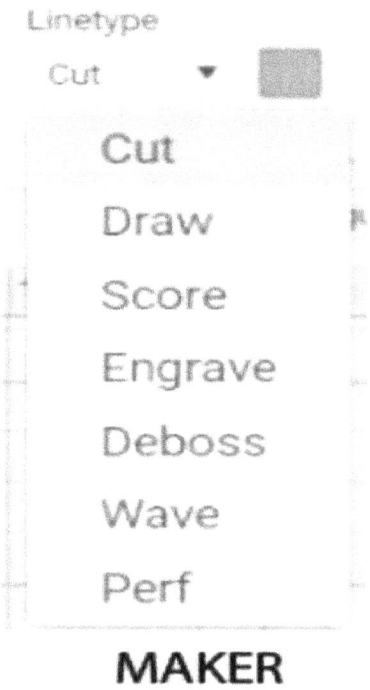

On the Cricut explore family Linetype, there are just three options.

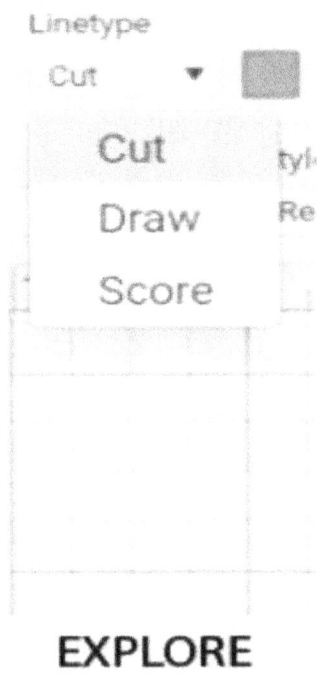

EXPLORE

Explaining the Linetype options tools.

- **_Cut:_** This is the default line type of all elements on your Canvas, except you upload a png image. When you press 'Make it' at the end of your design, this prompts your machine to cut those designs.

    The Cut option also helps you change the fill of elements in your project. These elements translate into colors of materials that you will use when cutting your project.

- **_Draw:_** This tool on the linetype helps you write on your design. When you select this option, you will be prompted to choose any of the Cricut pens available for you. Upon selection of a particular pen, the layers on your Canvas area will be listed with the color of the pen you picked. When the Draw tool is selected and you click on Make it, your Cricut will either write or draw instead of cutting. Also, this option doesn't color your designs at all.

- ***Score:*** The Score tool is an important version of the scoring line which is located on the left panel of your Canvas space. When this tool is selected and assigned to a layer, all the designs will appear dashed or scored.

    At the end of your project when you click on Make it, your Cricut will score the materials instead of cutting them.

- ***Engrave, wave, deboss, and perf:*** These are new tools added by Cricut to the Cricut Maker Machine. With these tools, you will be able to create amazing designs of different materials. They are still pretty new, so try them out when you can.

    One thing I know for sure about these tools is that they work with the Quick Swap Adaptive Tool.

The Fill tool

This option/tool is used mainly for patterns and printing. The Fill option gets activated only when you are using Cut as a linetype. When you have No Fill it means that you won't be printing any project.

The Print tool is the most important tool on your design Canvas because it makes it possible for you to print your projects and cut them.

When the Fill tool is active, when you click Make it, firstly, the files will be sent to your printer while your Cricut does all the cutting.

The Print type has two sub-options that allows you to perform magic on your Canvas. These options include Color and Pattern. When you explore these options you will be amazed at the project you will create

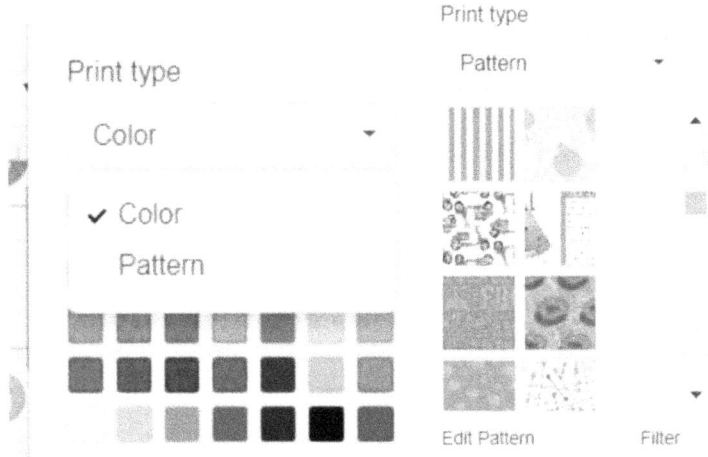

c. **Select all:** This tool serves to help you select all the elements in your Canvas area. Sometimes it is a hassle to select elements individually, so this tool helps you make multiple selections at the same time.

d. **Edit:** The Edit icon when clicked on has three tools, Cut, Copy, and Paste. With these options, you can copy an element, paste a copied element, or cut off an unwanted element on your Canvas.

Once you have made a selection on your Canvas, the Cut and Copy tools get activated. When you have copied or cut an element, the Paste option gets activated.

e. ***The Align icon:*** If you have ever used another design tool, this will be an easy walk around for you. But if you have not, it's easy to get a hang of.

The Alignment icon is one you should master as it is very important while working on your project. The Alignment tool helps your project stay perfectly organized and on the same line.

The Align icon has a drop-down menu that contains other alignment tools.

Let's take a look at the functions on the Align drop-down menu.

Align: This particular tool allows you to align all the elements in your design. It is activated when you select two or more elements on your Canvas.

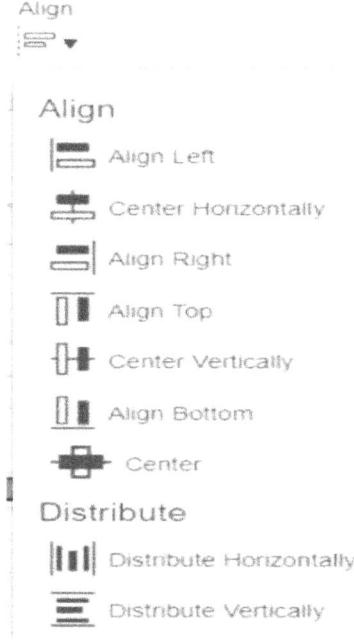

- *Align Left:* This function takes all the selected elements and aligns them to the left. Whichever element that is furthest at the left determines the alignment.
- *Center Horizontal:* Just like every other alignment option, this will align all the elements on your project horizontally, while the texts and images are centered.

- *Alight Right:* When you activate this option, all the elements on your project will be aligned to the right. Whichever element that is furthest at the right determines the alignment.

- *Alight Top:* This option aligns all the elements of your project to the top. Whichever element that is furthest at the top determines the alignment.

- *Center Vertically:* With this option, all the elements of your project will be aligned to the center. When working with columns and you want them organized and properly aligned, use this option.

- *Align Bottom:* This alignment option will align all the selected elements on your project to the bottom. Whichever element that is furthest at the bottom determines the alignment.

- *Center:* When this option is clicked on, it perfectly centers every element on your project: shapes, text, images.

- *Distribute:* The distribute option gives equal spacing to all the elements on your project. In Cricut Design Space, there is nothing as time-consuming as trying to manually allocate equal space between the elements on your project so, with this tool, all your problems are solved. For this tool to be activated, two or more elements must be selected on your project.

- *Distribute Horizontally:* This option will distribute the elements on your project horizontally. The furthest elements left and right on your project will determine the length of the distribution.

- *Distribute Vertically:* This option will distribute the elements on your project vertically. The furthest elements top and bottom on your project will determine the length of the distribution.

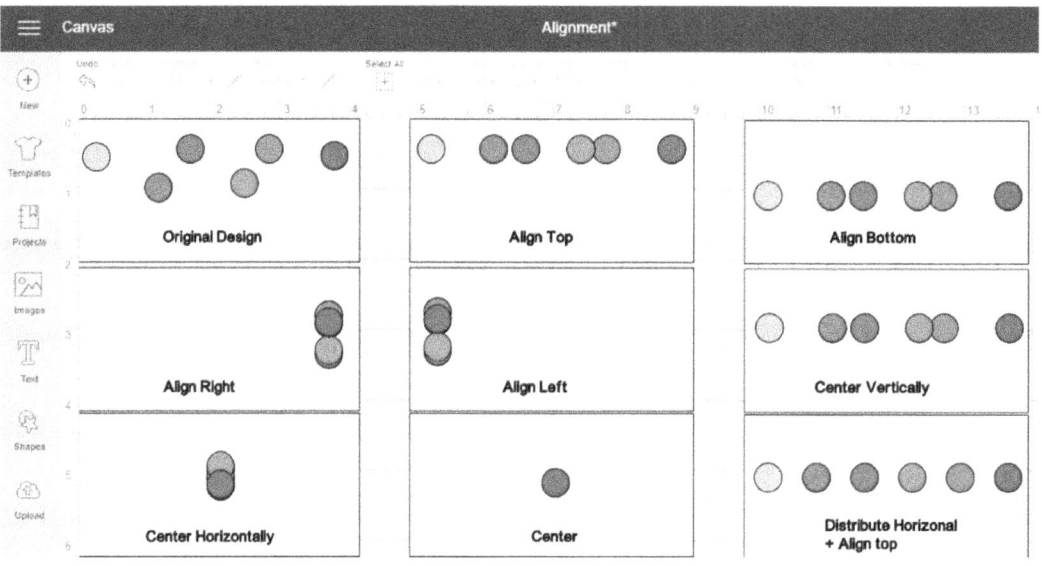

f. ***Arrange:*** The Arrange option helps put the elements on your project in the right place. When you are working on a project with multiple text, images, and designs, there is every probability that the new elements you add will be placed in front of others, but, in an actual sense, you want them placed at the back. The arrange option makes it easier to do that.

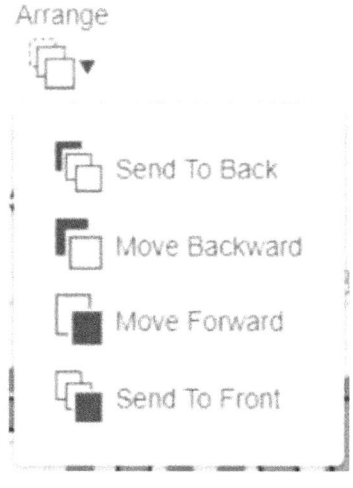

The Arrange option has other sub-options which includes:

- *Send Back:* This action will move all selected elements on your project to the back.

- *Move Backward:* This action will move all selected elements on your project one step back. This simply means that activating this item will just take the element(s) only one step back instead of all the way back behind other elements.

- *Move Forward:* This action will move the selected element(s) a step forward.

- *Send to Front:* This action will move the selected element(s) to the front of every other element on the project.

g. **Flip:** The Flip icon gives you the ability to reflect your designs on your Cricut Canvas.

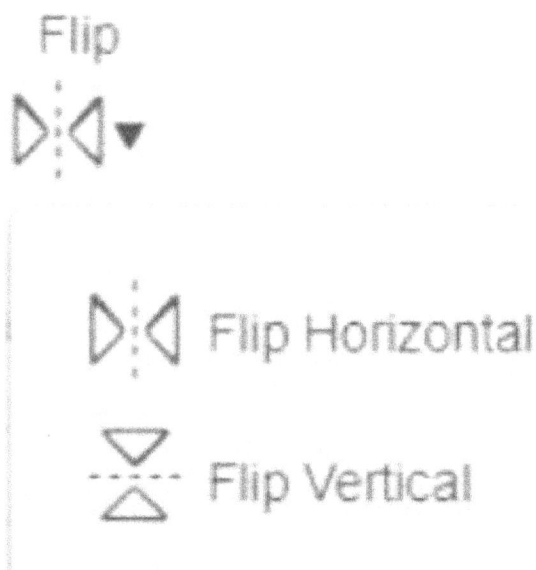

The Flip option has two sub-options:

- *Flip Horizontal:* This action when activated reflects the images on your design horizontally. The best way I can explain is that Flip horizontally helps you duplicate a design. When you have a design at the right and want to duplicate the same design at the left, Flip horizontally helps you to do that.

- *Flip Vertical:* This action perfectly helps you create a shadow effect on your design by duplicating the selected design vertically.

h. **Size:** Every element you introduce to your design Canvas (text, image, shape) has a size. Sometimes you may not want to alter the size, but the Size icon gives you the ability to modify elements to any size of your choice.

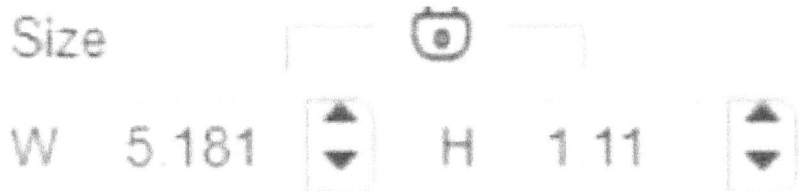

After modifying the size of an image, it is essential to click the lock icon on the size option. This is the way to tell your Cricut program that you don't want to keep those same dimensions as default.

i. **Rotate:** The rotate action helps you rotate an element to the desired angle. It can get tedious trying to get an image on your project to the right angle manually, but with the rotate option, it is very easy.

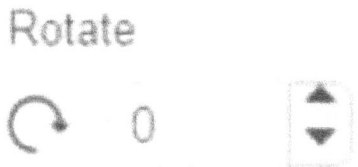

j. **Position:** This option shows you exactly where your elements are on a design Canvas area. With this tool, you can move elements on your project around by specifying where you want them to be.

This is pretty much an advanced tool, but a similar option to this is the alignment tool.

k. **Font:** This option gives you access to the different text fonts available for your design on Cricut. You can choose any font of your choice to work with.

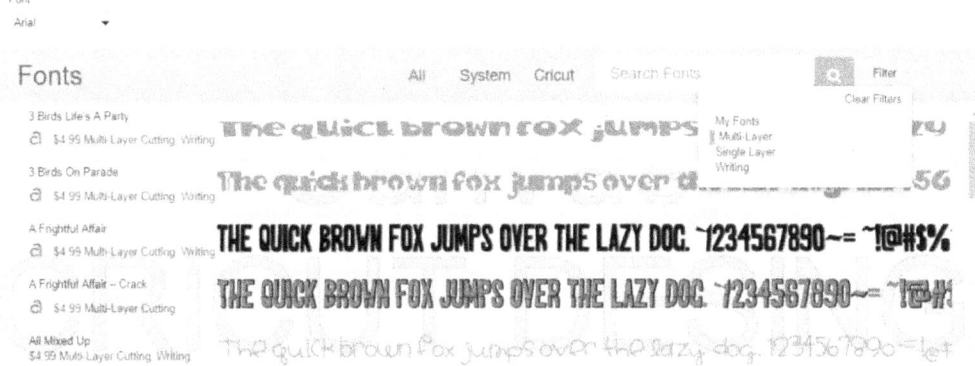

l. **Style:** The Style option works in hand with Fonts. Once you select a font of your choice, the next step is to choose the style. The style option has some sub-options.

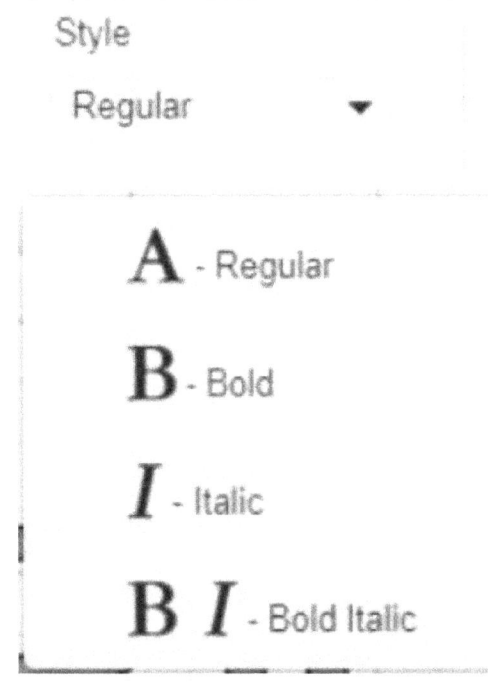

The Regular is the default style of your design Canvas. Bold makes your chosen font appear thicker. Italic makes your chosen font tilt to the right, while Bold Italic makes the italic font thicker.

m. ***Font Size, Letter Space, and Line Space:*** These three options are very amazing as it brings a sort of perfection to your projects.

- *Font size:* You can change the size of your text in the Font Size area.

- *Letter space:* While some fonts have considerable space between the letters others don't really have. The letter space option allows you to manage the spacing between letters.

- *Line space:* This option allows you to manage the space between the text lines in a paragraph.

n. ***Alignment:*** Don't get confused, this particular alignment is different from the other alignment explained initially. These alignment options work with paragraphs.

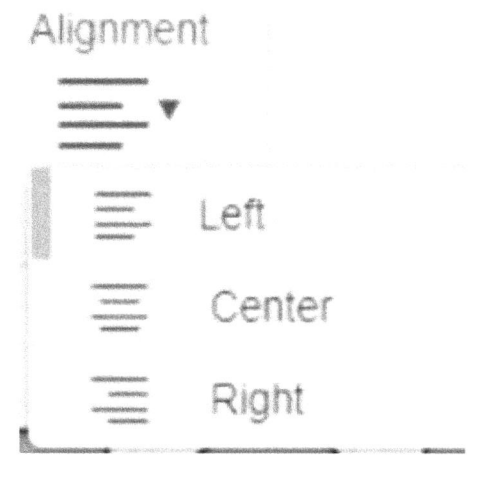

The Alignment option has other sub-options:

- *Left:* This action aligns selected paragraph(s) to the left.
- *Center:* This action aligns selected paragraph(s) to the center.
- *Right:* This action aligns selected paragraph(s) to the right.

o. **Curve:** Do you want to make your text shaped? This option is your best bet. The Curve option allows you to make your texts curved.

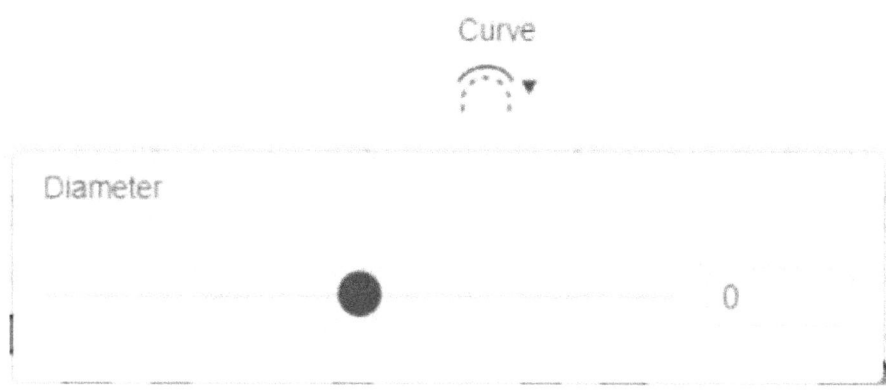

By moving the slider right or left it curves your texts upward or inward.

p. **Advance:** Don't get scared about this option, it is as easy as other options. Even though as a beginner you may not use it often, but once you get a hang of it you are good to go.

Chapter 3: Projects: How To Start A New Project

Starting a New Project - The Basics

When you are starting a new project, you'll want to know what that project will be, and what materials you will be using before doing anything else.

For example, if you want to cut vinyl letters to place on wood, you'll need to know all dimensions, so your letters fit evenly and centered on the wood. You'll need wood that vinyl can adhere to without the risk of peeling. And you'll want to be sure that your wood is sanded and finished according to your desire because you don't want any imperfections. You may find even with store-bought wood pieces advertised as ready-to-use, there are tiny imperfections.

You want to make sure when working with fabric that you know what inks or vinyl will adhere to the surface. You don't want any peeling or cracking to happen to your beautiful design.

When working with any kind of fabric, including Canvas bags, you'll want to pre-wash for sizing because shrinkage, after your design has been set, can cause the design to become distorted.

If you aren't sure exactly what you want to do, have something in mind so that you aren't wasting a lot of materials by trial and error. The cost of crafting materials can increase, so you'll want to eliminate as much potential waste as possible.

If you're new to Cricut Design Space, start with something simple. You don't want to get in over your head. That's the worst thing you can do when you learn any new craft. There are many used Cricut machines for sale, and while some users sell because they upgraded, others are users who gave up. You made the investment and you'll want to get a return on that investment.

Ready to conquer Cricut Design Space?

To keep up with any changes, you should subscribe to the company email list or check the Cricut website often.

Let's begin by clicking on New from our menu options. It's at the very top of the Canvas in the left corner.

An empty Canvas will appear. You might have previously started a project, and in that case, the machine will detect it in the queue, and you'll be asked if you want to replace the project. If you don't want to replace it, be sure you save all of your changes or you might lose them, and you don't want to lose all of your hard work. It's important to not rush so that you don't accidentally delete a project you want to be saved. When you've completed that action, you'll be returned to your new blank Canvas.

First, you want to name your project. Use a name that closely relates to it so you aren't getting projects confused. If you have a lot of projects, and you don't use a system to identify them, you might want to consider it.

As you can see from our illustration, everything you need is on the left, under the 'New' icon.

Different templates appear by clicking on the templates icon, however, these are only to get an idea of how your final project will look.

- Projects allow you to access the Make It Now™ platform. There are so many to choose from and you might find yourself spending a lot of time looking at them all.

- Images are just what they say. This is the icon you need to add an image or images to your project.

- Text is for writing the text if your project has words.

- Shapes allow you to add different shapes such as circles, squares, and hearts.

- Upload your images and/or begin cutting. This is the final design step!

If you know what your project is going to be, you can go to the Projects icon and begin to customize it or start cutting.

We have talked about subscriptions, and it should be noted that you can purchase a one-time design for a nominal fee. You can also purchase designs from Etsy and other craft sites.

When you've done your design, don't forget to save it. You will get the option of Save or Save as. You will get a message letting you know that your project was successfully saved. Save as will save your project as a new one and keep the old one under its name. You could need to rename your project with the Save as a feature.

It's easy to get so caught up in the design process and anxious to see the finished project that we can forget to hit Save. Your project should automatically save in the cloud, but if it doesn't, you'll have it. It's always better to be safe than sorry.

Now, you've brought your design to your screen. You want to give it a final look and make certain everything is where you want it. If you're ready to cut, click Make It.

If your Cricut machine isn't turned on do it now, and have all your materials ready. You'll want to follow the prompts. Set your material and load your tools and mat. Press the Go icon and wait. When the cutting is done, press Unload and carefully remove the mat.

Voila! Your project is finished. Wasn't that easy?

Basic Object Editing

The Canvas comes equipped with an editing toolbar that allows you to make corrections.

If you make a mistake, you can easily fix it. You can use the Undo and Redo buttons by clicking them the required number of times.

The Undo icon will let you get rid of something you don't like. It acts as an eraser, and each click will undo the previous action.

If you accidentally delete something, you can use the Redo button. This will restore your work.

Another editing tool is the linetype dropdown that will let you change to a Cut, Draw or Score object. It communicates with your machine so it knows what tools you're going to be using.

Cut is the default linetype you'll use unless you've uploaded a jpeg or png image. When you click on the "make it" icon, those designs will be cut.

Use Draw if you want to write on your design. You'll be prompted to select a pen, and you'll use this to write or draw.

Tip: This option won't color your designs.

You can use the Score feature to score or dash your design.

The Edit icon lets you Cut, Copy, and Paste from the Canvas. It functions with a drop-down menu and you use it by selecting the elements you want to edit from your Canvas.

The program also features an Align tool that will let you move your design around on the Canvas. If you've used a design program before, this should be easy for you to do. If you haven't, it can be tricky.

Functions of the alignment tool

The following are the functions you can use to move your design on the Canvas. You might want to practice using these until you're comfortable with them.

Align allows you to align all of your designs by selecting two or more elements on your Canvas.

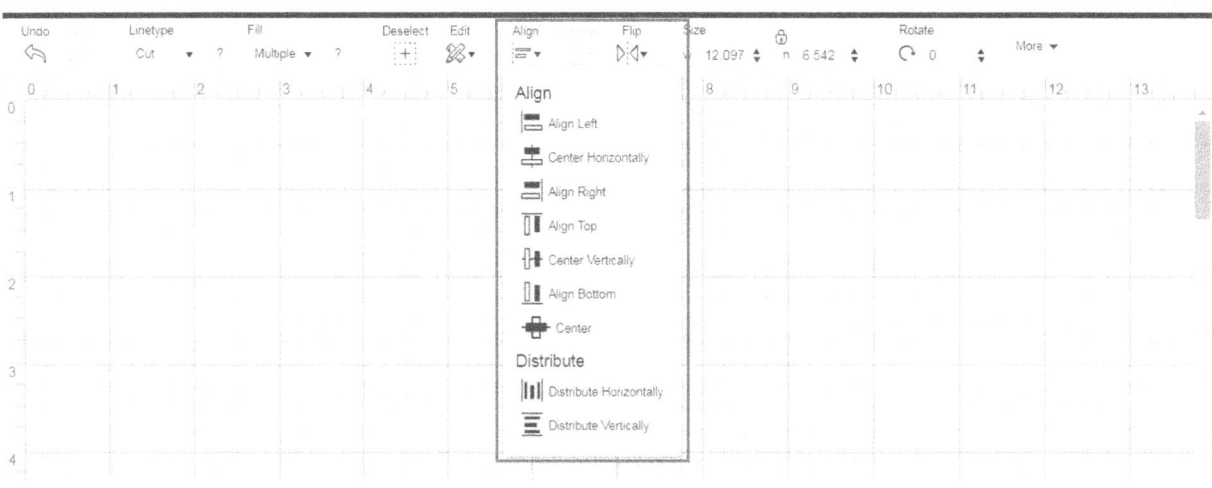

- Align Left will move everything to the left.

- Center Horizontal will align horizontally and will center text and images. This brings everything to the center.

- Align Right will move everything to the right.

- Align Top will move the designs you select to the top of the Canvas.

- Center vertically will align your selections vertically.

- Align Bottom will bring your selections to the bottom.

- Center will bring everything to the center, vertically and horizontally.

You can also distribute vertically and horizontally. This will give you some space between your design elements.

You can also flip, arrange, rotate, and size your design. All of these features are handy, and once you master them you can quickly align your design to your preference.

Using images in the design space

For starters, the Cricut Design Space library has over 60,000 images available for crafters to use in their crafts. Every update of Cricut brings about newly added images, so really, you are well equipped.

Selecting images for your project

As always, everything begins in your Design Space. Here, select New Project and then click on the Images tool located in your design panel. It will open up the images library to search for any image you want—either scroll or search for a specific image using the search bar.

Search using category

To make your search a lot easier, you can also search by using the Category function. Search for images using the Free this Week, Most Popular, and Recently Added options.

As you scroll down, you can also see the list of categories that are listed alphabetically. So essentially, you have plenty of different ways and options to find the perfect image for your design.

Search using cartridge

Before the latest updates came in, crafters using Cricut Design Space and Cricut Craft Room software could remember the physical cartridge to use with the Cricut machine. But now, you can do this via the Design Space. Practically, the Cartridge images arrange by theme, so this is another excellent way to find ideas for your project. If needed, you can also buy the entire cartridge, which is usually cheaper than buying a single image. Of course, this option makes sense only if you use the Cricut often, and you've explored all of those images on the Design Space and can't find what you want.

Filter your image search results

You can always use the Filter option only to show My Images, Uploaded, Free, Cricut Access, or Purchased at any point in your image search process. If you are not familiar with Cricut, you can easily find free images that allow you to test and try to design spaces before delving into buying prints.

About the images

As you go through your Design Space, you will see some images that have the Cricut Access symbol. It's usually a little green flag icon with an A on it. The images and fonts with this symbol are available only if you have subscribed to the Access subscriptions.

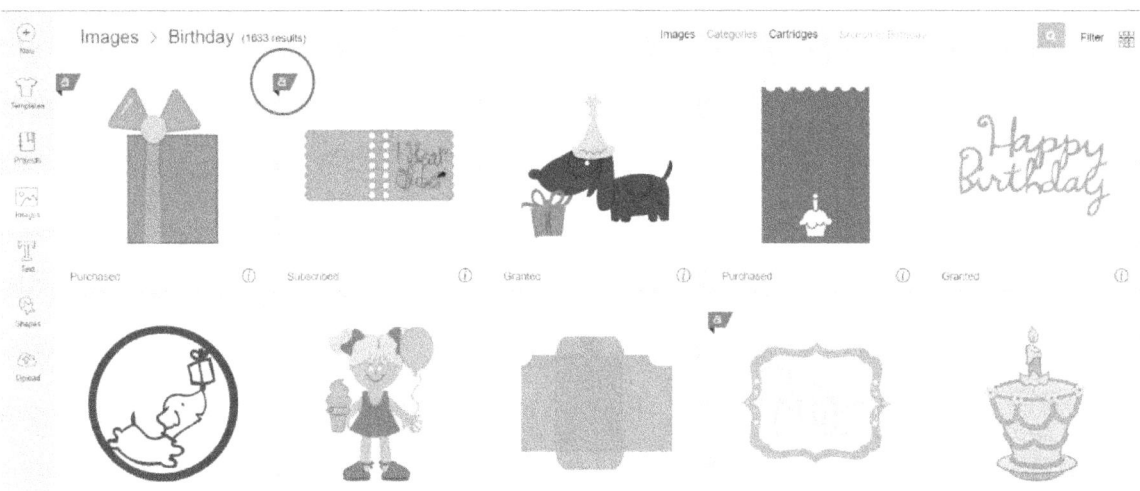

Suppose you are a heavy Cricut user, and you've explored all the images on the Library, or the photos on the Library are not according to your likeness or taste.

The other thing you want to know about the Images Library is the little italicized I on the right-hand corner for some images. After clicking it, you will see the image name, number, and the cartridge it belongs to. You can click on the link of the cartridge to see all images contained in the cartridge.

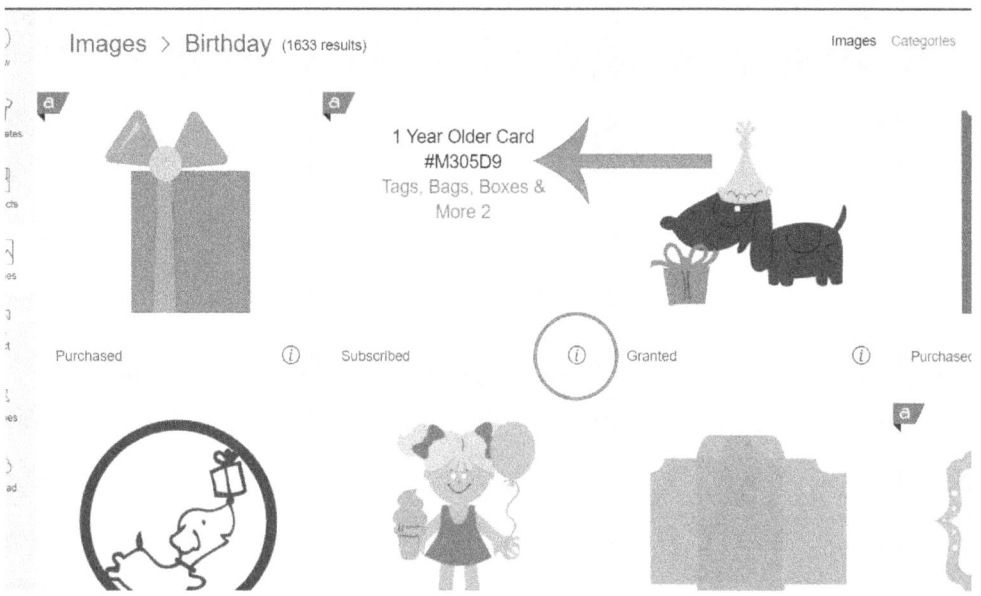

You would also see a printer icon on some of these images. It would mean that they design for ready-to-go use.

Adding images to your project

To select one or more images for your project, just click on each image. All you need to do is choose the photos you want, as many as you would like, and then click on Insert Images to include your Design Space images.

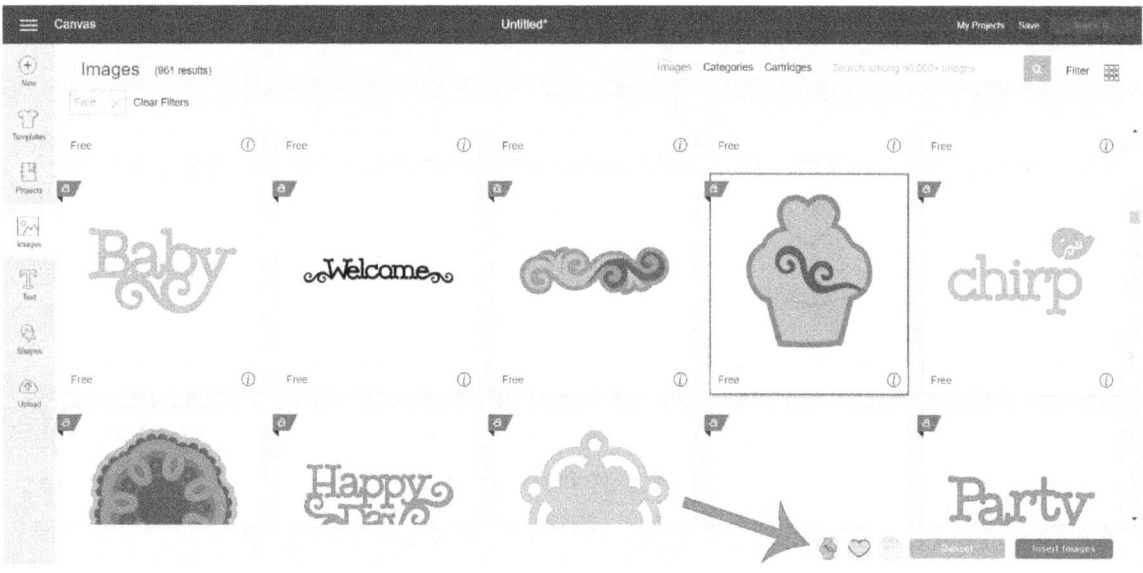

When the images are on your blank Canvas on Design Space, you can resize them or edit them according to how you want them on the design.

For any image that you select, there will be a box around it. You will see a red X mark in the upper left corner for you to delete the image. You can also rotate the image or even adjust the painting size according to your liking. You can also lock or unlock the image proportions. If you want to delete a photo, you no longer wish to work, just select the image, click the red X in the left top corner, select the image in the layers panel, and click the Delete button.

Searching and adding images for your project is extremely easy with the Design Space. Before you subscribe to the Access or getting a Cartridge, explore what Cricut has to offer first because with 60,000 over images you are bound to find something you like to do a beautiful project.

Project ideas to try

With Cricut, the ideas for projects are so vast, you'll be amazed at how much you can do. So, what are some ideas that could work for you? Here are a few that you can consider, and some of the best project ideas for those who are stumped on where to begin!

Easy Projects

Custom Shirts

Custom shirts are incredibly easy. The beauty of this is, you can use the Cricut fonts or system options, and from there, you can simply print it on. Personally, I like to use the iron-on vinyl, because it's easy to work with. Just take your image and upload it into Design Space. Then, go to the Canvas and find the image you want. Once you've selected the image, you click on the whitespace that will be cut– remember to get the insides, too. Make sure that you choose cut image, not print from cut image, and then place it on the Canvas to the size of your liking. Put the iron-on vinyl shiny side down, turn it on, and then select iron-on from the menu. Choose to cut, and make sure you mirror the image. Once done, pull off the extra vinyl to remove the vinyl between the letters. There you go! A simple shirt.

Vinyl Decals

Vinyl can also be used to make personalized items, such as water bottle decals. First, design the text– you can pretty much use whatever you want for this. From here, create a second box and make an initial, or whatever design you want. Make sure that you resize this to fit the water bottle, as well.

From here, load your vinyl, and make sure that you use transfer tape on the vinyl itself once you cut it out. Finally, when you adhere the lettering to the bottle, go from the center and then push outwards, smoothing as you go. It takes a bit, but there you have it–simple water bottles that children will love! This is a wonderful, simple project for those of us who aren't really that artistically inclined but want to get used to making Cricut items.

Printable Stickers

Printable stickers are the next project. This is super simple and fun for parents and kids. For this project, the Explore Air 2 machine works best.

With this one, you want the Print then cut feature, since it makes it much easier. To begin, go to Design Space and download images of ice cream or whatever you want, or upload images of your own. You click on a New Project, and on the left side that says Images, you can choose the ones you like, and insert more of these on there.

From here, choose the image and flatten it, since this will make it into one piece rather than just a separate file for each. Resize as needed to make sure that they fit where you're putting them.

You can copy and paste each element until you're done. Once ready, press Save, and then choose this as a Print then cut image. Click the big button at the bottom that says make it. Make sure everything is good, then press continue, and from there, you can load the sticker paper into the machine. Make sure to adjust this to the right setting, which for sticker paper is the vinyl set. Put the paper into there and load them in, and when ready, the press goes – it will then cut the stickers as needed.

From there, take them out and decorate. You can use ice cream or whatever sticker image you want!

Personalized Pillows

Personalized pillows are another fun idea, and are incredibly easy to make. To begin, you open up Design Space and choose a New Project. From here, select the icon at the bottom of the screen itself, choosing your font. Type the words you want, and drag the text as needed to make it bigger.

You can also upload images, too, if you want to create a huge picture on the pillow itself.

From here, you want to press the Attach button for each box, so that they work together and both are figured when centered, as well.

Then you press Make it – and you want to turn to mirror on, since this will be, again, on iron-on vinyl. From here, you load the iron-on vinyl with the shiny side down, the press continues, follow the prompts, and make sure it's not jammed in, either.

Let the machine work its magic with cutting and from there, you can press the weeding tool to get the middle areas out.

Set your temperature on the easy press for the right settings, and then push it onto the material, ironing it on and letting it sit for 10 to 15 seconds. Let it cool, and then take the transfer sheet off.

There you have it! A simple pillow that works wonders for your crafting needs.

Cards

Finally, cards are a great project idea for Cricut makers. They're simple, and you can do the entire project with cardstock.

To make this, you first want to open up Design Space, and from there, put your design in. If you like images of ice cream, then use that. If you want to make Christmas cards, you can do that, too. Basically, you can design whatever you want to on this.

Now, you'll then want to add the text. You can choose the font that you want to use, and from there, write out the message on the card, such as "Merry Christmas." At this point, instead of choosing to cut, you want to choose the right option–the 'Make it' option. You don't have to mirror this, but check that your design fits properly on the cardstock itself. When choosing material for writing, make sure you choose the cardstock.

From there, insert your cardstock into the machine, and then, when ready, you can press Go and the Cricut machine will make your card. This may take a minute, but once it's done, you'll have a wonderful card in place. It's super easy to use.

Cricut cards are a great personalized way to express yourself, creating a one-of-a-kind, sentimental piece for you to gift to friends and family.

Medium Projects

Cricut cake toppers

Cricut cake toppers have a little bit of added difficulty because they require some precise scoring. The Cricut maker is probably the best piece of equipment for the job, and here, we'll tell you how to do it. The scoring tool is your best bet since this will make different shapes even easier, as well. You will want to make sure you have cardstock and the cutting mat, along with a fine-point blade for cutting. The tape is also handy for these.

First, go to Design Space and choose the rosettes you want. From there, press 'Make it' and follow the prompts. It will then ask you whether you want the single or double wheel. Scoring shells are meant to create extra-deep score lines in materials, to get the perfect fold. The single wheel will make one crease, and the double wheel will make a parallel wheel that will crease–perfect for specialty items. Plus, the double wheel is thicker, so it's easier to fold.

Once you score everything, you remove it and replace the scoring wheel with the fine-point blade.

From here, you simply fold everything and just follow the line. This should make the rosette, and you can then use contrasting centers and create many of these to form a nice backdrop.

Cricut gift bags

Next are gift bags. Remember to put the foil poster board face-down on the mat itself, to help prevent the material from cracking and showing through to the white backdrop, when you fold them together after you score them.

To make these, you want to implement the template that you'd like to use in Design Space. From here, I do suggest cutting out the initial design first, and then putting it back in to create scoring lines, following the same steps. After that, you can take your item and fold along the score lines, and then use adhesive or glue to help put it all together. This is a great personalized way to do it, but it can be a bit complicated to work with at first.

Cricut fabric coasters

Fabric coasters with a Cricut maker are great, and they need only a few supplies. These include the maker itself, cotton fabric, fusible fleece, a rotary cutting mat or some scissors, a sewing machine, and an iron.

Cut the fabric to about 12 inches to fit the cutting mat – if it's longer, you can hang it off, just be careful.

From here, go to Design Space, then click shapes and make a heart. You can do this with other shapes, too. Resize it to about 5 inches wide. Press Make it, and you'll want to make sure you create four copies. Press continue, and then choose medium fabrics similar to cotton. Load the mat and cut, and then you do it again with the fusible fleece on the cutting mat, changing it to 4.75 inches. This time, when choosing the material, go to more, and select fusible fleece. Cut the fusible fleece, and attach these to the back of the heart with the iron and repeat with the second.

Sew the two shapes together, leaving a gap for stitching and turning. Clip the curves, turn it inside out, and then fold in the edges and stitch it.

There you go–a fusible fleece heart coaster. It's a little bit more complicated, but it's worth trying out.

Difficult Projects

Giant Vinyl Stencils

Vinyl stencils are a good thing to create too, but they can be hard. Big vinyl stencils are an excellent Cricut project, and you can use them in various places, including bedrooms for kids.

You only need the Explore Air 2, the vinyl that works for it, a pallet, sander, and, of course, paint and brushes. The first step is preparing the pallet for painting, or whatever surface you plan on using this for.

From here, you create the mermaid tail (or any other large image) in Design Space. Now, you'll learn immediately that big pieces are hard to cut and impossible to do all at once in Design Space.

What you do is to section each design accordingly, and remove any middle pieces. Next, you can add square shapes to the image, slicing it into pieces so that it can be cut on a cutting mat that fits.

At this point, you cut out the design by pressing Make it, choosing your material, and working in sections.

From here, you put it on the surface that you're using, piecing this together with each line, and you should have one image after piecing it all together. Then, draw out the line on vinyl and paint the initial design. For the second set of stencils, you can simply trace the first one and then paint the inside of them. At this point, you should have the design finished. When done, remove it very carefully.

And there you have it! Bigger stencils can be a bit of a project since it involves trying to use multiple designs all at once, but with the right care and the right designs, you'll be able to create whatever it is you need to in Design Space so you can get the results you're looking for.

Cricut quilts

Quilts are a bit hard to do for many people, but did you know that you can use Cricut to make it easier? Here, you'll learn an awesome project that will help you do this. To begin, you start with the Cricut Design Space. Here, you can add different designs that work for your project. For example, if you're making a baby blanket or quilt with animals on it, you can add little fonts with the names of the animals, or different pictures of them, too. From here, you want to make sure you choose the option to reverse the design. That way, you'll have it printed on correctly. At this point, make your quilt. Do various designs and sew the quilt as you want to.

From here, you should cut it on the iron-on heat transfer vinyl. You can choose that, and press Cut. The image will then cut into the piece.

At this point, it'll cut itself out, and you can proceed to transfer this with some parchment paper. Use an EasyPress for best results and push it down. There you go, an easy addition that will definitely enhance the way your blankets look.

Step-by-step guide on some Cricut projects

Felt roses

Materials needed

- SVG files with 3D flower design.
- Felt sheets.
- Fabric grip mat.
- Glue gun.

Steps

1. First of all, upload your flower SVG graphics into the Cricut design.

2. Having placed the image in the project, select it, right-click, and click Ungroup. This allows you to resize each flower independently of the others. Since you are using felt, it is recommended that each of the flowers is at least 6 inches in size.

3. Create several copies of the flowers, as many as you wish, selecting the colors you want in the Color Sync Panel (by dragging and dropping the images on to the color you would want them to be cut on). Immediately you're through with that, click on Make it on the Cricut Design Space.

4. Click on Continue. After your Cricut Maker is connected and registered, under the Materials options, select Felt.

5. If your rotary blade is not in the machine, insert it. Next, on the Fabric Grip Mat, place the first felt sheet (in order of color), then, load them into your Cricut Maker. Press the Cut button when this is done.

6. After they are cut, begin to roll the cut flowers one by one. Do this from the outside in. Make sure that you do not roll them too tight. Use the picture as a guide.

7. Apply hot glue on the circle right in the middle and press the felt flowers that you rolled up on the glue. Hold this in place and do not let it go until the glue binds it.

8. Wait for the glue to dry, and your roses are ready for use.

Custom coasters

Materials needed:

- Free pattern templates.

- Monogram design (in Design Space).

- Cardstock or printing paper.

- Butcher paper.

- Lint-free towel.

- Round coaster blanks.

- Light grip mat.

- Easy Press 2 (6" x 7" recommended).

- Easy Press mat.

- Infusible ink pens.

- Heat resistant tape.

- Cricut bright pad (optional) for easier tracing.

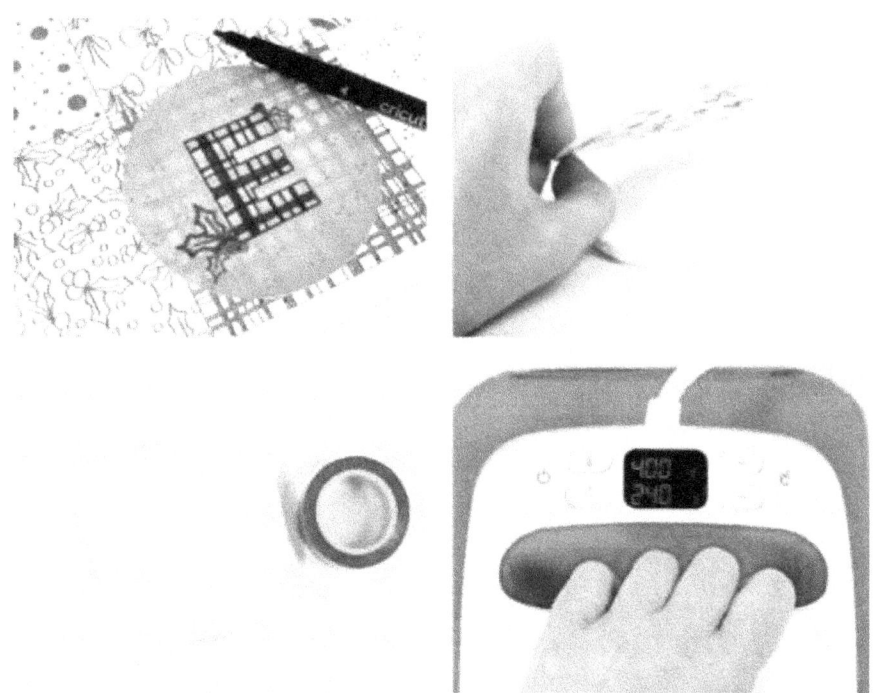

Steps

1. In Cricut Design Space, open the monogram design. You can click Customize and choose the designs that you want to cut out or just go ahead and cut out all the letters.

2. Click on Make It.

3. On the page displayed, click on Mirror Image to make the image mirrored. This must be done whenever you are using infusible ink. For your material, choose Cardstock. Place your cardstock on the mat and load it into the machine; then press the Cut button on the Cricut machine.

4. After the Cricut machine is done cutting, unload it, and remove the done monograms from the mat.

5. Trace the designs onto the cut-out. If you have a Cricut Bright Pad, you can use it to carry out this step much more easily, as it will make the trace lines easier to identify. Tracing should be done using Cricut infusible ink pens.

6. Use the lint-free towel to wipe the coaster. Ensure that no residue is left behind to prevent any marks left on the blank.

7. Make the design centered on the face down coaster.

8. Get a piece of butcher paper which is about an inch larger on each side of the coaster and place on top of the design.

9. Tape this butcher paper onto the coaster using heat resistant tape, to hold the design fast.

10. Set the temperature of your Easy Press to 400 degrees and set the timer to 240 seconds.

11. Place another butcher paper piece on your Easy Press mat, set the coaster on top of it, face up.

12. Place another piece of butcher paper on top of these. Place the already preheated Easy Press on top of the coaster and start the timer.

13. Lightly hold the Easy Press in place (without moving) or leave it in place right on the coaster –if on a perfectly flat surface–till the timer goes off.

14. After this is done, gently remove the second Easy Press, then turn it off.

15. The coaster will be very hot, so you should leave it to get cool before you touch it. When it is cool, you can peel the design off of it.

Customized doormat

Materials needed

- Cricut machine.

- Scrap cardstock (The color does not matter).

- Coir mat (18" x 30").

- Outdoor acrylic paint.

- Vinyl stencil.

- Transfer tape.

- Flat round paintbrush.

- Cutting mat (12" x 24").

Steps

1. Create your design in Cricut Design Space. You can also download an SVG design of your choice and import it into Cricut Design Space. Make sure that your design is the right size; resize it to ensure that this is so.

2. Next, you are to cut the stencil. You do this by clicking Make it in Cricut Design Space when you are done with the design. After this, you select Cardstock as the material. Then, you press the Cut button on the Cricut machine.

3. When this is done, remove the stencil from the machine and weed.

4. Next, on the reverse side of the stencil, apply spray glue. After this, attach the stencil to the doormat, exactly where you want your design to be; then, pick up the letter bits left on the cutting mat, and glue them to their places in the stencil on the doormat.

5. The next step is to mask the parts of the doormat which you do not want to paint on. You can do this using painter´s plastic.

6. Now, it's time to spray-paint your stencil on the doormat. Keeping the paint about 5 inches away from the doormat, spray up and down, keeping the can pointing straight through the stencil. If it is at an angle, the paint will get under the stencil and ruin your design. Spray the entire stencil 2-3 times to make sure that you do not miss any part and that the paint is even.

7. You're just about done! Now, remove the masking plastic and the stencil and leave the doormat for about one hour to get dry.

T-Shirts (Vinyl, Iron On)

To make custom t-shirts using your Cricut machine, you will need to use iron-on or heat transfer vinyl. Ensure that you choose a color that contrasts and matches well with your t-shirt.

Materials needed

- Cricut machine.
- T-shirt.
- Iron on or heat transfer vinyl.
- Fine point blade and light grip mat.
- Weeding tools.
- Easy Press (regular household iron works fine too, with a little extra work).
- Small towel and Parchment paper.

Chapter 4 Advanced Tips And Techniques

The design Canvas platform

The following are ways you can work smarter on the design Canvas platform:

1. **Making use of cartridges for searching similar images:** Most times, the numerous outcomes of images gotten from the search bar in the image library can overwhelm a Cricut user. Whenever an image is searched, too many dissimilar results pop up. It, most of the time, makes it difficult to single out one favorite image out of these results. And sometimes, when a favorite image is found, more similar images are always wanted. To stop this from happening again, ensure that you make use of the cartridge of the image you're searching for. The easiest and fastest means of accessing a cartridge of an image is by clicking the small information (i) icon that is located at the bottom right of the image on the Design Space image library. By doing that, the image's details will be revealed. A green link will also appear, giving you access to every image of equal similarity. Knowing this will enable you to start matching or coordinating images, which is more effective than the outcomes from the search bar.

Photo credit- cricut.com

2. **Cutting, Drawing, or Scoring Lines:** In the past, Cricut users had to search for designs that had specific attributes for drawing and scoring a line (instead of cutting.) Not anymore, those days are behind all Cricut users. With the latest upgrade that has been made by Cricut on the Design Space, a user can comfortably change lines from cutting to drawing to scoring by merely making use of the easy-to-use Line type menu positioned at the topmost toolbar.

If you observe closely, you'll discover that almost all designs are tagged as Cut on the Design Space Canvas. Nonetheless, you can easily modify the outline of the image to be either scored (by utilizing the scoring wheel or) or drawn (by using pens.) All you need to do is to make sure that the layers of your design are ungrouped and unattached so that the way the project design will be created will change.

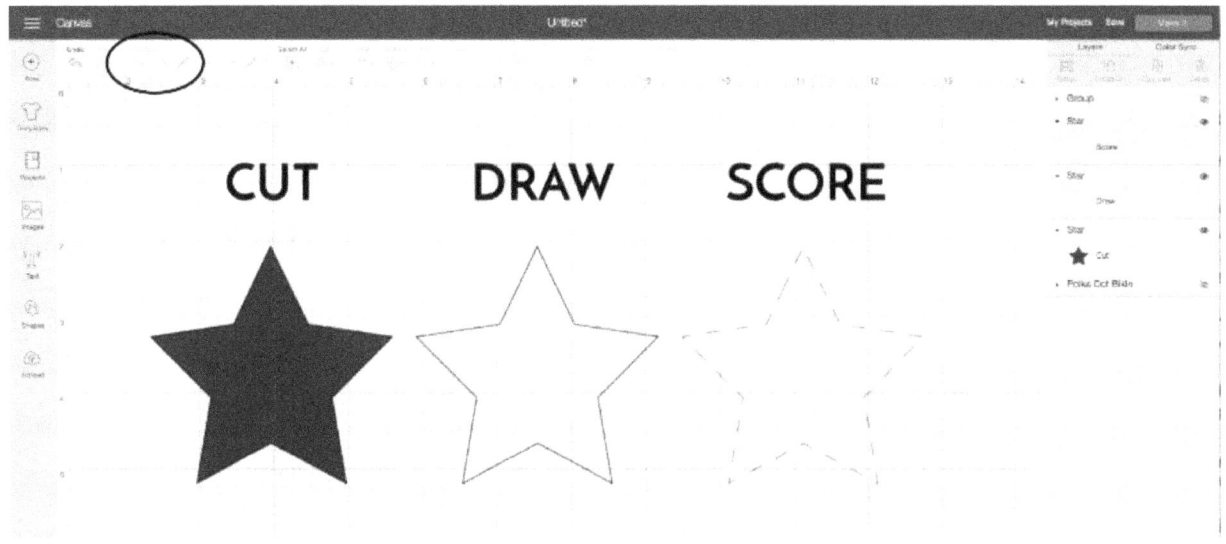

Photo credit- cricut.com

3. **Color Management:** If you can maximize the use of the Color Synchronization tool, you can significantly save much time working on different projects. This will likely ensure that you are using colors that match across various designs. A lot of times, when you work on a lot of designs on the design Canvas simultaneously, you may end up with several shades of similar colors. Instead of choosing all the single layers autonomously to recolor, go to the Color Sync tool positioned on the tool panel on the right side. The colors you will find on this panel are the ones that are presently in use. Notwithstanding, you can also drag active layers that are currently on the design by using your mouse and dropping it in a new color that hasn't been used on the design. If you desire to maintain the use of matching colors throughout your project designs, or you wish to have some layers with the same color in order to cut more efficiently, making use of the Color Sync is the fastest and most comfortable means of doing it.

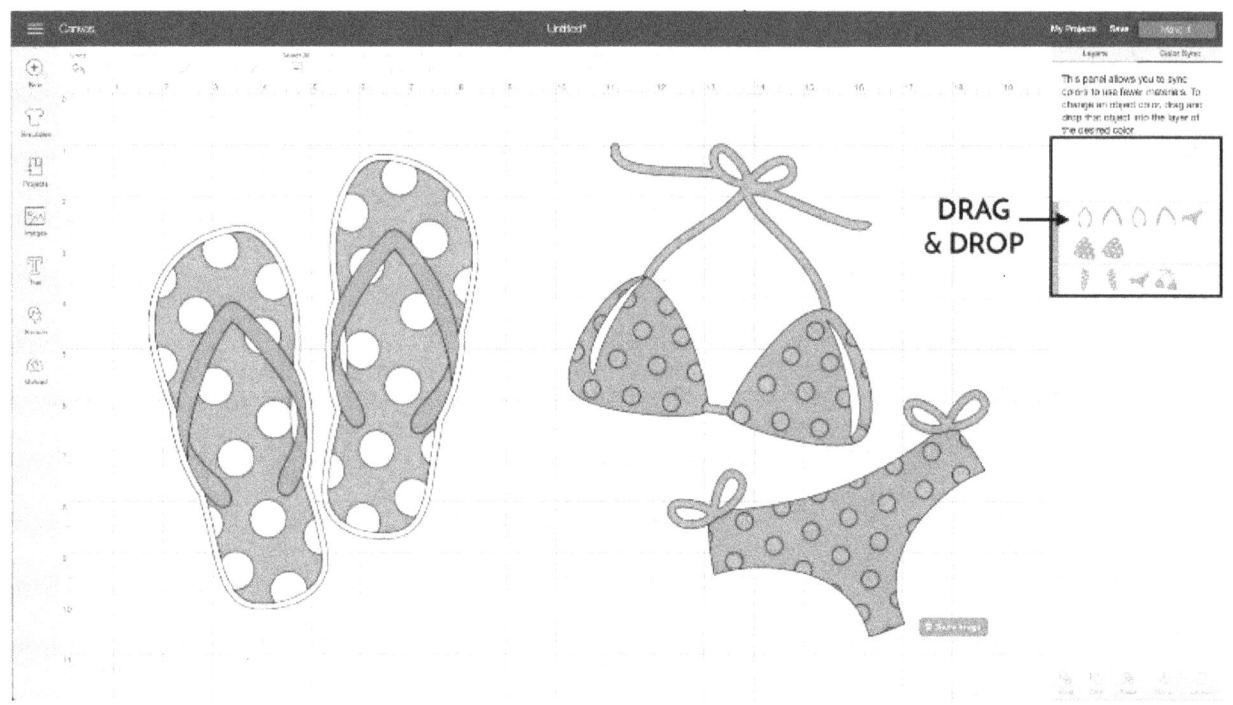

Photo credit- thehomesihavemade.com

4. **Applying the Hide tool:** A lot of users find themselves crowding the Canvas area with too many redundant images while they work on their projects. And they end up cutting all the elements on the Canvas area when the time comes to cut out their projects. There're likewise some times when you will wish or have to cut out some portions of the design you're working on. Instead of getting these unnecessary images deleted off your Canvas screen, you can just hide them by clicking the little eye icon positioned by the right side of the layers panel beside the image. You should note that any image you hide won't be permanently disconnected from the Canvas. However, it will not be added with the rest of the images when moving your project for cutting. You may also toggle the Hide icon on/off. This will make it easier to cut the parts needed only, and also keep an organized and clean design Canvas at the same time, without getting the images you still want to work on mixed up.

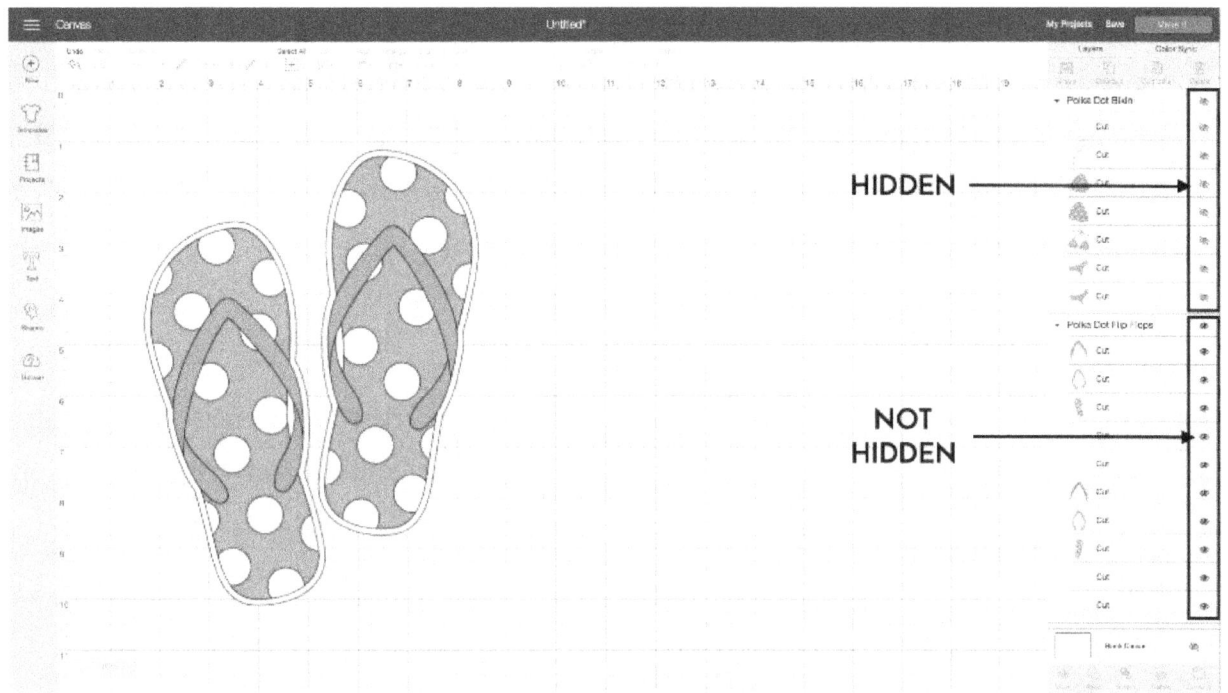

Photo credit- thehomesihavemade.com

5. **Adjust Image Patterns:** The Fill tool located at the topmost toolbar allows you to modify the way you fill images. Picking a single layer from the panel, colors can be switched, or the image interior can be given a different pattern.

There're quite a lot of pre-loaded patterns that can be used to fill images so as to make the project more stimulating without having to depend on patterned scrapbook or cardstock. Even though there're numerous designs to choose from, the scale and orientation of the chosen pattern can also be altered by clicking Edit Pattern located in the Pattern menu under the Fill panel. It is important to note that you can only use this function through the Print then cut method.

6. **Utilizing Keyboard Shortcuts:** Almost every computer program has keyboard shortcuts. Microsoft, Adobe, CorelDraw, and so on, they all have keyboard shortcuts. And just like them, the Design Space has keyboard shortcuts too. There are shortcuts for virtually every command you can think of, shortcuts for Copy, Cut, Paste, Duplicate, Undo, Delete, and many more. These functions are at the corner of every image,

positioned at the topmost toolbar by the right side of the Layers panel. A lot of time can be saved by using as many shortcuts as possible. You can even try making use of functional keyboard shortcuts that work on other computer software out there. Most of these keyboard shortcuts are common; you can make use of Ctrl+C for copying, Ctrl+X for cutting, Ctrl+V for pasting, Ctrl+Z to undo mistakes, etc.

The Cut screen platform

A lot of Cricut users tend to think they won't be able to go further with their project editing once they send it for cutting after designing. They believe the editing ends immediately after clicking on the Make it button. But there are still so many actions and editing that a user can carry out on the Cut screen platform. And if done wisely, you will be able to save a lot of time and spare some materials.

1. **Moving mages around a single mat:** Even though the Design Space software automatically brings all your images and designs on the surface of the mat according to color and orientation, it, most times, does not arrange them exactly the way you would want them. Nevertheless, these items can be moved around the mat surface while you're still on the Cut screen.

   To reorganize your items on the mat surface, you can just start dragging and dropping the images where you need them to be. If you want, you can also rearrange by moving and rotating a cut however you want them on the mat. You can rotate the images by using the handles at the uppermost right corner of the Cut screen.

   By making these adjustments, you won't only be able to make your work more perfect than the default settings would make it, you will also have your cut wherever and however you desire it. Your project looks better with these adjustments, especially when you're working on a scrap or an oddly-shaped material. Just make sure that your Cut screen gridlines are fit into the gridlines of your mat to ensure that your design fits the material correctly wherever it is placed.

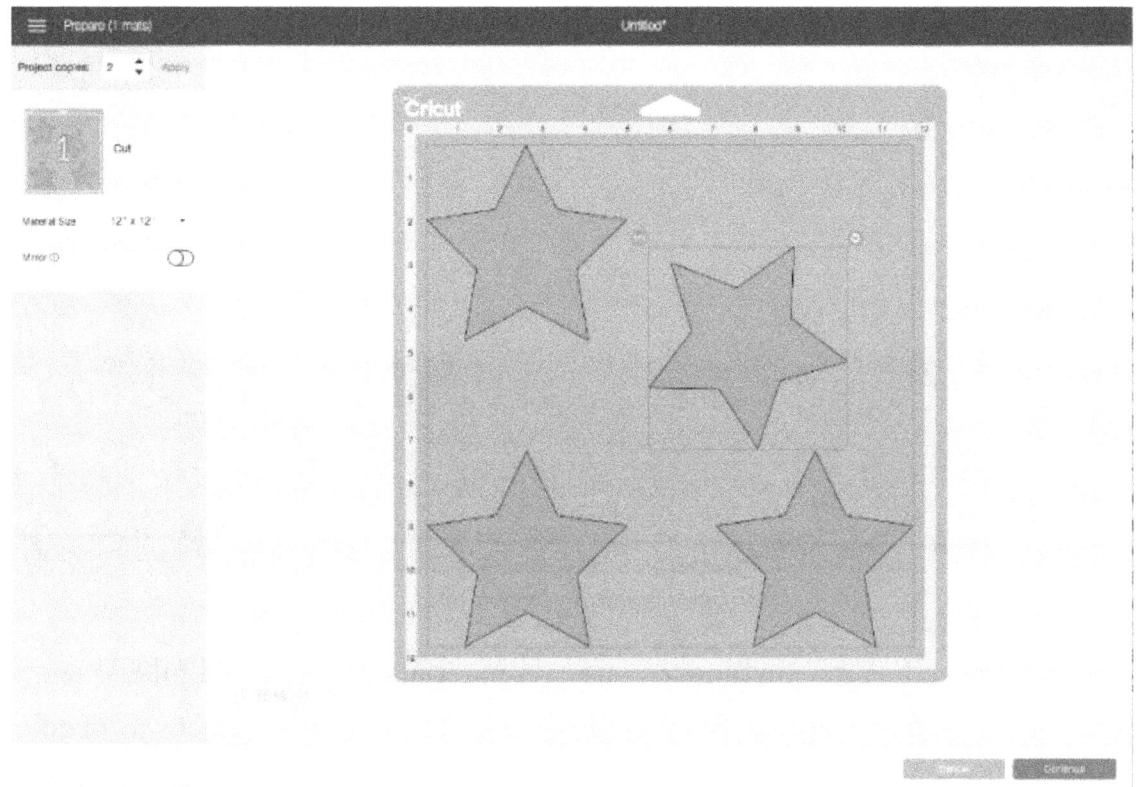

Photo credit- thehomesihavemade.com

2. **Moving images from a mat to another:** Although your images can be moved around just a single mat, you can likewise move the images from a mat to another without having to go back to the design Canvas to change colors. This can be done by clicking the three tiny dots positioned at the uppermost left side corner of that image you're currently working on. Once you've done that, select the Move to Another Mat option. Then you will be allowed to choose the mat you want that image to be on. You'll easily notice the change.

Photo credit- thehomesihavemade.com

This feature can be used anytime to conserve materials. If you're skillful enough, you can arrange all your images to fit into a single mat. This is also a perfect way of quickly changing the colors on designs without having to exit the Cut screen to manually modify the color of the designs.

3. **Re-cut or Skip Mats:** This feature will really prove useful to you if you just know how to use it on the Cut screen. After sending your designs for cutting, the remaining processes don't require much attention. As long as your Cricut machine is fed with the correct paper color and size just exactly as the Cut screen illustrates it, you shouldn't worry about the results; your project should come out precisely the way you designed it. Nonetheless, you may find yourself wanting to re-cut a particular mat after cutting it the first time or wishing to skip the mat that is next in line. The good news is, that can be done easily without you needing to exit the Cut screen.

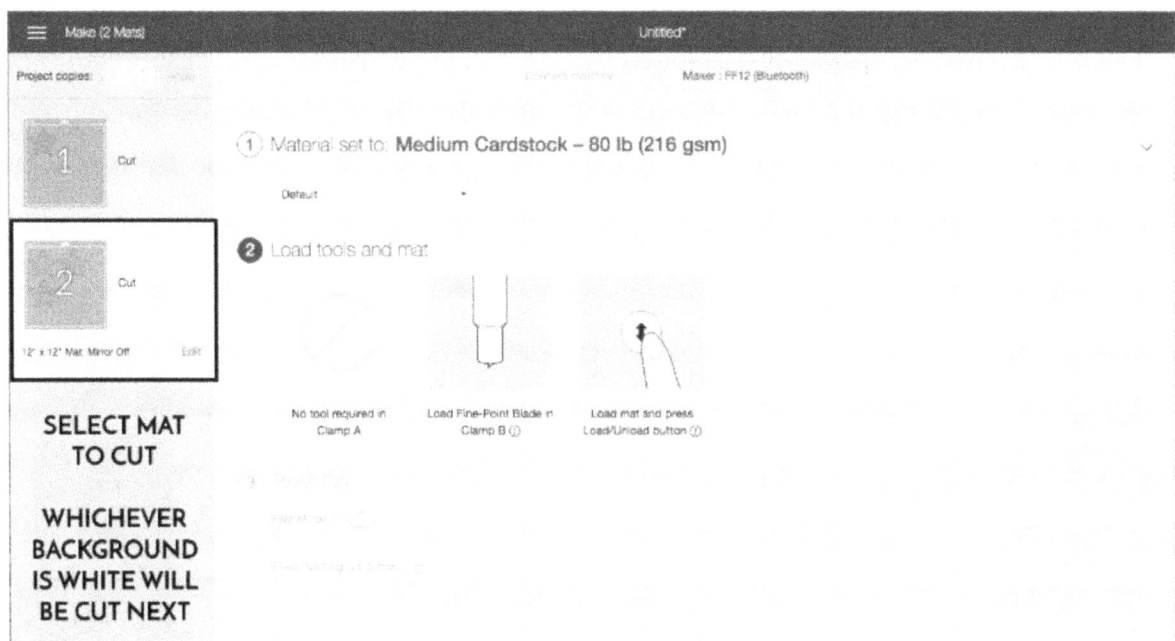

Photo credit- thehomesihavemade.com

However, you need to do this before you load your mat into the machine. You're free to select a particular mat you wish to cut manually by merely clicking or selecting the mat by the left-hand side of the Cut screen. The mat you handpicked will be skipped automatically by the cutting machine.

Moreover, if there is a particular mat you would like to re-cut, even after there're cut-marks all over it showing that the mat has been worked on already, return to the Cut screen and select that particular mat you want to manually re-cut. The Cricut machine will handle the rest automatically. However, much care must be taken when you re-cut or skip mats. Ensure you always double-check if what you're loading into the machine fits perfectly into the emphasized mat on the Cut Screen. A lot of Cricut users make mistakes so many times whenever they re-cut or skip mats without full attention.

4. **Saving commonly used materials:** Many Cricut users feel stunned always when they learn about this particular feature after using the Cricut software for a long time. They realized how much they'd missed! You're certainly missing so much if you're not making use of the Custom materials option. A lot of people, especially those people

making use of the Explore Air 2 series, do not make use of this feature unintentionally because their Cricut machine is set to Vinyl, Iron-in, Cardstock, etc. Only people that use the Cricut Maker machine can notice the Custom materials function within the Design Space easily since there is no available option to choose the material you are cutting.

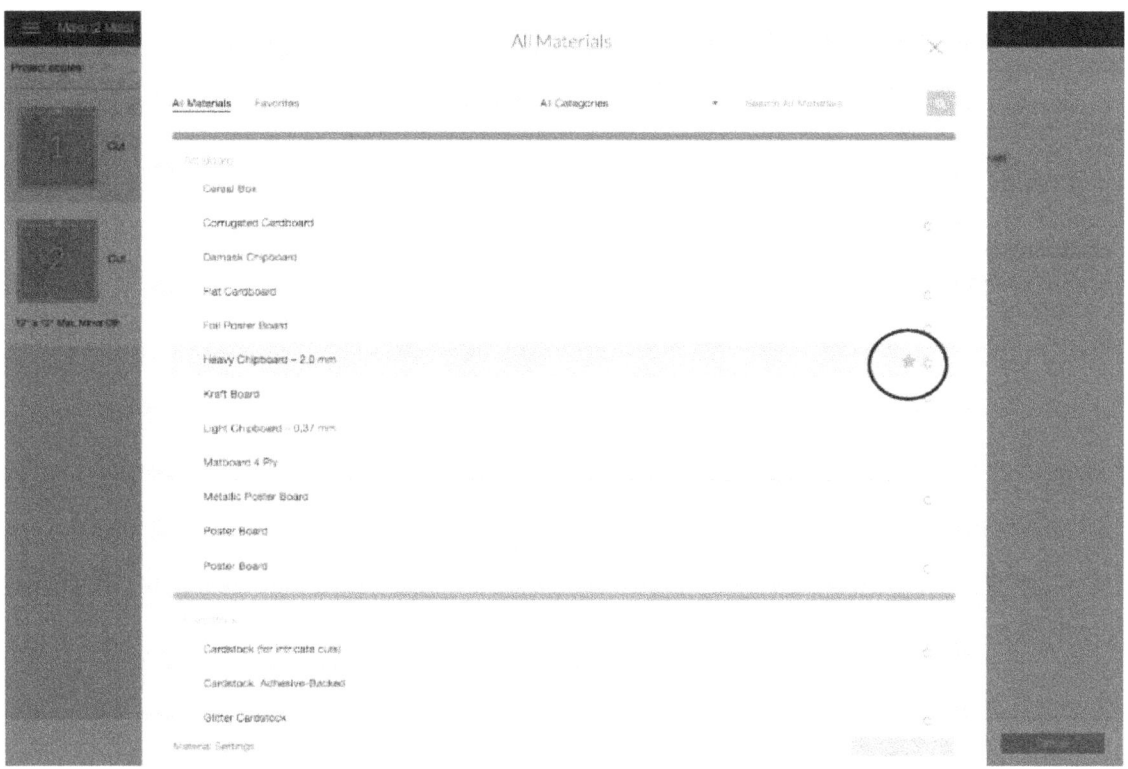

Photo credit- cricut.com

You don't have to go through the stress of strolling through more than a hundred custom materials so as to find the common Cardstock, Vinyl, and Iron-on Vinyl settings over and over again. You can just add each one of these to the Favorite box. It shouldn't take you more than a few minutes to stroll through the Materials menu and locate the materials that you make use of regularly. Just click on the star positioned under the Materials menu, and then proceed to select Favorites instead of Popular on that same menu. Once you've done that, all that will be left is just a menu showing all the materials you mostly cut. That is way easier and comfortable, right?

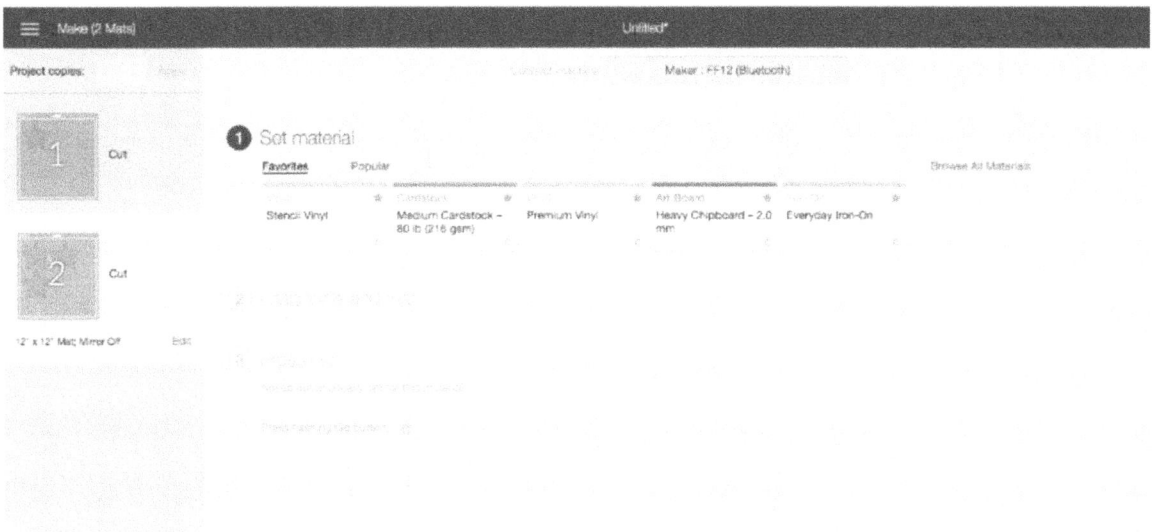

Photo credit- cricut.com

5. **Connecting Two or More Cricut Machines Simultaneously:** Even though a typical Cricut user doesn't often make use of more than a single Cricut machine, it's possible to connect more than one machine to your Design Space account at the same time. You can do this by either using Bluetooth when using a wireless machine model or using a USB with your PC. Moreover, you shouldn't worry about getting your machines and your designs mixed up during the cutting session. The number of Cricut machines you connect to your Design Space doesn't matter. The first step you'll take when you reach the Cut screen is to select which machine you want to use to cut your design. You will find this function in a drop-down menu located at the top. With this step, Cricut ensures that its users can stay assured that they're using the intended machine for their project all the time.

6. **Easily Adjusting Cut Pressure:** Even though it looks fantastic to have the capability of modifying your materials' settings, sometimes all that is required is an extra or lesser pressure to allow your Cricut machine to efficiently cut through the material you set. If you want to adjust the cut pressure, once you've selected your material of choice on the Cut screen, adjust the pressure by using the drop-down menu provided at the top. You can choose to decrease, increase, or make use of the default pressure. Using this

technique, you can effortlessly and swiftly change your cutting depth without having to rummage around the custom settings of your material.

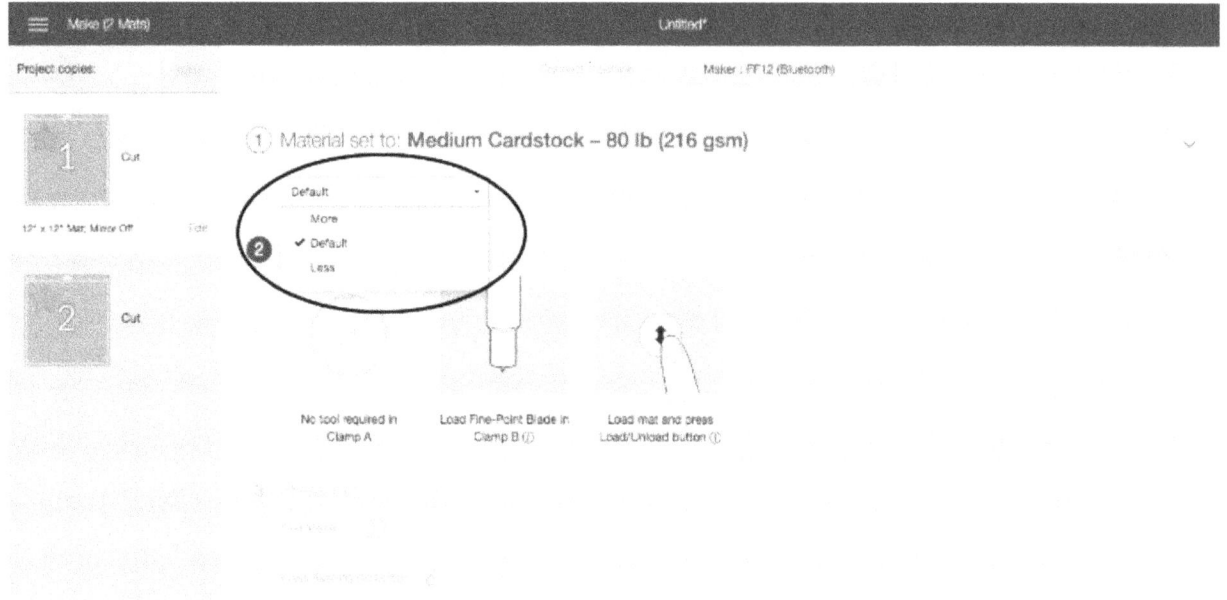

Photo credit- cricut.com

7. **Mirror Setting:** There're times when Cricut users have to do their design cutting in reverse, particularly when they are working on projects with Iron-on. This process of reversing is known as Mirror. Although your designs can always be flipped on the Canvas screen horizontally, there is also an option provided to mirror designs while using the Cut screen.

This setting doesn't only enable you to mirror the images or mats you want to flip; it also allows you to create and adjust your designs without having to flip them on the Canvas screen. It gets easier to view and customize your designs on the mat.

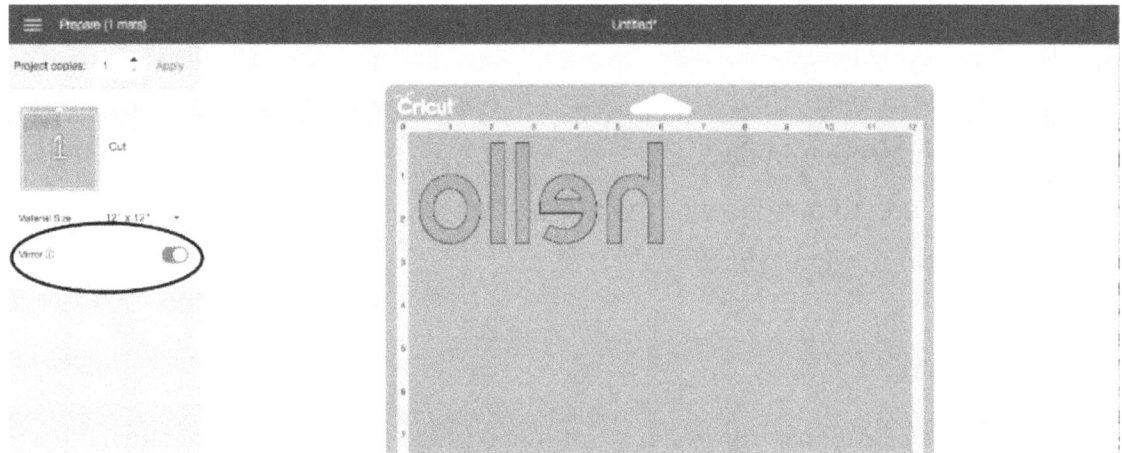

Photo credit- thehomesihavemade.com

8. **Filling your mat by adjusting project copies**: A lot of Cricut users don't get to use this cool Auto-fill function, either by unawareness or unavailability. This function can only be accessed on Cricut machine models that are old. Using the old machine models, a single star can be put on your Canvas, and you can select your paper size manually, and then select Auto-fill without stress. Once you click on Auto-fill, your Cricut machine will fill up the paper with stars automatically, fitting in as many stars as your paper can comfortably take. Even though you will not find this function in the most recent Design Space, there is an easy way of doing almost the same thing the function does.

There is a particular option located at the uppermost part of the Cut screen once you reach the Cut screen platform where the settings of your project copies can be done. This function allows you to cut for as much time as you want on the Design Canvas. Although it could take some time to figure out the exact number of project copies you need to fill your mat, it's way faster than duplicating your designs on the Design Canvas.

All the tips and techniques that have been given so far should be carefully studied. Some of them may look subtle, but you shouldn't overlook them if you don't want to end up wasting your time or materials. Many full-time Cricut users are always on the hunt for information on how they can save time and materials while on the Design Space. The information is in your hand right now, what you do with it is now your decision.

Using advanced design space tools

There are some many Design Space tools that will look mysterious to a beginner or new user. Some will almost seem meaningless and redundant. However, these tools are not useless or worthless; you just don't know how to make use of them yet. The following are some of the advanced tools on the Design Space.

The Flatten tool

The Flatten tool has a lot of usefulness. It's not just a tool that flattens; it performs more than one function. Below are some of its functions:

- The Flatten tool changes multi-layered pictures into one single-layered image.
- It is used to convert an image to a printable image, to enable it for print-and-cut.
- It removes every cut line from an image.
- It retains every color of a multi-layered image.

How to make use of the Flatten tool

- Pick the layers that you want to flatten by clicking on Select All, or by pressing and holding the Ctrl key on the keyboard while clicking on the layers.
- When you've selected all the layers you want, click on Flatten positioned at the lower right corner.
- Once you've done that, your image becomes flattened. All you will see on the Layers panel is one layer with a text that says, Flatten.

The Color Sync tool

Like the Flatten tool, the Color Sync tool also has more than one function for Design Space users who know their way around it. Below are some of its functions:

- The Color Sync tool can be used to recolor shapes, layers, etc.

- It can be used to match the colors of all layers on the Canvas.

- It is very useful for consolidating material colors.

- It saves a user so much time and materials.

This feature wasn't available in the old version of the Design Space. But now that it is available in the new version, why not make exploits with it? This tool makes it much more comfortable to synchronize colors in a project so a user can cut them all on a single material. All you have to do is open the Color Sync panel located at the right side of the screen, and then start dragging and dropping all the shapes respectively into the selected layer you wish for it to synchronize to. If you desire to cut every star in chartreuse, for example, then just drag every other star to that same layer at the Color Sync panel. It feels so much easier to do this, and knowing they are all going to have the same color is comforting!

Sketching on the Design Space

One of the most interesting facts about using the Cricut Explore model is that users can also upload images that they have drawn themselves! There are two techniques of doing this, one is by making use of Illustrator, and the other is by making use of the Design Space. And since we're discussing about the Design Space, I'll only mention how to do so on the latter. The following are the processes:

- You first need to have the intended image on your computer by importing it. So, if you've hand-drawn what you want on a piece of paper or your tablet, the next step is to scan it to your computer, snap it with your mobile device and send it to your computer, or save and send it to the computer through your tablet. Whichever way you want to do it, ensure you save it as a png or jpeg file.

- Convert the sketch using the Design Space by first uploading the image, making use of the Upload tab by the left side.

- You will be requested to choose the image type; you should select the option that fits your image background. Proceed by clicking Continue and let your image be saved as a Cut image, and then click Save. You will notice that your image is now a Cut file.

And that's how you upload and work with your sketch on the Design Space. With this function, you can let your creativity run wild! There are so many things you can do with your hands! Since you're not limited by the Design Space platform, don't ever let your imagination be limited!

Chapter 5 Other Tips & Tricks

There are so many tricks that can help you use your Cricut machine better and faster to ensure that you are getting the most out of it.

Each machine has tips and tricks to make it work better. We tell you what sites you can go on and what stores you can go to find supplies as well. Many people assume that the only place that you can go to get this kind of supplies is a crafting store. A crafting store is one of the best places that you can get the supplies because they do offer discounts in certain cases and they offer great quality for the products you want. However, they are not the only store that gives high-quality products, and we'll let you know where you can go and to get supplies of high-quality but do not cost an arm and a leg. People do not know that you can go into other stores because the craft world can come with a stigma that you are supposed to shop only in crafting stores. This is not true, however, and we will tell you how to get great supplies.

We give you tips on how to clean your machine and what not to do which is going to help you to be able to understand just how easy it is to damage your machine. These machines can be very temperamental and doing the wrong thing can damage them in a way that makes it so you might have to buy another machine. As these machines are a hefty investment, you do not want to break it on accident, and we have given you tips for how to avoid this.

There are also tips on things you can use instead of the supplies that are listed here. Meaning, if you are in a pinch and you run out of your regular supplies, there are things that you can use instead. We also give you some great tips on how to get the best quality of work from your machine and how to keep your machine running at its best. This is going to be great for you as an owner because this means that you are going to be able to make your machine last longer. For the people that do not have information about their machine, and they do not know how to take care of their machine, their machine is going to wear out much quicker. So, let us dive into our tips and tricks!

- Look in other places besides craft stores to find supplies. Some great examples are sites like eBay or look into clearance sales. One of the best places that people have found to be a great place for supplies is 'Dollar Tree'. You can find vinyl, fabric, or boards to use.

- Another tip that ties into the Dollar Tree is that you can find supplies for transforming your craft room into how you want it and finding tools to keep your supplies organized.

- Curling is a big problem with projects, and this next tip is going to show you how you can avoid it by remembering not to peel the paper away from your cutting mat. Peel the cutting mat away from the paper instead. Roll your mat backward away from the material that you're cutting. This is especially true if you are cutting paper. If you do this, you will get a nice cut and flat project. If you do not do this, then it can curl massively and shred along with tearing.

- Keeping your mats clean is also going to be a great way to make them last longer so you do not have to replace them as often and waste your money. A great tip for keeping those mats clean is to use your lint roller. Make sure that you have removed all the little papers and roll away. The lint roller trick is especially beneficial if you have been cutting glitter cardstock. Since this does not remove everything, you should be aware of that, but it will get rid of most things.

- Freezer paper makes great stencils and you can get it for only a dollar!

- Keeping your blades separate and organized will help too. Having separate blades for vinyl or fabric will help the blades stay sharp and the way you need them to longer. Keeping the blades separate is also going to help you be more organized. If you want, you can use a permanent marker on each of the blades so that you know what blade is for what particular material you want to cut with them. It is like owning a pair of fabric scissors. You would not use fabric scissors to cut paper, so instead, keep your blades sharp by keeping them separate. You can make a small mark which blades are for what material. If you do not want to use the marker on them, you can make a chart. Just remember to replace the cap so that they are not getting mixed up.

- You can also spray paint on your vinyl if you need color and don't have it, just make sure it's a Rust-oleum metallic spray and give it a quick spray. Make sure the vinyl isn't cut and dry it before cutting. This is going to help ensure that you have the proper cutting techniques and you have the proper settings in place. This also ensures that you are not wasting materials, time or money.

- Besides Cricut pens, there are a variety of other options that work for Explore machines. They include American Crafts, Recollection, Sharpies, or even Crayola.

- You can also use your system fonts in your projects. You can go to sites that offer fonts to find a lot of amazing ones for free and then you can use them for your machine.

- If you have a smaller or more intricate design you can use a weeding box. This is especially helpful if you're cutting multiple designs on one mat.

- Make sure that your dial is set to the correct setting for materials. It is very easy to forget that this is in the wrong setting and then the cut can be wrong.

- Load your mat correctly. Both sides of the mat need to be able to slide under the rollers or the mat will not cut in the correct manner.

- When you can no longer make a smooth cut or an effective cut, you need new blades. Be careful when replacing them because you can cut yourself pretty badly.

- You can clean your cutting mats with baby wipes as well. They need to be water-based and using them to keep your mats clean can help them stay sticky longer. Make sure that these baby wipes have no fragrance. If they are not water-based, they will damage the mat and you will not be able to use it again.

- Keep the plastic sheets that come with your mats and you can protect the mats between uses. This helps your mats last longer so that you can use them repeatedly.

- If you are not sure about the correct cut setting, run a small test cut first. This is especially true if you have a larger project. Doing this is going to make sure that you are not wasting expensive materials that you want and need. It will also make sure you understand what cuts can do to materials.

- Your vinyl needs to be placed the right way up on the cutting mat. The heat transfer vinyl should always be placed shiny side down.

- When you are cutting heat transfer vinyl, you need to remember to mirror the design. This is crucial because if you do not, then you will be cutting incorrectly, and your project could be ruined as a result.

- The Cricut toolset is not a necessity, but it can certainly help, and it can be a great thing to have on hand when you're mastering your machine. It also has many different items that can make your crafting easier and less of a hassle.

- Many card projects require that you have a stylus. If the machine you bought is part of a bundle it can have the stylus inside it already, but some may not. This is something to ask the person at the store when you are buying one because the stylus can really help.

- Make sure that you do a practice project before a real one as well because this will let you get adjusted to your machine and make sure that you do not waste materials on your first project. When you buy your machine, there should be a practice project already in place.

- Make sure that your blade is placed correctly. If it is placed too high, it may only cut part of the way through, but if it is down to low, it will ruin your mat. A test cut will make sure it is in the right spot therefore could save you a lot of frustration.

- Many people forget that the pen is in their machine after finishing a project and that can be a big no-no. The reason for this is because if the lid is not on it, it will dry out and the pens can get very expensive. So be sure to put the pen cap back on and make sure it is all the way on.

- Keeping some supplies on demand is a good idea as well, particularly if you're going to be working with vinyl and cardstock. Since most projects use vinyl, you could have some of that on hand along with a pack of cardstock and things of that nature.

- Know which machine has which options on it. The machines are different and can come with different settings as well.

- When your mat loses its stickiness, you may think that you have to buy a new one. You do not, however, at least in most cases, because there are tips you can use here too. Clean your mat and see if that works and then tape your project down to hold it in place. Not over an area that needs to be cut but just over a few edges. A tack paint that is medium tape is good for this and shouldn't damage the cardstock.

- A trick for installing fonts into your computer, you may need to sign out of the app and then back in before your new font will show up. If this does not work, then be sure to restart your computer.

- The deep cut blade is a handy tip here as well. Having the deep blade means you can cut through thicker materials like chipboard, felt, and leather. It is compatible with the Explore Air 2. Just make sure when you get this blade, you get the housing for it as well.

- If you have a project that cuts on two different materials (such as a pink cardstock and a purple cardstock), you can do this at the same time by positioning the designs you will be cutting in different areas of the Canvas on your app. Click Attach, then position the materials in the same spot on the map. This tip can be applied to Design Space for desktop and web.

If you use all of these tips, you will be able to use your machine to your heart's content and make any project. You will also be able to save money so that you're not spending a fortune on supplies every time you run out. Utilize these to your benefit and enjoy being able to use your machine with better knowledge.

Chapter 6 Common Problems And How To Solve Them

Material tearing or not cutting completely through

This is the biggest problem with most Cricut users. When this happens, the image is ruined, and you've wasted material. More machines have been returned or boxed up and put away due to this problem than any other.

But don't panic, if your paper is not cutting correctly there are several steps you can take to try and correct the problem.

Most important is this: Anytime you work with the blade TURN YOUR MACHINE OFF. I know it's easy to forget this because you're frustrated and you're trying this and that to make it work correctly. But this is an important safety precaution that you should remember.

Make simple adjustments at first. Turn the pressure down one. Did it help? If not, turn the blade down one number. Also, make sure the mat is free of debris so the blade rides smoothly.

Usually the thicker the material, the higher the pressure number should be set to cut through the paper. Don't forget to use the multi-cut function if you have that option. It may take a little longer to cut 2, 3, or 4 times, but by then it should cut clean through.

For those of you using the smaller bugs that do not have that option here is how to make your multi-cut function. After the image has been cut, don't unload the mat just hit load paper, repeat last, and cut. You can repeat this sequence 2, 3, or 4 times to ensure your image is completely cut out.

If you are using thinner paper and it is tearing try reducing the pressure and slowing down the speed. When cutting intricate designs, you have to give the blade enough time to maneuver through the design. By slowing it down it will be able to make cleaner cuts.

Clean the edge of the blade to be sure no fuzz, glue, or scraps of paper are stuck to it.

Make sure the blade is installed correctly. Take it out and put it back so it's seated firmly. The blade should be steady while it's making cuts. If it makes a shaky movement it's either not installed correctly, or there's a problem with the blade housing.

Be aware that there is a deep cutting blade for thicker material. You'll want to switch to this blade when you're cutting heavy card stock. This will also save wear and tear on your regular blade. Cutting a lot of thick material will wear your blade out quicker than thinner material and cause you to change it more often.

Machine freezing

Remember to always turn your machine off when you switch cartridges. When you switch cartridges leaving the machine on it's called "hot swapping" and it can sometimes cause the machine to freeze. This is more of an issue with the older models and doesn't seem to apply to the Expression 2.

You know how peculiar electronic gadgets can be, so give your machine a rest for five or ten minutes every hour. If you work for several hours continuously, your machine might overheat and freeze up.

Turn the machine off and take a break. Restart it when you come back and it should be fine. Then remember not to rush programming the machine and give it an occasional rest.

Don't press a long list of commands quickly. If you give it too much information too quickly it will get confused in the same way a computer sometimes does and simply freeze up. Instead of typing in one long phrase try dividing up your words into several cuts.

If you're using special feature keys make sure you press them first before selecting the letters.

Power problems

If you turn your machine on and nothing happens the power adapter may be at fault. Jiggle the power cord at the outlet and where it connects to the machine to make sure it's firmly connected. Ideally, you want to test the adapter before buying a new one. Swap cords with a friend and see if that fixed the problem. Replacement adapters can be found on eBay by searching for a Cricut adapter power supply.

The connection points inside the machine may also pose a problem; here is how to test that. Hold down the plug where it inserts into the back of the machine and turn it on. If it powers up, then the problem is inside the machine and the connection points will have to be soldered again.

If the machine powers up but will not cut then try a hard reset. See the resource section for step-by-step instructions on resetting your machine.

Here are a few tips especially for Expression 2 users. Have you turned on your machine, you watch it light up and hear it gearing up but when you try to cut nothing happens? Or you're stuck on the welcome screen or the LCD screen is unresponsive.

Well here are two quick fixes to try. First, try a hard reset sometimes called the rainbow screen reset to recalibrate your die cutter. If that does not resolve the problem you're going to have to restore the settings.

To help cut down on errors try to keep your machine updated. When an update is available, you should receive a message encouraging you to install the latest version.

For those of you using third-party software that is no longer compatible with the Cricut you probably already know that updating your machine may disable that software.

When you cut heavy paper and your Expression 2 shuts down try switching to the normal paper setting and use the multi-cut function.

Carriage will not move

If the carriage assembly does not move, check to see if the belt has broken or if the car has fallen off the track. Provo Craft does not sell replacement parts, which is nuts, so try to find a compatible belt at a vacuum repair shop.

If the wheels have fallen off the track, remove the plastic cover, and look for a tiny screw by the wheel unscrew it. You now should be able to move the wheel back on track.

Unresponsive keyboard

If you are sure you are pressing the keys firmly, you have a cartridge inserted correctly and a mat loaded ready to go, but the keypad is still not accepting your selection, the problem may be internal.

You will have to remove the keyboard and check if the display cable is connected to the keypad and to the motherboard. If the connections are secure then you have a circuit board problem and repairs are beyond the scope of this book.

An important reminder, please do not attempt any repairs unless your machine is out of warranty.

Weird LCD screen

The LCD screen is now showing strange symbols or is blank after doing a firmware update. Try running the update again making sure your selections are correct.

When the image you choose is bigger than the mat or paper size you selected, the preview screen will look grayed out instead of showing the image. So, increase the paper and mat size or decrease the size of your image.

Also, watch out for the gray box effect when using the center point feature. Move the start position down until you see the image appear. The same thing may happen when using the fit to length feature. Try changing to landscape mode and shorten the length size until the image appears.

Occasionally using the undo button will cause the preview screen to turn black; unfortunately, the only thing to do is turn the machine off. Your work will be lost and you have to start again.

Cartridge errors

Sometimes dust or debris accumulates in the cartridge port; gently blow out any paper fiber that may have collected in the opening. Make sure the contact points are clean and that nothing is preventing the cartridge from being read properly.

With any electrical machine overheating can be a problem. If you get a cartridge error after using your machine for a while turn it off and let it cool down for about fifteen minutes.

If this is the very first time you're using the cartridge and you get an error I'm sure you know the trick about turning the cartridge around and inserting it in backward.

If you thought you could use your Imagine cartridges with your Expression 2, think again. You will get an error message because you can only use the art cartridges that you can cut with, the colors and patterns cartridges are for printing.

Even brand-new items fresh out of the box can be defective. If you see a cartridge error 1, 2, 3, 4, 5, 6, 9, or 99 call customer service and tell them the name, serial number, and error message number and they may replace the cartridge.

Trouble connecting to your computer

All Cricut machines come with a USB cord that lets you connect to your computer and allows you to use the other products like the Cricut Design Studio software, Cricut Craft Room, or the Cricut Gypsy with your machines.

Double check your USB connection and try another port.

Check to see if you may have a firewall or antivirus software that is blocking the connection.

See if you're running the latest firmware. You may need to update. Older machines update via firmware (Personal Cutter, Expression, Create, and Cake) the newer (Expression 2, Imagine, and Gypsy) use the Sync program to update.

When anything else fails

I know that no one wants to hear this. But there are going to be times when you may have to resort to calling customer service. This is especially true if your machine is still under warranty. You don't' want to do anything that might void the warranty on a truly defective machine.

Sadly, Prove Craft is known for its long wait times and sometimes less than stellar service. Stick it out and demand that your machine is fixed or replaced.

After a while, you may notice some of your projects coming out in a condition that is less-than-crisp.

Ensure your machine is on stable footing

This may seem pretty basic but ensuring that your machine is on a level surface will allow it to make more precise cuts every single time. Rocking of the machine or wobbling could cause unstable results in your projects.

Ensure no debris has gotten stuck under the feet of your machine that could cause instability before proceeding to the next troubleshooting step!

Redo all cable connections

So, your connections are in the best possible working order, undo all your cable connections, blow into the ports or use canned air, and then securely plug everything back into the right ports. This will help to make sure all the connections are talking to each other where they should be!

Completely dust and clean your machine

Your little Cricut works hard for you! Return the favor by making sure you're not allowing gunk, dust, grime, or debris to build up in the surfaces and crevices. Adhesive can build up on the machine around the mat input and on the rollers, so be sure to focus on those areas!

Check your blade housing

Sometimes debris and leavings from your materials can build up inside the housings for your blades! Open them up and clear any built-up materials that could be impeding swiveling or motion.

Sharpen your blades

A very popular Cricut trick in use is to stick a clean, fresh piece of foil to your Cricut mat, and run it through with the blade you wish to sharpen. Running the blades through the thin metal helps to revitalize their edges and give them a little extra staying power until it's time to buy replacements.

Another way to do this is to make a ball of foil, remove the blades from the housing, and stick them into the ball of foil several times until you notice a shine on the blade. This can give you a better idea of how sharpened your blades are becoming before you finish up with them, and it seems like a more expedient way to sharpen several blades in one sitting, but the reviews seem to be equally as positive as letting your machine do the work for you on one blade at a time.

Conclusion

The following step is to utilize your new found wisdom on the cutting edge craft project designing and creation offered by "Cricut". You are now poised to follow the detailed instructions described in this manuscript to create your own personalized and one of a kind craft projects that reflect your creativity and serve as an exhibit of your expression.

The possibilities that the Cricut machine has to offer are endless. Every craftsman, beginner, or professional creates beautiful craft pieces according to their level of expertise regarding the Cricut Machine, and after reading this manuscript, you will not be left out. This manuscript has deliberated enough information that you are already ready to go and perform a great artwork of which the world will be proud. So get to work straight away and start creating beautiful crafts. Owning this type of machine is a prime opportunity for many people to develop their expertise in craftsmanship, and it's incredible if you want to venture out and try new things as a crafter because you can add so many new items to your portfolio.

As a result, this machine can literally offer never-ending opportunities for a crafter.

In this manuscript, we've discussed how to set up your Cricut machine as well as the advantages of owning one, and we gave you all the information you need to be able to use it efficiently and effectively. It is very typical to get overwhelmed when you own a Cricut machine because of all the information. Still, we told you exactly what you need to know to get started and start creating impressive and innovative projects. There's so much information out there, and the best part is that most of it is free, which means you have more opportunities to get images and things you need to craft, but it also means you get a much bigger chance to get ideas for your projects.

Most people don't even know where to get information about their machine or the items they can use to start crafting, but this manuscript has all the information you need from describing the Cricut machine's most basic function to reflecting ideas for experienced users. We have also shown you that once you have the required skills and the right resources, you can cut even more with the Cricut machines, so you are aware of this as well. In this way, we've made sure you can never forget exactly what you can cut using this machine. However, if you're ever confused, there's a whole part in this manuscript on how to set up your machine and how to set up your design space. We have also included some helpful hints and tips to make sure you have some great ideas on how to make it easier for you to use this machine and the supplies, and you can use all of these tips to your advantage. If you follow the tips you've found in this manuscript, you're going to be able to find supplies easier, keep your mats cleaner, use your machine way better, maintain your machine considerably better, and even gain some amazing storage tips and actually make your craft space a place you can be proud of and feel happy and content while you're working. The ability to do that will help boost both your craftsmanship and your emotions.

Cricut Design Space is a web-based program just as a partner application and now a beta Desktop software that permits you to make, transfer, and oversee records to work the Cricut Maker and Cricut Explore machines. You can get to the application remotely in individual machines, utilizing your PC, tablet, and even cell phone. Cricut Design Space™ additionally permits you to get to a library of tasks and files to download.

CRICUT PROJECT IDEAS

Introduction

A Cricut machine permits us to do projects with insane exactness since it replaces what we would routinely cut with either scissors or an x-acto. Including inconspicuous speed and quality. You can get to their library of the plan by subscription by paying per project OR (and this is the thing that I like the most) you can transfer your records and work of art! This little force wonder permits creatives a smooth, experience as we've never had before. With the Cricut machines, you can make not just paper crafts or modifying clothing with vinyl, carving, or stenciling. In any case, cut texture and more than 100 different materials. The people at Cricut are additionally altering the business by carrying sublimation printing to crafter's fingertips with perhaps the most recent discharge, Infusible Ink! The introduction of Infusible Ink items have been a distinct advantage because Infusible Ink heat moves are always implanted into your base material. They keep going as long as the undertaking itself. No chipping, no stripping, no splitting, and no wrinkling—ever! So, to summarize, a Cricut machine is your envisioned right hand with regards to making!

Cricut Design Space is a web-based program just as a partner application and now a beta Desktop software that permits you to make, transfer, and oversee records to work the Cricut Maker and Cricut Explore machines. You can get to the application remotely in individual machines, utilizing your PC, tablet, and even your cell phone. Cricut Design Space™ additionally permits you to get to a library of tasks and files to download.

Imagine if Pinterest had a baby with an otherworldly site that fundamentally does all your creating for you. That is the Cricut Design Space. Cricut Design Space is a web-based program that lets you peruse pages and pages of predesigned extensions to structure your projects on your work area, computer, tablet, and phone. Cricut Design Space houses more than 75,000 pictures, 400 fonts, and more than 800 predesigned Make It Now projects. The Make It Now areas are far accomplished for you, and all you need to do is to click "Go."

Cricut Design Space additionally lets you transfer your JPEG and SVG files just as your fonts. It's a workhorse. Talk has it the Design Space can likewise foresee the winning lottery numbers for the following ten years. That is false.

What Is Cricut Access?

If you somehow happened to mosey on over to Cricut Design Space right this second... proceed... I'll pause.

Did you mosey?

Presently, without a Design Space Subscription, you'll pay about a buck for each picture you use, and about $3-7 for each Make It Now venture you buy. It'll fundamentally work as an "individual" administration. You'll pick what you need, and you'll pay for it. I loathe that thought. I detest paying for things.

Cricut Access is the service for all you folks who likewise prefer not to pay for things. Cricut Access gives you access to a vast number of pictures, text styles, full cartridges, and Make It Now extensions at no extra expense. Here is how it works:

What Do I Get?

Well—it'll rely upon which Cricut Access participation you pick–don't stress–they're all extraordinary.

Monthly:

- Pay $9.99 on a month-to-month premise and get boundless access to more than 400 fonts and 75,000 pictures... no compelling reason to follow through on individual costs for every textual style you love.
- 10% off of all requests on the Cricut website and 10% off of licensed images.

- The simplicity of scanning for Cricut Access pictures because of the convenient minimal green flags that direct you to all photographs, cartridges, textual styles, and activities that are saved for your account.

Yearly:

Just like the month to month subscription. When you pay for an entire year, you save money!

Premium:

Identical benefits as the month-to-month and yearly subscriptions, with that special reward of more reserve funds like FREE transporting on orders over $50!

What Don't I Get?

There are a few pictures, fonts, and activities that won't be remembered for your Cricut Access membership, however, you do get 10% off any Design Space content that you'd need to pay for out of pocket

Cricut Access membership doesn't permit you to utilize your 10% markdown on the renewal of your Cricut Access memberships... shucks.

How Much Does It Cost?

Now, how about we talk dollar bills! There are two options:

- You can pay for the entire year without a moment's delay for $95.80, which comes to about $7.99 per month OR
- You can pay $9.99 per month for your membership with the alternative to drop whenever.

Whichever way you go, you'll have boundless access to a vast amount of substance and all that could be needed to start creating. I like to take the "pull out all the stops" alternative and pay for everything in advance. That way, come June, I've disregarded that $95.80, and I incline that I am merely getting everything for free!!!! (I know everyone will be with me on this).

For What Reason Should I Care?

Here is how I see it: if you possess a Cricut Explore Air or Cricut Maker, at that point, Cricut Access is the best way to go. You burned through all that cash on a great machine so you would do well to utilize it. Try not to let it sit in the corner and transform into a brightening rack. Set that awful kid to work! It will astound you, and in a matter of hours, you'll be snared. With my Cricut Access participation, I concoct many reasons under the sun to utilize my machine. You'll discover pictures that you never knew existed, and you'll have a fabulous time using them in imaginative manners.

Amazing—and remember, you'll get 10% off every one of those provisions from the Cricut website, which incorporates mats, cutting edges, vinyl, Easy Press machines, and tools among loads of different things.

Chapter 1. Cricut Design Space Project Ideas

Craft Ideas for Your Cricut Cutting Machine

Want any Cricut ideas for the cutting software for your Cricut? Cricut personal electric cutters are revolutionizing handcrafts, and the amount of creative and beautiful things they can suddenly do are astounding people around the world.

The way a Cricut works is simple: just load one of the many cartridges available into the cutter, choose what color card stock you'd like to work with for that particular design, and cut away. Each cartridge has a number of thematic designs-anything from seasonal designs to favorite superheroes-and Cricut users can choose from each cartridge one or more designs. Then, the designs cut out are fixed on.

- Fitting the wall
- Scrapbooks
- Photo frames
- Custom greeting cards-you call them-as with a Cricut, anything is possible.

Maybe the most endearing idea for Cricut craft would be a Cricut calendar. With each month, a separate page might be created, and each of these separate pages could be decorated with different designs. July, for instance, will be trimmed with the designs used in the Seasonal Cartridge Independence Day, while February is the obvious choice for the Seasonal Cartridge Love Struck. However, the fun isn't stopping there, and the Mother's Day Cartridge would be perfect for May, while the Easter Cartridge is a natural April. Cricut-land is unique to December, and Cricut handlers have numerous sets of designs to choose from, like the Joys of the Season Cartridge besides the Snow Friends Cartridge.

What would life be without scrapbooks to document our most precious belongings of every single waking moment: our children? Scrapbooks can be customized to each and every child with the Cricut cutting machine, and what could be better than, for mother and daughter or father and son, to settle down together and choose with which images they wish to decorate their own pictures. Cricut also knows that boys and girls are different and that while the boys probably won't like using the Once Upon a Princess Cartridge, they'd definitely go wild over the Batman: The Brave and The Bold Cartridge. On the other hand, little girls would probably turn their dainty noses up at the Robotz Cartridge but love the Disney Tinker Bell and Friends Cartridge. For Cricut scrapbooking ideas, you never will be at a loss.

Nevertheless, your Cricut layout ideas are not only limited to photos, and there are also alphabets available-such as the Sesame Street Font Cartridge, and the Ashlyn's Alphabet Cartridge-that would be handy whenever it's time to customize a gift. Ideal gifts should include pictures of beloved pets-or even vinyl wall-hangings commemorating a special event such as that overseas trip-all embellished with beautiful and colorful Cricut cut-outs of course. Cricut provides for every possibility, and at this time they Create a Critter Cartridge and the Seasonal Cartridge Summer in Paris would be perfect to accompany your Cricut home decor. Birthdays, Christmas, Graduations, Bar Mitzvahs, baby showers: the list of presents is boundless, and that does not even comprise those ventures "made for fun." Cricut has cartridges that can be thought of to match every single occasion-and every single project. Completing a Cricut project together is also a great way for a family to bond with each other, and the beautiful things made together can be treasured for a lifetime. With a personal electric cutter from Cricut, only the sky and your imagination is the limit.

Awesome Cricut Card Ideas for Your Family

Now that you own a Cricut cutting tool, why waste another penny on a store-bought greeting card. For the Cricut, you charged a lot so let's put it to work. Here are just a couple of Cricut Card Ideas that will get you started and let you use some of your chosen Cricut cartridges. The next calendar holiday coming up is Easter. I think of how your family and friends will react when they receive a handmade greeting card made by YOU when I think of what Cricut card ideas I can come up with. Now that you've got your Cricut cutting machine, and a variety of Cricut cartridges, adding your personal touch to a card is so easy.

If the Cricut Doodle charms cartridge is one of the Cricut cartridges you have, you can make a really cute handmade Easter Bunny greeting card or an Easter Basket filled with colored eggs. Or maybe the Cricut Wild Card cartridge is another one of your Cricut cartridges so you can make a Filigree Easter Egg card. One of my Cricut Card suggestions is if you have your Imagination Cartridge on the Cricut Extension. You can make a card in a basket with a Bunny coloring the Easter eggs or a bunny. As far as all the Cricut card ideas I could come up with for Easter are concerned, they do not all need to have bunnies or eggs on them. Here is an example of using another of your Cricut cartridges, A Walk in My Garden cartridge. You can use this Cricut cartridge to make beautiful daffodils, hyacinths, or tulips to be your card theme. You are the Easter card maker, show off your talent, and have fun.

Then there's Mother's Day, the next big card day. Think of how your Mom would feel her child receiving a personalized greeting card. You are going to make her day entirely. Using your wonderful Cricut cutting machine, no matter what Cricut cartridges you have, you will be able to find something that will put a smile on her face, and of course you will do all this. It could be as simple as a basic flower from the cartridge of the Plantin School Book that you cut on a card in different sizes and layers, and then add the words Happy Mother's Day or the Best Mommy in the World. The best thing about your Cricut cutting machine is that it gives you thousands of Cricut card ideas and all the Cricut cartridges that are available to you. You can see your cards look so good that you cannot wait to send them out or start selling them. I'm going to get busy making my very own Cricut cutting machine with my handmade greeting cards, how about you?

What is the Imagine Cricut Machine?

One of its kind is the Cricut Imagine machine which ProvoCraft publicized at the CHA. It is currently the only machine that allows the user to use the same device to both cut and print, saving a lot of time and money. With HP inkjet printing technology, you can select a pattern from a vast cartridge collection, get it printed and cut it in one go.

To Scrapbookers, What Does It Mean?

A great way to improve and add pizzazz to all kinds of arts and crafts projects, including scrapbooking and card making, is to use cut-outs and shapes in different colors. These diets that are also called that consist of a variety of materials such as paper, foils, card stock, transparencies vellum, and thin plastics. Today, with most labor-intensive and automated cutters on the marketplace, examples are the Sizzix and Cricut Expression, you need to prepare ahead and select your die-cut color before cutting. In other words, the color of your design will be the color of your choice of paper (or cloth, or stock). Besides that, you may need to change paper colors frequently when creating complex or intricate designs.

Other systems, like the Wishblade, allow you to print the desired shape using an ordinary inkjet printer instead of running the printed page through the cutting machine. The biggest problem with that is that it's a two-step process, using two different machines, which requires the user to set up registration marks correctly so that the machine knows exactly where to cut. This is often a process of trial and error, and the outcomes are not always satisfactory. Thus, there is a need for a program that allows the user to print an image without manual registration and cut the image. This is where the Cricut Imagine comes in to fill a huge market gap and generally open up a whole new world of possibilities for scrapbookers, card makers, and paper craftsmen.

Primary Features of Cricut Imagine

- You can fill any form with beautiful patterns with Cricut Pattern and Cricut Color Cartridges, by adding.
- The designs have more dimension and variety.
- You can use all preceding Cricut Imagine cartridges. But new cartridges will also be released to operate exclusively with this new unit, as was the case by means of the Cricut Cake.
- Cricut Imagine also supports equally the Gypsy and Design Studio software.
- Use of an LCD touch-screen navigation system to easily access all the information.

- New Cricut Imagine cartridges include: 12 new Cricut Imagine Art cartridges and 12 new Cricut Imagine Colors & Model cartridges.
- The paint and pattern generator on-board help you to choose colors, sizes, and more.
- The Cricut Imagine machine will cut shapes from .25" to 11.5" and works up to 12" x 12" large-format papers.
- Like Cricut and other previous devices, the Imagine doesn't require a device to operate.
- Share the same blade and blade housing as other Cricut types of machinery, making it relaxed for users to advancement short of having to purchase it all over again.
- Mat, which is significantly improved, is the only difference.

That means no more purchasing loads of costly scrapbook paper, changing colors of paper between cuts, or dealing with manual registration marks. Everything you need in one simple system to use that does everything for you and allows your creativity to soar. The Cricut Imagine is unique, not only to the art industry, but also to the technology community. There is currently no other tool that embodies both printings and cutting the way the image does.

Chapter 2. List Of Materials That Can Be Used With Compatible Cricut Machines

Certain materials can be cut on various Cricut machines, but it does vary from machine to machine. The newer machines have more functionality with more materials. No matter the machine though, there are some materials you may have thought of, like those listed on the Cricut website, while there are others you may not have thought of. Just like you may not have thought of some out-of-the-box ideas for projects to do!

Main Materials

Cricut Website is a treasure-trove of information for both the new and experienced Cricut user. One helpful feature is the list and store for materials. The items listed for sale on the website include:

- Cling for windows
- Washi sheets
- Vinyl
- Vellum
- Transfer Tape
- Poster board
- Iron-on materials
- Foils
- Leather-like materials
- Craft foam

- Papers, including cardstock
- Etc.

Within these categories, multiple items are also listed. For example, under vinyl, items are included like basic vinyl, transfer vinyl, and adhesive vinyl. Ultimately, the Cricut website lists over 100 different materials that the machines can cut, many of which they sell on the site. This is very convenient if you want to guarantee the materials will work with the machine and you do not want to waste their time shopping around for things.

Other people prefer to try more out-of-the-box materials and projects to test their creative powers and those of their machines.

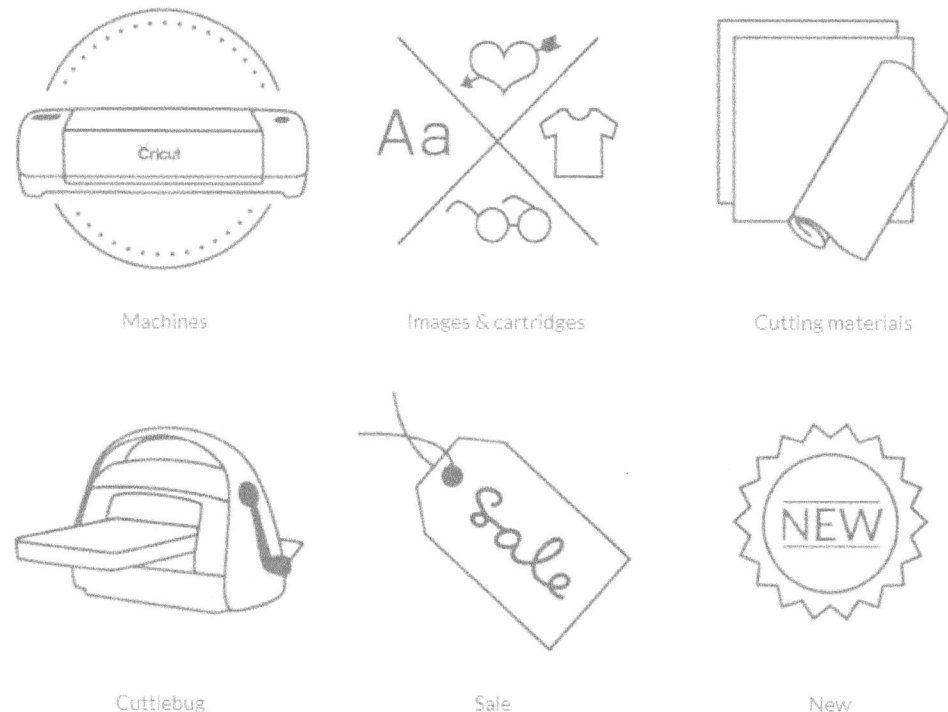

Alternative Materials

While vinyl and paper are the most popular materials to cut with your Cricut, that material is just the "tip of the iceberg," so to speak. There are so many other materials crafters have used successfully with their Cricut machines. Below is a list of some of the items to consider:

- Balsa Wood

Balsa is a quick-growing, American tree. The thin wood it produces is often used in model making or rafts. This is because it is very lightweight and slightly pliable. Craft projects from balsa wood include favor tags for weddings or parties, rustic-looking placeholders for the table, or a natural-themed sign for a door or wall.

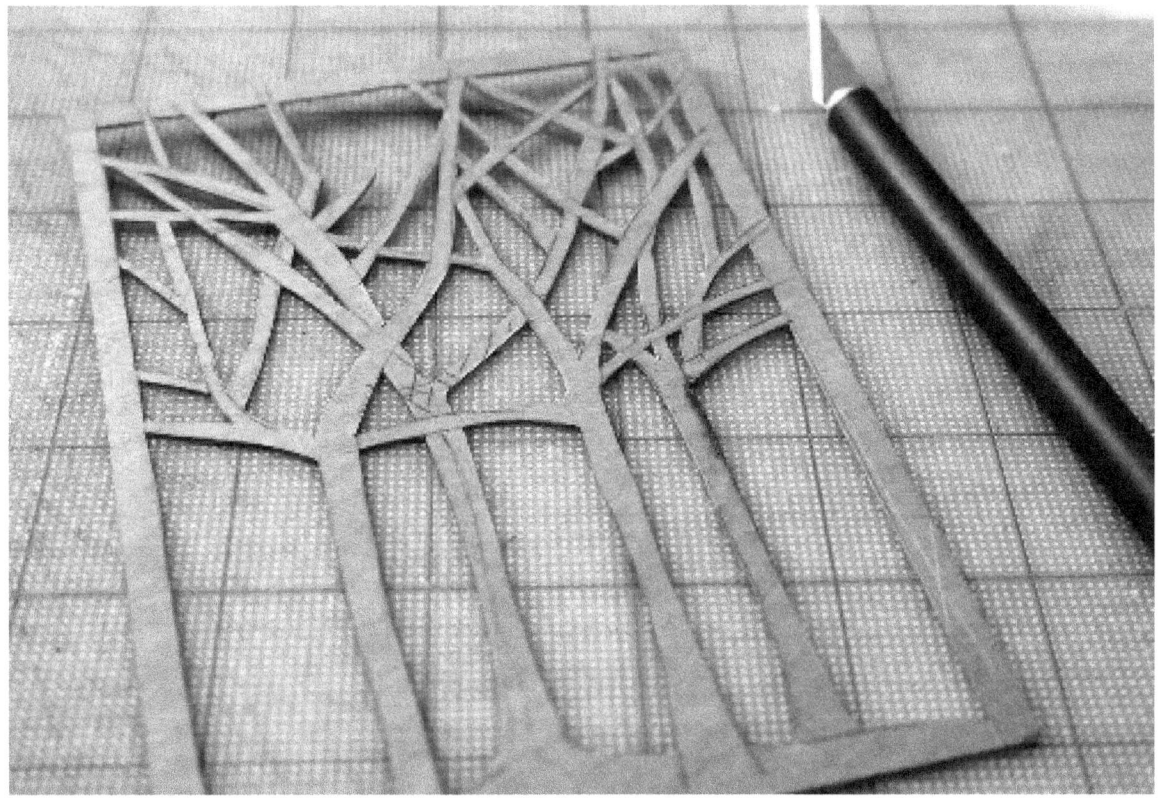

- Pens

While this is not exactly an unusual material, it is an often-under-used tool. These pens can not only be functional but can create beautiful sketches.

For some projects, a pen can be used to include creating coloring pages, placemat designs for children at restaurants or holidays (of course, these are great for adults, too!), or monogrammed jewelry. For example, a metallic initial can be printed on a circular piece of leather and strung on a necklace for an instant, personal statement piece of jewelry.

A mandala made with a pen and paper

- Duct Tape

The popularity of duct tape as a fashion or crafting item has blossomed over the past few decades, producing projects from wallets to prom dresses. It is still a material that some Cricut DIY-ers underestimate.

This material can be durable and fashionable. Projects made using Duct Tape include Bold and textured gift tags for packages or an art portfolio that showcases the vibrancy and precision of the artist with the added touch of this material.

- Fabric

Fabric is not an unusual material for some Cricut users, but because the variety of fabric available to choose from is so vast, it needs to be mentioned again because there are some techniques and materials that are a little more unusual. For example, cutting a lace-like pattern into fabrics can immediately add a color palette of fancy lace to any project. This also makes it possible to have the same lace pattern on a variety of complimentary fabrics or colors.

- Faux Leather and Leather

Cricut does not sell real leather. They offer a variety of different leather-like or "faux" leathers. "Faux" means "fake".

Depending on your preference, you can use either material. Despite what you choose, both are good materials to cut with the Cricut. Custom jewelry, like necklace pendants or earrings, are simple and stunning projects. These make beautiful and personal gifts or add the right touch to a special outfit. Leather can also be used for making fashionable bracelets or cuffs.

Having an intricate cut on a lovely piece of leather or faux leather, the bracelet can be attached to an adjustable band. Hair bows or bows to add to clothing or handbags are also possible. For a hair bow, hot glue a hair clip to the back when the bow is finished. Use hot glue or another adhesive to attach the bow to clothing or a purse. Other hair accessories can be made, like flowers and other shapes.

These can be attached to hair clips, like the bows, or attached to hard or stretchy headbands. Leather can also be used as an embellishment to pillows or other fabrics, like chair backs, or made into manly coasters.

- Felt

Felt is another multi-functional material that you can use for a host of projects. Because this item is fairly sturdy but has good flexibility, it is perfect for just about anything.

In addition, it comes in all different colors and is relatively inexpensive. Some unique projects that can be made from felt include garlands of multi-layered flowers to hang over a window curtain or above a bed, a textured phrase attached to a pillow, an interactive tree-shaped advent calendar, banners, ornaments, and cupcake or cake toppers.

- Magnets

Magnets can be used for more than just the fridge, and thankfully Cricut is there to help create new and fun ways to make magnets for all these different purposes. Be selective about the type of magnet you choose to cut.

Thick and solid magnets do not work well for these projects, but the thinner sheets of magnets are good for fun crafts.

Some ideas that are outside the fridge-box include; a magnet to be attached to the dishwasher that indicates if the machine is loaded with dirty or clean dishes, magnetic busy boards such as a mermaid scene with underwater characters or a race track with cars and spectators (do not forget a trophy for the first across the finish line!). Magnetic words to spell out messages on the side of the car or, yes, on the fridge, or school pride or mascots to attach to the car.

- Cling vinyl for windows

Custom decals for holidays or to create a statement on the car or a mirror can cost a lot of money if it is bought from a store or ordered custom from a shop.

Instead, use your Cricut to get crafty. Consider making a saying or image and stick it to the window.

Chapter 3. Materials For Cricut Machines

Cricut machines have been designed to handle a wide variety of materials. Most of the machines can work with a majority of materials, but they do have specialties among them. Read on for more information on the Cricut Explore One, Cricut Explore Air 2, Cricut Maker, and Cricut EasyPress 2 and the materials that work best with each.

Cricut Explore One

This machine only has one carriage, so you might find yourself swapping out tools more often than with the other machines. This machine can cut over 100 different materials. It can also write and score. Here's a sampling of some of the most common materials used with the Explore One machine.

- Vinyl—Vinyl, outdoor vinyl, glitter vinyl, metallic vinyl, matte vinyl, stencil vinyl, dry erase vinyl, chalkboard vinyl, adhesive foils, holographic vinyl, printable vinyl, vinyl transfer tape, iron-on vinyl, glitter iron-on vinyl, foil iron-on, holographic iron-on, printable iron-on for light or dark fabric, flocked iron-on vinyl, and neon iron-on vinyl
- Paper—Cardstock, glitter cardstock, pearl paper, poster board, scrapbook paper, vellum, party foil, cereal boxes, construction paper, copy paper, flat cardboard, flocked cardstock and paper, foil embossed paper, freezer paper, kraft board, kraft paper, metallic cardstock and paper, notebook paper, paper grocery bags, parchment paper, paper board, pearl cardstock and paper, photographs, mat board, rice paper, solid core cardstock, watercolor paper, and wax paper

- Fabric—Burlap, canvas, cotton, denim, duck cloth, faux leather, faux suede, felt, flannel, leather, linen, metallic leather, oilcloth, polyester, printable fabric, silk, and wool felt
- Specialty—Adhesive foil, adhesive wood, aluminum sheets, aluminum foil, balsa wood, birch wood, corkboard, corrugated paper, craft foam, duct tape, embossable foil, foil acetate, glitter foam, magnet sheets, metallic vellum, paint chips, plastic, sticker paper, shrink plastic, stencil material, tissue paper, temporary tattoo paper, transparency film, washi sheets and tape, window cling, wood veneer, and wrapping paper

Cricut Explore Air 2

The Explore Air 2 can cut the same materials as the Explore One. The difference is that it has two carriages instead of one, so it's easier to swap between tools. It's also a bit faster than Explore One. The Air machines have wireless and Bluetooth capabilities, so you can use the Cricut Design Space on your phone, tablet, or laptop without connecting directly to the machine.

Cricut Maker

The Cricut Maker has about 10x the cutting power of the Explore machines. It includes a rotary blade and a knife blade, so in addition to all the above materials, it can cut into more robust fabrics and materials. With the sharper blades, it's also better at cutting into more delicate materials without damaging them. Here's a list of some of the additional materials the Maker can cut.

- Acrylic felt
- Bamboo fabric
- Bengaline
- Birch
- Boucle
- Broadcloth
- Burlap
- Velvet
- Calico
- Cambric
- Canvas
- Carbon fiber
- Cashmere
- Challis
- Chambray
- Chantilly lace
- Charmeuse satin
- Chiffon
- Chintz
- Chipboard
- Corduroy
- Crepe paper
- Cutting mat protector
- Dotted Swiss
- Double cloth
- Double knit
- Dupioni silk
- EVA foam
- Eyelet
- Faille
- Fleece
- Foulard
- Gabardine
- Gauze
- Gel sheet
- Georgette
- Gossamer
- Grois point
- Habutai
- Heather
- Heavy watercolor paper
- Homespun fabric
- Interlock knit
- Jacquard
- Jersey
- Jute
- Kevlar
- La Coste
- Lycra
- Mesh
- Metal
- Microfiber
- Moleskin
- Monk's cloth
- Muslin
- Nylon
- Organza
- Handmade paper
- Plush
- Sailcloth
- Satin silk
- Seersucker
- Sequined cloth
- Bonded silk
- Tafetta
- Tulle
- Tweed
- Velvet
- Wool crepe

Cricut EasyPress

The Cricut EasyPress 2 is a small, convenient heat press. It works with any type of iron-on material and can adhere to fabrics, wood, paper, and more. Cricut also offers Infusible inks that are transferred to the material using heat. The EasyPress is a great alternative to iron, as it heats more quickly and more evenly.

Crafting Blanks

The objects you decorate using your Cricut can be referred to as blanks. This can be absolutely any object, and it can be something you stick vinyl to, etch, paint, draw on, write on, or anything else you can think of. They're called blanks because they provide a mostly blank surface to be decorated, though they can also have colors or designs.

Some popular blanks are cups, mugs, wine or champagne glasses, travel mugs, tumblers, and other such drinking vessels. Craft stores will usually sell these, but you can find them at almost any store. They don't need to be considered a "craft" supply for you to use. Most stores have a selection of plain cups and mugs or travel mugs and tumblers with no designs on them. As long as you can imagine a Cricut project with it, it's fair game.

Drink wares aren't the only kitchen or dining-related blanks. Get creative with plates, bowls, and serving utensils. Find blank placemats or coasters at most stores. Decorate mason or other types of jars. Dry goods containers, measuring cups, food storage containers, pitchers, and jugs—anything you can put in your kitchen can serve as a great blank for your projects.

Clothing is another popular choice for Cricut projects. T-shirts are easy to make with iron-on vinyl, and you can find cheap blanks at any store or a larger selection at craft stores. In fact, craft stores will typically have a large selection of clothing blanks, such as t-shirts, long sleeve shirts, ball caps, plain white shoes, plain bags, and so on. Thrift stores or consignment shops can be an unusual option as well. You could find a shirt with an interesting pattern that you'd like to add an iron-on to or something similar.

Glass is fun to work with and has a ton of project options with your Cricut machine. Glass blocks can be found at craft or hardware stores. Many stores that carry kitchenware will have plain glass cutting boards, or you can find them online. Craft stores and home goods stores could sell glass trinkets or décor that you can decorate. You can even buy full panes of glass at your local hardware store and have them cut it to your desired size.

There are plenty of blanks related to electronics, as well. Electronics stores, online stores, and some craft stores offer phone and tablet case blanks. They might be clear, white or black, or colored. Portable battery packs are another option as well. Many times, these blanks are significantly cheaper than already decorated ones, or you can buy them in bulk for a lower price. Get your phone case for a cheaper price and customize it how you like.

Book covers make great blanks, as well. Customize the cover of a sketchbook, notebook, or journal. Repair the cover of an aged book, or create a new book cover for a plain one that you have. If you have old books that you aren't going to read, create a new fake cover for them and use them as décor.

Chapter 4. Easy Cricut Project Ideas

DIY Leather Cuff

The Materials:

You do not need many materials for this project. All you need to create your own DIY leather bracelet is:

- A minor piece of leather.
- A rope or cord.
- Curved nose pliers for jewelry (or old classic fine nose pliers also works!).
- Deep cut blade for your Cricut Explore.
- Small jump rings (2) (optional).

To develop the design, I selected an image of the concept space that I was looking for "lace." I had fun with the size and cut on the paper to check its size before cutting the most expensive skin. After reaching the perfect size, I pressed cut. My stomach may have flip flops while I was waiting!

I have to be completely honest here. I was hurt when I took the rug. The design, which was a bit complex, was cut perfectly everywhere. I didn't need to touch a single cut. (The only that can be carried out differently next time is to put the smooth side of the leather on the carpet so that the fibers of the fabric do not adhere to the carpet when the skin is removed!)

DIY Leather Bracelet

Once the pattern is cut, simply make the size of your cord or chain for the bracelet. I used 6 links on every side of the pattern and included the chain to the skin with small jump rings. You can tie the links directly to the skin, but my ties were very rigid and they didn't want to tear the skin to try and move. The jump rings were much more flexible.

How to Cut Leather with Cricut Explore:

To cut the skin with Cricut Explore, you must have:

- A Cricut Explore Air or Cricut Explore One
- Cross transfer belt
- Cross hatch
- Leather tools (this is my favorite type of leather for fabrication because it is sturdy and fits perfectly, but you can also use other types of leather for this project).

Instead, we will use Cricut Transfer as a buffer between the leather and the cutting mat. It's a pretty easy and fast addition that will save you money and frustration.

Cut the transfer tape to the size of your skin, then glue it on the skin part. Finally, place it on the cutting mat with the transfer tape as a cushion.

Once you've loaded the skin into your machine, be sure to set the selector to "Custom". You can select "Skin Group" from the drop-down menu.

For my project, I used some leather keys with my own sources, as well as free forms of Cricut Design Space. We just created letters, reproduced one of the letters, and then soldered with a rectangle.

Once the cut is complete, you can peel off the transfer tape and reveal a clean tapestry cap underneath. No more pieces of skin ruining your carpet

Leather Keychain

Now that you've cut your leather, it's time to put in your key!

You will need:

- Leather Monogram
- Small talk
- Leather glue
- Bull clips (not shown)

Pass one side of the leather monograms onto the key ring, then fold the leather in half and remove each side with leather glue. Use bull sleeves to hold the sides together until the glue is completely dry.

Add some color to your keys with acrylic leather paint. I created a color inlay effect to embed a diagonal band with washi tape.

Cutting of custom material

For the custom bass wood configuration, I made a cutting pressure of 220 and a multiple cavity of 4x. Important Tips! Be sure to reflect your image in the drawing space before cutting. The raft wood is a very red wood and the white rolls leave traces in the wood. When reflecting on the image, you can use the back that will be nice and smooth!

The cards came out very clean this time!

Wood Raft Paper

So, I have all my letters once my size is finished and ready to put on my canvas. (I used an 18 x 24" black cloth.

The Design

I used homemade acrylic paint and a sample paint remover to paint the letters of agglomerates. The "BE" received a layer of white paint and I left the wood letters on the tray.

Painting Paper

I love the contrasting colors of the bright colors in black and white and it harmonizes with the colors I have in the room.

3D Letters

Once all the letters were in place, I glued them onto the fabric with hot glue. I couldn't be happier with the end result!

3D Literature Sign: Have Courage, be Kind

Playroom Beware: It really illuminates the children's study area and combines with DIY magnetic tangrams on the wall.

Cricut Iron-On Picnic Blanket

Make your own round blanket with bright palm leaf details.

Starting with today's Cricut Ironing Picnic Blanket, which contains one of the latest images available in the Cricut Design Space Access service. As soon as I saw this Monstera leaf, he knew he was going to do something about it.

Use your Cricut Explore to create this Iron Cricut Smooth Cricut with vibrant and modern colors

Here's what you'll need:

- Explore Cricut
- Subscription to Cricut Design Space Access (optional, but excellent)
- Iron the shapes of Monstera leaves in bright colors with Cricut fuse material (I used wheat, raspberry, pink blush, lime, and sun yellow).
- 70" round white tablecloth
- Pom-pom trim
- Canvas glue
- Iron game
- Iron

Use your Cricut Explorer to create this brightly colored Cricut picnic blanket.

Step 1

Fold the coat in half, this will make the job easier. Arrange all the crowd shapes as you want in the final drawing.

Use your Cricut Explore to create this Iron Cricut Smooth Cricut with vibrant and modern colors

Step 2

Iron each shape slowly pays attention to the intersection of the shapes to avoid accidentally injuring one shape on the plastic support of the other.

Step 3

I turn the tablecloth and use the fabric to glue the tassel thread over the entire edge of the tablecloth. Leave to dry for a few hours.

Tips for Using Iron Materials

For all the shapes that come out of the edge, fold it under and iron on the bottom of the coat

Don't use steam! Use a dry hot iron to iron any shape.

Use your Cricut Explore to create this Iron Cricut Smooth Cricut with vibrant and modern colors.

Glitter Monogram Cushion DIY

What you need:

- Cricut Explore Air Machine
- Cricut design space cost
- Iron Cricut in the color/style of your choice
- Cricut instruments
- iron
- table
- Scissors
- The rule of thumb/tape
- insert cushion
- pillow

1. Take your table and measure. Determine the desired size for your monogram to find out what size to get in my design space. My pillow measured 18 inches square (from the H&M store, nice and affordable things!), and I decided to make my monogram no more than 10 inches.
2. Begin by making your own monogram in the Cricut design space. I made my design with the Monogram KK font from the DaFont website. The best thing is it is free! You can download it here. Write the letters of your monogram with the text tool and select the Monogram KK character. And then select Isolated Letters. This will ensure that your 3 letters are separate so that you can move and resize independently.
3. Put your letters to the desired size. For my monogram, I made our last initial (B) larger, 8 inches high. I made our first initials (E and J) every 6 inches tall. I put a 10 × 10 frame on my canvas to keep a reference to the height or width of the template. I like the appearance of these monograms when the letters overlap and interchange. So, I made sure each letter was played or overlapped in one way or another.
4. Once I appreciated my design, I selected the 3 levels of letters and clicked on Weld. This makes it possible to combine all overlapping edges into one large piece!
5. Now they are ready to cut! Make sure you remove or hide your square path if you created it to guide you. Click on the green IR button in the upper right corner of the design space to create your project. It looks like this:
   Cricut GO button
   The Cricut program puts the drawing on a page so you can cut the project. Be sure to select "Picture mirror (on the rail)" on the next panel.
6. Put the iron on the equipment on your Cricut cutting mat. Place the non-matte or glossy or colored sideways on the side of the rug. For my mission, I select the shiny silver material. Be sure to select Iron on the dial of your Cricut machine. Then click on IR on your Cricut and see its magic!
7. After you cut your template, carefully remove any items that are not part of your template using your Cricut tools or your fingers. My design was very ornate and this part took a while. Be sure that you are inside a room that is well lit to see what you are doing. After removing all the unnecessary parts, you will be ready to stretch!

8. Warm up the iron and iron your model on the pillow, using a piece of cloth to protect it from the iron and your gift pattern. I used a Turkish towel, but you can wear an old shirt or whatever you have on hand.

   My pillow was a smooth and shiny material and took a little longer to look longer than I expected. I had to turn over my iron for planting. Imagine that each type of fabric is different, so keep that in mind when making your project.

   Each time during ironing, I took the fabric and started removing it from the adhesive panel. If he still employed his employer, he would accompany him again. Just keep on booting until your design adheres! Once everything is glued, remove the entire adhesive style.

Chapter 5. Paper-Based Projects

Christmas Greeting Cards

You may have been aware before now that there are 50,000+ predesigned images in the Cricut Design Space library and Christmas is by the corner. Therefore, you have a lot of activities marking the season. Greeting cards are a great way to show that you care especially for your friends and family. The images in the library can create super amazing Christmas greeting cards you can send as gifts and for sales during Christmas.

Knowing there are many images you can play in the library is one thing, the other thing is knowing how to use these images to create beautiful and super amazing greeting cards with your Cricut Explore Air 2 machine. I want to show you how you can use your Cricut Explore Air 2 machine to do this using this step by step approach.

The materials for this project include a Cricut Explore Air 2 machine, computer or smartphone, cardboard papers, glue, a pair of scissors, Cricut writing pens, and micro glaze.

I want to believe that you know what Micro Glaze is but if you don't know, Micro glaze is a protective cream wax for coating art works especially papers. Since this project involves papers majorly, Micro glaze is important to produce a colorful print out with a little shine on it.

1. Go to your Design space app. open it and log into your account.
2. Go to Insert Images, click it, and type 'cards' in the text field to view hundreds of free images.
3. Tap or click on Insert shapes then select Square.
4. Go to the edit panel and click the Unlock button to unlock it.
5. Select the size of the card you wish from the available sizes.
6. Click the Ok button.

7. To produce a card, you wish to fold, score line at the middle of the square. To score a line in the middle, click on the inserted images to select it and view the score line. Go to the top middle position of the square, click it and drag it down to the bottom line of the square. To make sure that the score line is at the middle of the square, draw a box over the score line, click the Align button at the top of the Canvas and then click Center.
8. Attach the score line to the square by selecting the square and the score line together, then click Attach in the Layer's panel. Do not be surprised if the shapes change color when you select it. Blue color indicates that the shape is selected, otherwise, it is white.
9. Adjust the color of the square.
10. Again, select the shapes, unlock it, then drag it down till the shapes cover 50% of the square.
11. Adjust the shapes and colors on the square to your wish then move to the next step.
12. Click the Text button on the left pane to pop up a text box where you can input whatever text you wish, type 'Merry Christmas' in the text field, or any text that sends your desired message to the recipient
13. Highlight the text then edit the text size, fonts, shape, and other properties of the text as you wish on your screen. Alternatively, you can use the pre-designed cards in the Design Space, edit them to obtain the final image that tickles your fancy, especially when you don't have the time and energy to start your design from the beginning. The only challenge with this is that you cannot share the files with anyone when there are copyrighted images on it. If you must share, then adjust any shared images in your design.
14. Once you are satisfied with your design, click the "Make it" button on the top right corner of your screen to cut your design out.
15. Check the preview of your design on the virtual mat to see the arrangement on the mat. If you are satisfied with the arrangement, click Continue.
16. Place the color marker in the left compartment. To do this, open the clamp of accessory A, remove the cap of the marker, push the marker inside accessory A till a clicking sound is heard then clamp the accessory.

17. Place your cardboard paper on the mat and then load it into the machine.
18. Press the Load/Unload button then press the flashing Cricut button to start cutting your shape.
19. Repeat steps 15-17 for all the layers you designed. Note that an extra layer will be required for the outer cover of the card.
20. When you're done printing and cutting your design, remove from the mat gently so that the tiny details don't get messed up or broken.
21. Apply a little micro glaze on the printed surface to protect the printout.
22. Arrange the layers together inking the edges where necessary then fold the score line properly. Make sure that you apply glue to the printed paper before attaching it to the card.

Christmas Tag

Christmas gift tags have been around for a very long time and will still be around as long as Christmas is still being celebrated. It is a beautiful way to customize your Christmas gifts and very cheap to make. The step by step approach to making an amazing Christmas tag for the season is as follows:

1. Let me start with the materials for this project which include: Cricut Explore Air 2 machine, White cardstock, Cricut pen (.4 fine point tip), ribbon, and weeding tool.
2. Create a New Project in your Design Space.
3. Upload your images for the Christmas tag, text messages, snowflakes, or any designed image you wish to use on the tag unto your Canvas.
4. Resize your tag to your desired value. I want to believe you can do that? At the Layer's panel, remember?
5. Zoom the tag if the size is really small on the screen so that you don't strain your eyes trying to see your design.
6. Place your snowflake on the front of your Christmas tag then align it to the center horizontally.

7. Resize the snowflake appropriately to fit into your Christmas tag.
8. Slice the snowflake and repeat the same process for the Christmas text message.
9. Change the image to white and select the color of the Cricut pen to Black 0.4 tip.
10. Attach all of them and click on the Go button on top.
11. Turn your dial to custom and select "Cardstock Intricate Cuts 0.27mm."
12. Place your cardstock paper on the Standard Grip mat and then load the mat by pressing the power button on your Cricut Explore Air 2 machine.
13. Insert your fine 0.4 fine pen in accessory A and press the flashing Cricut button to begin the writing and cutting process.
14. When the machine finishes its job, unload the mat by pressing the Load/Unload button again.
15. Color any part of the text that needs adjustment because the Cricut Explore Air 2 machine will not color the font for you.
16. Use a weeding tool to gently remove your Christmas tag from the mat.
17. Finally, use the ribbons to tie the Christmas tag to your desired position on your handcraft wall, or door, or any position you wish to place it in your house.

The good thing about the Christmas tag project is that you have the freedom to add any image of your choice to give it a personal message and appeal. Of course, it is super simple to do and will encourage you on to share the love this Christmas season.

Monogrammed Christmas Ornament

A monogram is an image made by combining two or more overlapping graphemes or other letters to form one symbol or logo. A monogram is a unique way to give identity to the owner of a property which is something we all like to do. Of course, we all have properties in different forms, and what better way to find them than a monogram customized using your darling Cricut Explore Air 2 machine.

The Cricut Explore Air 2 machine can engrave monograms on materials including acrylic ornaments. These beautiful pieces of ornaments are beautiful to behold and gives the crafter such an amazing feeling of satisfaction and creativity.

The tools required for this project include Cricut Explore Air 2 machine, Chomas Creations Engraving Tool, Cricut Design space, a piece of an acrylic coaster, and painter's tape.

The Chomas Engraving Tool is used to engrave and etch materials with the help of a die cutting machine like your darling Cricut Explore Air 2. It is the second most important material for this project and it is easy to install on your Cricut Explore Air 2 machine.

Chomas Engraving Tool

Use the step by step approach described below to engrave your monogram on an acrylic coaster. It is super simple and will serve as amazing decorations for your room during the Christmas celebration and even as a gift to family and friends.

1. Select a monogram in Design Space and insert it into Canvas
2. Insert a circle into the Canvas or any proper shape for this project, but the circle will be preferably considering the shape of the ornament.
3. Weld the shapes into one color.
4. Set the size of the shape to that of the ornament plate you wish to use.
5. Place the monogram into the circle and resize the monogram to fit into the circle in a way that appeals to you.
6. To cut the coaster, send the design to the virtual mat and make sure that your design is in the right place where you wish Cricut Explore Air 2 machine to cut on the coaster, then use the next steps I to h to cut the coaster.
7. Set the coaster on the Strong Grip mat at the right place and secure it.
8. Load the mat by pressing the Load/Unload button on the machine.
9. Press the flashing 'C' Cricut button to start cutting the coaster.
10. When the cutting is done, press the Load/Unload button to unload the mat and remove the coaster that has been cut from the mat.

11. The next thing is to set the cut coaster unto the mat again at the precise position, then secure it firmly with painter's tape. Of course, the painter's tape should be underneath the coaster.
12. Replace the cutting blade with the Chomas engraving tool on the right-hand side of the adaptive tool. Make sure the coaster material is not touching the White Star Wheel while the machine is engraving it.
13. Repeat steps 2-3.
14. Finally, press the Load/Unload button to unload the mat showing your beautifully engraved monogram on the coaster.
15. Clean up by wiping dirt off the ornament, then hang it in your preferred place.

Chapter 6. Cricut Projects With Vinyl

Giant Vinyl Stencils

Vinyl stencils are a good thing to create, too, but they can be hard. Big vinyl stencils make for an excellent Cricut project, and you can use them in various places, including bedrooms for kids.

You only need the Explore Air 2, the vinyl that works for it, a pallet, sander, and of course, paint and brushes. The first step is preparing the pallet for painting, or whatever surface you plan on using this for.

From here, you create the mermaid tail (or any other large image) in Design Space. Now, you will learn immediately that big pieces are hard to cut and impossible to do all at once in Design Space.

What you do is a section of each design accordingly, and remove any middle pieces. Next, you can add square shapes to the image, slicing it into pieces so that it can be cut on a cutting mat that fits.

At this point, you cut out the design by pressing "Make It", choosing your material, and working in sections.

From here, you put it on the surface that you are using; piecing this together with each line. You should have one image, after piecing it all together. Then, draw out the line on vinyl, and then paint the initial design. For the second set of stencils, you can simply trace the first one, and then paint the inside of them. At this point, you should have the design finished. When done, remove it very carefully.

And there you have it! Bigger stencils can be a bit of a project since it involves trying to use multiple designs all at once; but with the right care and the right designs, you will be able to create whatever it is you need to in Design Space, so you can get the results you are looking for.

Cricut Quilts

Quilts are a bit hard to do for many people, but did you know that you can use Cricut to make it easier? Here, you will learn an awesome project that will help you do this. To begin, you start with the Cricut Design Space. Here, you can add different designs that work for your project. For example, if you are making a baby blanket, or quilt with animals on it, you can add little fonts with the names of the animals, or different pictures of them, too. From here, you want to make sure you choose the option to reverse the design. That way, you will have it printed on correctly. At this point, make your quilt. Do various designs and sew the quilt as you want to.

From here, you should cut it on the iron-on heat transfer vinyl. You can choose that, and then press "Cut." The image will then cut into the piece.

At this point, it will cut itself out, and you can proceed to transfer this with some parchment paper. Use an EasyPress for best results and push it down. There you go, an easy addition that will definitely enhance the way your blankets look.

Cricut Unicorn Backpack

If you are making a present for a child, why not give them some cool unicorns? Here is a lovely unicorn backpack you can try to make. To make this, you need ¾ yards of a woven fabric—something that is strong, since it will help with stabilizing the backpack. You will also need half a yard of quilting cotton for the lining. The coordinating fabric should be around about an eighth of a yard. You will need: about a yard of fusible interfacing, some strap adjuster rings, a zipper that is about 14 inches and does not separate, and some stuffing for the horn.

1. To start, you will want to cut the main fabric; you should use straps, the loops, a handle, some gussets for a zipper, and the bottom and side gussets.
2. The lining should be done too, and you should make sure you have the interfacing. You can use fusible flex foam, to help make it a little bit bulkier.
3. From here, cut everything and then apply the interfacing to the backside. The flex-foam should be adjusted to achieve the bulkiness you are looking for. You can trim this, too. The interfacing should be on the backside; then add the flex foam to the main fabric. The adhesive side of this will be on the right-hand side of the interfacing.
4. Fold the strap pieces in half and push one down, on each backside. Halve it, and then press it again; stitch these closer to every edge, and also along the short-pressed edge, as well.
5. From here, do the same thing with the other side, but add the ring for adjustment, and stitch the bottom of these to the main part of the back piece.
6. Then add them both to the bottom.
7. At this point, you have the earpieces that should have the backside facing out. Stitch, then flip out and add the pieces.
8. Add these inner pieces to the outer ear, and then stitch these together.
9. At this point, you make the unicorn face in the Design Space. You will notice immediately when you use this program that everything will be black, but you can change this by adjusting the desired layers to each color. You can also just use a template that fits, but you should always mirror this before you cut it.
10. Choose vinyl, and then insert the material onto the cutting mat. From there, cut it and remove the iron-on slowly.

You will need to do this in pieces, which is fine because it allows you to use different colors. Remember to insert the right color for each cut. At this point, add the zipper, and there you go!

Custom Back to School Supplies

This tutorial will show you how to use your iPad to create and convert designs for your Cricut machine to cut!

Materials needed:

- Vinyl
- Standard Grip Mat
- White Paper
- Markers (including black)
- Pencil Case
- 3 Ring Binder
- iPad Pro (optional)
- Apple Pencil
- Cricut Design Space App
- Drawing app (e.g. ProCreate)
- ProCreate Brushes

Instructions:

1. The first thing to do is to convert your kid's drawing into an SVG file that the Cricut Design Space recognizes. This will be done by tracing it in the ProCreate app.
2. Get your child's design—it should not be too complex, to minimize weeding.
3. Open the Procreate app on your iPad.
4. Create a new canvas on ProCreate. Click on the "Wrench" icon and select "Image."
5. Next, click "Take a Photo." Take a picture of the design. When you are satisfied with the image, click "Use It."
6. On the Layer Panel (the two squares icon), add a new layer by clicking the "Plus" sign.
7. In the Layers panel, select the layer containing the picture and click the "N." Also, reduce the layer's opacity so that you can easily see your draw lines.

8. From your imported brushes, select the "Marker" brush. To avoid the need to import a brush, choose the inking brush. You can resize the brush in the brush settings under the "General" option.
9. On the new layer, trace over the drawing.
   a. Click on the "Wrench" icon, click "Share," then "PNG."
   b. Next, "Save" the image to your device.
   c. Alternately, use your black marker and trace the drawing on a blank piece of paper, then take a picture of it, using your iPad or phone.
   d. The next stage is to cut the design out in Cricut Design Space
   e. Open up the Cricut Design Space app on your iPad.
   f. Create a 'New Project'.
   g. Select "Upload" (located at the screen's bottom). Select "Select from Camera Roll" and select the PNG image you created in ProCreate or the image you traced out.
   h. Follow the next steps.
   i. Save the design as a cut file and insert it into the canvas. Here, you can resize the design or add other designs.
   j. Next, click "Make It" to send it to your Cricut.
   k. Choose "Vinyl' as the material.
   l. Place the vinyl on the mat and use the Cricut to cut it.
10. Now, you can place the vinyl cutouts on the back, to make your child stand out!

Gift Tags

Materials needed:

- Cricut machine
- Variety of cardstock, and a vinyl
- A ready-made Design Space project, for tags that say 'I love you'
- Glitter pen of your choice
- Account for Design Space

Instructions:

1. Follow the prompts to draw, and then cut each layer as the project needs.
2. Glue two paper layers together. "Align" the heart-shaped hole at the top of the tag.
3. Add your vinyl, and then burnish it to make sure it will adhere properly, and thoroughly.
4. Add ribbon or twine to the hole, for the tag.

Paper Pinwheels

Materials needed:

- Cricut Maker or Cricut Explore
- Standard Grip mat
- Patterned cardstock in desired colors
- Embellishments
- Paper straws
- Hot glue

Instructions:

1. Log into the "Design Space" application and click on the "New Project" button on the top right corner of the screen to view a blank canvas.
2. Let us use an already existing project from the Cricut library and customize it. So, click on the "Project" icon and type in "Paper Pinwheel" in the search bar.
3. Click on "Customize" to further edit the project to your preference, or simply click on the "Make It" button and load the cardstock to your Cricut machine, and follow the instructions on the screen to cut your project.
4. Using hot glue, adhere the pinwheels together to the paper straws, and the embellishments as shown in the picture above.

Rugrats T-shirt

The materials that you will need for this project are:

- The Explore Air, or the Maker
- An iron
- A small piece of fabric or linen cloth
- T-shirts
- A Rugrats file (SVG file)
- Supplies from the Cricut company which are:
- Access membership
- The standard cutting mat
- Weeder
- Scissors
- An iron-on lite (vinyl)
- An iron-on glitter

The instructions that you need to make this design are listed here:

1. Open your design in the Design Space.
2. Choose a color scheme you want to use.
3. Attach your images to cut.
4. Place your vinyl onto the cutting mat, and be sure that the shiny side is down.
5. Load your mat into the machine.
6. Click the "Go" button to start the cutting process. Make sure that your image is mirrored. You will have to check the box that says "Mirror Image."
7. Weed your cut design.
8. Repeat the process with the different pieces of your images using different vinyl pieces to add color.
9. Place the image on the shirt how you want it to look.
10. Iron, be careful. Focus on the corners of your design. It should peel easily.

These shirts are a really great way for you to get creative and have fun. Does your child like unicorns or superheroes? You can do this, too! With the Cricut machine, you are only limited by your own creativity. There are thousands of designs that you can use for T-shirts: from movies, cartoons, anime, your favorite childhood characters, and anything else you can imagine including favorite animals and quotes.

Chapter 7. Project To Create Fabric Cuts (Part 1)

Adorable Christmas Tea Towels

Instructions:

- I opened Cricut Design Space and began a fresh project. The Design Space Image Library has over 60,000 pictures, so it's simple to begin designing your project in no time.

- Press the image you want to work with and the software inserts it into a fresh project document. I chose these wonderful hand-lettered "Merry and Bright" and "Merry Christmas" designs for my towels and arranged them for vinyl heat transfer sheets.
- Explore Air's favorite features are dial settings.
- With Cricut Explore Air, you just turn the knob to grab stuff you're working with, and the machine looks after the straightforward peasy.
- Set the "Iron-on" dial, and you're prepared to cut.
- Place a sheet of vinyl heat transfer, load it into the device, and press the cut button.
- Use Cricut Weeder to remove the excess vinyl from the design.
- I put the vinyl on my folded tea towel, covered it with a cloth, and ironed it in the instructions of the package.
- Once the vinyl heat transfer has been strongly adhered to, and discard plastic backup.
- I slipped a piece of cardstock under the towel top and used silver, gold, and champagne-colored fabric paint to add some shiny polka dots. Allow the paint to dry completely before removing the paper layer below.

Mommy Is on a Break "Socks"

Using my Cricut to create these socks, I began opening the Cricut Design Space. I typed the sentences into the design, played the size, and spaced a bit until I was sure my socks fit.

Then I loaded the heat transfer vinyl into the Cricut and sent the Cricut the cutting design. Don't forget to mirror your iron-on image design, so the text isn't backward in your project.

While cutting the vinyl, I cut some dense paper to produce inserts for my clothes to help "spread them out" while ironing on the design. The inserts were about 3" wide and 7" long, and I put them down to the toe in my shoes, so the bottom was flat.

I removed the background vinyl once the vinyl was sliced, then placed the vinyl sentences on my socks' soles.

I used my iron vinyl heat-press, but you can use iron instead.

After pushing the vinyl onto the clothes, I let them cool for a minute, pull the inserts out, and put them on. These were a super comfortable couple of socks already.

Fabric Heart Coasters Using Cricut Maker

Supplies:

- Cricut Maker
- Cotton fabric with coordinating thread
- Fusible fleece Rotary cut and mat or
- Iron Sewing Machine

Instructions:

Step 1

- Cut fabric to 12″ width to fit on the cutting board. If your fabric is longer than matting, no problem. It can hang the edge.

Step 2

- Open and add a fresh project. Click "forms" and insert a heart-shaped pop-up window.
- Reduce the heart to 5.5″. Click the top-right corner "Make." Change "Project copies" to 4 in the top-left corner and click "Apply."
- Click "Continue" in the bottom right corner. Set the material to "Medium cotton."

- Load and cut the mat with the fabric.

Step 3

- Repeat Step Two, but this time put the fusible fleece on the cutting mat. You'll also alter the heart shape to 5,375. Click "View more" when choosing content and type "fusible fleece" in the search bar.
- Cut two fusible fleece hearts.

Step 4

- Attach a fusible fleece heart to the tissue core with a warm iron. Repeat the second fleece heart.
- Sew heart forms together to create fabric heart coasters with a Cricut.

Step 5

- Sew together two heart forms (one with a fleece attached). Leave a tiny gap in turning to stitch.

Step 6

- Clip the curves below.

Step 7

- Turn the heart right. Press warm iron fold opening corners and click again.

Step 8

- Heart stitch, edge 1/4".
- Consider using two distinct fabrics, such as pink/white stripes and pink/white floral fabric. They're reversible after all.

Cricut Iron Shirt on Vinyl

Making a T-shirt needs two significant measures. First, you must decide what to say. I recommend you attempt to stick with one color. Sayings, sentences, or words are ideal.

Second, you must take on which shirt you'd like the saying. I produced my lovely sister's "fries before guys" shirt. She went to Target and discovered her smooth, flowy blouse.

Make sure the shirt could be ironed because you're going to use an iron on it. Here are a few things you'll need: Cricut Explore Air 2, Iron-on Vinyl

How to Cut Iron-On Vinyl:

- You'll begin with your picture. You can upload an image from the computer or create an image in Cricut Design Space.
- Open Design Space Cricut.
- Choose your canvas by left-clicking "Canvas." It's a shirt type baseball tee, so I chose that. Set the shirt size under "Canvas" on the right.
- Left-click "Upload picture." By browsing your files, pick your image, and choose what it is. For this project, and most iron-on projects, select "Simple Cut."

- Now press the space you'd like to cut out. Remember every letter's inside. That's enjoyable for some reason. It brings me back to my Microsoft Paint days when I used Bucket. Remember this?
- The next step is crucial. (Most are essential, but it's simple to miss.) Select "Cut Image"—NOT "Print," then "Cut Image." (Printing is a distinct project form.) Place this picture on your canvas and size it to your liking.
- Place iron on the shiny side of your mat and turn the button to Iron-on, or select Iron-on from the drop-down menu.
- Click "Cut."
- Ok, that's another significant, easy-to-miss move. Click "Iron-On Mirror" before hitting "Go."
- After cutting, remove surplus vinyl around the edges. Use your weeding tool to remove the parts in letters.
- Customizing your t-shirt How to Iron on Vinyl to T-shirt Now iron it on. Set your iron to "Cotton," or the hottest environment. Ensure there's no steam.
- Start warming the material. Put iron on the shirt for 15 seconds.
- Place your iron-on vinyl wherever you want. Put a pure cotton cloth on top of the plastic. That's important, so you don't melt the plastic on your shirt.
- Put iron on the press cloth for about 30 seconds. Flip your jacket over, do the same thing across the shirt.
- Now you'll take the sticky portion and separate it from the vinyl. Do this while it's hot. It'll be much more straightforward. If a piece doesn't come off, place the iron on the portion you're attempting to pick up, and it should pull off.
- Now plastic should be separated from vinyl. Put the press cloth back on and run with the iron, so you know it's wonderful.

DIY Striped Nautical Tote Bag

Supplies:

- Cricut
- Glitter Iron-On Vinyl in blue
- Fabric Medium DecoArt
- Americana Acrylic Craft Paint

Instructions:

Step 1

- Use a weeding tool to get rid of all the surplus vinyl around your anchor picture

Step 2

- Tape a striped pattern on the canvas tote bag

Step 3

- Mix one portion of the color medium with one part of the acrylic. Next, remove the painter's tape

Step 4

- Let the paint dry entirely, then use a warm iron. Alternatively, the brand new Cricut Easy Press to apply the glitter iron-on anchor picture.

Tooth Fairy Pouch

Supplies:

- Array of Pens
- Tons of products such as SportsFlex iron-on vinyl,
- Weeding tool
- Embossed foil paper,
- Also, holographic sparkle XL scraper

Instructions:

- Begin by opening a Blank Canvas in the Design Space.
- Kindly go to Images in the left Design Panel and search for the word "tooth." You can also check the file by typing in #M22992CA. It's the middle tooth in the screenshot below: then click on the face and white tooth spots in the Layers panel and delete them, leaving the gray piece.
- We'll cut the tooth in iron-on white vinyl, but using the gray layer makes it simpler to see what we're doing.
- Then, using the Design Panel text tool, type your child's name.
- Then we want to make this a Cricut font with a description. To do this, go to the font drop-down menu and right-click "Filter" and select "Multi-Layer." This will narrow your decisions down to more than one layer of fonts.
- Then pick the one you like. I chose Piper's Alphalicious Short Stack, Miles' Cherry Limeade. Change letter spacing if you think letters are too distant. Copy and paste a second name copy.
- In the Layers Panel, visualize the outline layer by pressing the "eye" icon.
- Then delete the primary font layer, leaving the outline.
- Then choose both name and tooth and click on "Slice" at the bottom of the Layers Panel. Slice the tooth and name.
- Delete the purple letters (there will be two—the portion of the letters outside the tooth and the portion of the letters inside the tooth. Then delete the gray messages, leaving you with an overview of the letters. Then insert the other name you recorded previously on top of the tooth to make sure everything fits together.
- Having your two parts adhered together you are done. I enjoy this project because Cricut Design Space is readily customizable—no additional files are needed.

Leather Geometric Buffalo Pillow

Supplies:

- Cricut Maker
- Cricut 12x 14″
- Cardstock Cricut
- Cutting Mat
- Cricut Fine Point Blade Glue or Tape Runner

Instructions:

- Use the connection above to resize the flowers to the size you need, then click "Make It."
- Once cut, you can collect any parts you want. I hotly attached my toothpicks to the top of my cake. For the term topper, I used bigger wood skewers to stand above the flowers. Instead of flowers, this would be super sweet with mini paper rosettes.
- Use paper and your Cricut maker to create custom cake decor. With every addition to the tools the maker utilizes, the Cricut Maker has already made it so much easier to create the possibilities.

Customized Pillow with Cricut

Supplies:

- Protective Sheet Pillow Cover
- Cricut Machine
- Glitter Iron-On Vinyl
- Cricut EasyPress Mat
- Insert Cricut Access
- Iron-On

Instructions:

Step 1

- Open the Cricut Design Space on your smartphone. Click "New Project" from the Home tab.

Step 2

- Select the text icon at the lower part of the screen and choose your required font. Type your last name and drag the box corner to make it bigger or lower to suit your pillow

Step 3

- Next, pick the Text icon to insert a second line of text for your "Est. Year."
- Drag and center properly under your last name

Step 4

- Next, pick both textboxes simultaneously and press the attach button. Appears when you click the Actions button. This will connect the two text boxes for focused cutting.

Step 5

- Next press the "Make It" button, and the screen appears. You'll want to make sure the Mirror's "on."

Step 6

- To switch off and on the mirror environment, press the picture at the top left corner. The screen above appears. Switch "on."

Step 7

- Mirror button—The mat will now display your mirrored picture, and you're prepared to load your Iron-On Vinyl SHINY SIDE DOWN onto your mat. Click and follow the prompts.

Step 8

- Once the design is sliced, weed the surplus vinyl and center your pillow cover design.

Step 9

- Next, set the EasyPress timer and temperature for your shirt material. Refer to EasyPress Settings Chart.

Step 10

- Cover the structure with the Iron-On Protective Sheet and top the protective sheet with the EasyPress and click the Cricut button. Remove once it's beeped. Flip through your pillow cover and heat back 10 to 15 seconds.

Step 11

- Cool the iron-on and merely remove the sheet.

Chapter 8. Project To Create Fabric Cuts (Part 2)

Let's start these projects using fabric as the base material. You will learn to create a variety of projects that you can further customize as you follow the instructions below and have unique designs of your own.

Fabric Headband

Materials needed— "Cricut Maker" or "Cricut Explore", FabricGrip mat, gray polka dot fabric, thread, black or decorative elastic, home sewing machine.

- Click on the "Projects" icon and type in "fabric headband" in the search bar.
- Click on "Customize" to edit the project to your preference further or simply click on the "Make It" button and load the fabric to your "Cricut" machine by placing the right side down on the mat and follow the instructions on the screen to cut your project.
- For assembly, measure your head where you would wear the headband and minus 15 inches from the measurement then cut the elastic at that length to use underneath the headband.
- Place the right sides together and pin the elastic inside with the ends sticking out that can be pinned at the end of the headband.
- Use the sewing machine to sew around the outside edge of the headband leaving a 0.5-inch seam. Then sew over the ends of the elastic while it is between the two headband pieces leaving 2 inches opening unsewn along one side of the headband.
- Clip around the seam allowances with snips and turn the headband right side out. Use the end of a spoon to turn the edges of the headband out then use an iron to press and solidify the shape.

- Top stitch around the edge of the headband with a quarter-inch seam allowance for a finished look and close the turning hole.

Forever Fabric Banner

Materials needed— "Cricut Maker" or "Cricut Explore", FabricGrip mat, glitter iron-on (black, pink), "Cricut EasyPress", weeder, pink ribbon, canvas fabric, sew able fabric stabilizer, sewing machine, and thread.

- Log into the "Design Space" application.
- Click on the "Projects" icon and type in "fabric banner" in the search bar.
- Click on "Customize" to edit the project to your preference further or simply click on the "Make It" button. Place the trimmed fabric on the cutting mat removing the paper backing then load it to your "Cricut" machine and follow the instructions on the screen to cut your project. Similarly, load the iron-on vinyl sheet to the "Cricut" and cut the design, making sure to mirror the image.
- Carefully remove the excess material from the sheet using the "weeder tool," making sure only the design remains on the clear liner.
- Using the "Cricut Easy Press Mini" and "Easy Press Mat" the iron-on layers can be easily transferred to the fabric. Preheat your "Easy Press Mini" and put your iron-on vinyl design on the fabric and apply pressure for a couple of minutes or more. Wait for a few minutes prior to peeling off the design while it is still warm.

Fabric Flower Brooch

Materials needed—"Cricut Maker" or "Cricut Explore", FabricGrip mat, printable iron-on, "Cricut EasyPress", weeder, fabric pencil pouch, and inkjet printer.

- Log into the "Design Space".

- Click on the "Projects" icon and type in "fabric pouch" in the search bar.
- Click on "Customize" to edit the project to your preference further or simply click on the "Make It" button and follow the prompts on the screen for using an inkjet printer to print the design on your printable vinyl and subsequently cut the design.
- Carefully remove the excess material from the sheet using the "weeder tool".
- Using the "Cricut Easy Press Mini" and "Easy Press Mat" the iron-on layers can be easily transferred to the fabric. Preheat your "Easy Press Mini" and put your iron-on vinyl design on the fabric and apply pressure for a couple of minutes. Wait for a few minutes before peeling off the design while it is still warm.

Flower Brooch

Materials needed—"Cricut Maker" or "Cricut Explore", FabricGrip mat, aqua fabric, liquid starch, iron and ironing board, brooch fastener, needle, ivory thread, button cover kit with wire loop back (size 20).

- Log into the "Design Space" application and click on the "New Project" button.
- Click on the "Projects" icon and type in "fabric brooch" in the search bar.
- Click on "Customize" to edit the project to your preference further or simply click on the "Make It" button.
- Prior to cutting the fabric, press the fabric pieces, and follow the instructions on liquid starch to prepare the material for the application. Place the fabric pieces with the printed sided down on the cutting mat, then load it to your "Cricut" machine and follow the instructions on the screen to cut your project.
- Use the button cover kit to cover one button and run a stitch along the center circle of the smallest flower. Then pull the thread to cinch in the center. Repeat this for the other flowers.

- Carefully layer the flowers together concentrically and stitch together in the center. Lastly, stitch the covered button to the center of the stitched flower, then stitch the brooch fastener to the back of the flower.

Leather Flower Hat

Materials needed—"Cricut Maker" or "Cricut Explore", standard grip mat, Cricut Faux Leather, button, strong adhesive, and hat.

- Log into the "Design Space" application and click on the "New Project" button on the top right corner of the screen to view a blank canvas.
- Click on the "Projects" icon and type in "leather flower hat" in the search bar.
- Click on "Customize" to edit the project to your preference further or simply click on the "Make It" button and load the faux leather to your "Cricut" machine by placing it face down on the mat and follow the instructions on the screen to cut your project.
- For assembly, glue tabs on each flower together to give shape to every single layer and let dry.
- Glue all the flower layers on top of one another with the biggest layer at the bottom. Once the flower dries completely, glue a button on the center of the flower. And finally, glue the flower to the hat.

Floral Mousepad

Materials needed—"Cricut Maker" or "Cricut Explore", FabricGrip mat, printable fabric, mousepad, adhesive.

- Log into the "Design Space" application and click on "New Project."

- Click on the "Images" icon on the "Design Panel" and type in "#MB145E" in the search bar. Select the image and click on the "Insert Images" button at the bottom of the screen.
- Edit the project to your preference or simply click on the "Make It" button and load the vinyl sheet to your "Cricut" machine and follow the instructions on the screen to print and cut your project.
- Once you have the printed fabric cut, use the adhesive to adhere it to the mousepad.

Jellybean Burp Cloth

Materials needed—"Cricut Maker" or "Cricut Explore", FabricGrip mat, fabric (light gray, teal), rotary cutter, turning tool, sewing machine, and thread.

- Click on the "Projects" icon and type in "jellybean burp cloth" in the search bar.
- Click on "Customize" to edit the project to your preference further or simply click on the "Make It" button. Place the trimmed fabric on the cutting mat then load it to your "Cricut" machine and follow the instructions on the screen to cut your project. (Pay attention to the direction of the print for each fabric piece).
- With the right sides together, pin the two bean pieces together and sew with a 6mm seam around the edge of the bean pieces, leaving a 1-2-inch opening for turning in the middle straight area.
- Clip all curves generously and use a chopstick to turn the fabric pieces' right side out through the turning hole. Press all seams.
- Lastly, top stitch the entire shape and close the turning hole as well.

Personalized Coaster Tiles

Materials needed—"Cricut Maker" or "Cricut Explore", standard grip mat, "Cricut" iron-on lite, freezer paper, "Cricut Easy Press Mini", "Easy Press" mat, weeding tool, pillow cover, screen print paint, paintbrush.

- Click on the "Images" icon on the "Design Panel" and type in "#MED91E0" in the search bar. Select the image and click on the "Insert Images" button at the bottom of the screen.
- Edit the project to your preference or simply click on the "Make It" button and load the freezer paper with the non-shiny side up on the mat to your "Cricut" machine and follow the instructions on the screen to cut your project.
- Using a weeder tool, remove the negative space pieces of the design. Carefully place the stenciled quote on the pillow.
- Using the "Cricut Easy Press Mini" and "Easy Press Mat", iron on the design to the pillow. Preheat your "Easy Press Mini" and put your design on the desired area and apply pressure for a couple of minutes or more. Remove the freezer paper and let it dry overnight.
- Set the paint with the "EasyPress" once again and enjoy your new pillow!

Chapter 9. Project With Glass

Projects and Ideas with Glass Vinyl cut with your Cricut machine can help you create beautiful glass projects. There are several different ways you can use it, as well. Any glass object can be a blank for these projects. You might already have some things in your kitchen that you'd like to decorate. These make wonderful gifts, too—no one will believe that you made them yourself and that they're not expensive gifts.

Glass etching cream is an interesting product that lets you easily create etched glass projects. There are several different brands that you can find at craft stores or online. You may be able to find them at hardware stores as well.

Read the instructions carefully and follow them exactly, to get your desired results and to be safe. It is actually an acid that eats away at the glass to create the etched effect. This may vary between brands, but often, stirring the cream around during its setting time will make the etching more pronounced. This will be a permanent effect on the glass.

Besides etching, you can also create beautiful glass projects using vinyl.

Outdoor vinyl, which is permanent, is the best choice if you want the design to stay put through use and washing. Removable vinyl will be temporary, and you can peel it off; it won't survive being washed. Window-cling vinyl sticks to glass via static, so they are quite temporary but can easily be changed out and reused.

Etched Monogrammed Glass

Etched Monogrammed Glass Glasses are one of the most-used things in your kitchen, and it's impossible to have too many of them. It's actually quite easy to customize them with etching, and it will look as if a professional did it. Simply use glass etching cream that you can find at any craft store! Be sure to read the instructions and warning labels carefully before you begin. The vinyl will act as a stencil, protecting the parts of the glass that you don't want to etch. Be sure to take your time to get the vinyl smooth against the glass, especially where there are small bits. You don't want any of the cream to get under the edge of the vinyl. You can use the Cricut Explore One, Cricut Explore Air 2, or Cricut Maker for this project.

Supplies Needed:

- A glass of your choice—make sure that the spot you want to monogram is smooth
- Vinyl
- Cutting mat
- Weeding tool or pick
- Glass etching cream

Instructions:

1. Open Cricut Design Space and create a new project.
2. Select the "Image" button in the Design Panel and search for "monogram."
3. Select your preferred monogram and click "Insert."
4. Put the vinyl on your cutting mat.
5. Direct the project to your machine.
6. Utilize a weeding device or pick to remove the monogram, leaving the vinyl around it.
7. Remove the vinyl from the mat.
8. Carefully apply the vinyl around your glass, making it as smooth as possible, particularly around the monogram.
9. If you have any letters with holes in your monogram, carefully reposition those cutouts in their proper place.
10. Following the instructions on the etching cream, apply it to your monogram.
11. Remove the cream and then the vinyl.
12. Give your glass a good wash.

Live, Love, Laugh Glass Block

Glass blocks are an inexpensive yet surprisingly versatile craft material. You can find them at both craft and hardware stores. They typically have a hole with a lid so that you can fill the blocks with the items of your choice. This project uses tiny fairy lights for a glowing quote block, but you can fill it however you'd like. The frost spray paint adds a bit of elegance to the glass and diffuses the light for a softer glow, hiding the string of the fairy lights.

Holographic vinyl will add to the magical look, but you can use whatever colors you'd like. This features a classic quote that's great to have around your house, but you can change it. You can use the Cricut Explore One, Cricut Explore Air 2, or Cricut Maker for this project.

Supplies Needed:

- Glass block
- Frost spray paint
- Clear enamel spray
- Holographic vinyl
- Vinyl transfer tape
- Cutting mat
- Weeding tool or pick
- Fairy lights

Instructions:

1. Spray the entire glass block with frost spray paint, and let it dry.
2. Spray the glass block with a coat of clear enamel spray, and let it dry.
3. Open Cricut Design Space and create a new project.
4. Select the "Text" button in the Design Panel.
5. Type "Live Love Laugh" in the text box.
6. Use the dropdown box to select your favorite font.
7. Arrange the words to sit on top of each other.

8. Place your vinyl on the cutting mat.
9. Send the design to your Cricut.
10. Use a weeding tool or pick to remove the excess vinyl from the design.
11. Apply transfer tape to the design.
12. Remove the paper backing and apply the words to the glass block.
13. Smooth down the design and carefully remove the transfer tape.
14. Place fairy lights in the opening of the block, leaving the battery pack on the outside.

Unicorn Wine Glass

Who doesn't love unicorns? Who doesn't love wine? Bring them together with these glittery wine glasses! The outdoor vinyl will hold up to use and washing, and the Mod Podge will keep the glitter in place for years to come.

Customize it even more with your own quote. You could use a different magical creature as well—mermaids go great with glitter too! Customize this to suit your tastes or to create gifts for your friends and family. Consider using these for a party and letting the guests take them home as favors! You can use the Cricut Explore One, Cricut Explore Air 2, or Cricut Maker for this project.

Supplies Needed:

- Stemless wine glasses
- Outdoor vinyl in the color of your choice
- Vinyl transfer tape
- Cutting mat
- Weeding tool or pick
- Extra fine glitter in the color of your choice Mod Podge

Instructions:

1. Open Cricut Design Space and create a new project.
2. Select the "Text" button in the Design Panel.
3. Type "It's not drinking alone if my unicorn is here."
4. Using the dropdown box, select your favorite font.
5. Adjust the positioning of the letters, rotating some to give a whimsical look.
6. Select the "Image" button on the Design Panel and search for "unicorn."
7. Select your favorite unicorn and click "Insert," then arrange your design how you want it on the glass.
8. Place your vinyl on the cutting mat, making sure it is smooth and making full contact.
9. Send the design to your Cricut.
10. Use a weeding tool or pick to remove the excess vinyl from the design. Use the Cricut BrightPad to help if you have one.
11. Apply transfer tape to the design, pressing firmly, and making sure there are no bubbles.
12. Remove the paper backing and apply the words to the glass where you'd like them. Leave at least a couple of inches at the bottom for the glitter.
13. Smooth down the design and carefully remove the transfer tape.
14. Coat the bottom of the glass in Mod Podge, wherever you would like glitter to be. Give the area a wavy edge.
15. Sprinkle glitter over the Mod Podge, working quickly before it dries.
16. Add another layer of Mod Podge and glitter, and set it aside to dry.
17. Cover the glitter in a thick coat of Mod Podge.
18. Allow the glass to cure for at least 48 hours.

Chapter 10. Other Ideas For Advanced Level

Asides from using the Cricut to make projects for your home, there is the extra advantage of creating stuff to adorn yourself. These include your earrings, bracelets, necklaces, and other adornments.

Earrings

It is possible that you might have been interested in making earrings while using your Cricut but you do not have the technical know-how. Do not stress further, this part is going to give you a step by step breakdown of how to go about this.

Materials and Tools needed:

- Cricut Machine
- Cricut Blade (comes with the machine)
- Faux leather
- Metallic Vinyl
- Purple Standard Cutting Mat

- Transfer Tape
- Nose Pliers
- Spatula
- Earring Hooks
- Scissors
- Hole Punch
- Scraper or Cricut EasyPress

The steps include:

1. You should be logged on to your Design Space on your personal computer or iPad.
2. Once you are logged in to your Design Space, there is no limit to what design of earrings you can make. Create a new project and select the "Insert Image" option. You can then use the "Search" option to obtain any shape of your desire.
3. Once you have found your desired shape, you should then insert it. How your iron-on accents would look like depends on your decision.
4. You can then use the "Slice" and "Weld" options found in the Layer Panel to make different slice shapes for your earrings.
5. Upon completing your design, you should select the "Make It" option. It is also important to be certain that you have your second mat mirrored as your cutting material is iron-on. Your first mat should be the Faux Leather while the second should be the Metallic Iron-On.
6. Start with a piece of Cricut Metallic Leather and position it on a Strong Grip mat in a sweeping manner, apply pressure to have the leather stick to the mat. In the case when the mat and leather do not stick together, you should use masking tapes to hold firm the sides of the mat and leather together.
7. The start wheels should then be moved to the far-right side of the machine. The Fine-Point Blade should then be replaced with the Deep-Cut Blade. The Deep-Cut Blade is to ensure proper and full cutting of the material.
8. In your Design Space, click on "Make," and then have Faux Leather chosen as the material option for cutting.

9. Have the Mat placed into the Cricut machine and you should proceed to cut? When the cut is finished, remove the mat, and with the most care, you should then have the excess leather removed and this has the earrings left alone on the mat.
10. The star wheels should then be returned to the initial position from which they were moved while the blades should be switched back to Fine-Point Blade from the Deep-Cut Blade. For the earring that you have decided on, you should cut a sufficiently sizable portion of iron-on and then have it applied on the mat.
11. The Cricut weeding tools should then be engaged to weed the specific earrings by having the excess vinyl peeled back with great care. The earring should be covered with a sheet of transfer tape, and then the vinyl should also be burnished on the transfer tape. The hearing should then be cut into pairs as the white paper that backs them is removed. Leather earrings left on the purple mat will be perfectly lined up with the vinyl.
12. The vinyl should then be positioned on top of the earrings and then the vinyl is to be burnished on the leather. This can be done with the scraper or by heating up your Cricut EasyPress—the recommended settings for the EasyPress varies as the base material you are using determined the temperature you will be using.
13. You should then have the transfer tape peeled off so as to have your earrings uncovered. You should then live off the mat each earring with your Spatula.
14. You should then attach the metal hooks to your earrings. You should open your eyes in the earring using a pair of needle-nose pliers. This should be done gently and also the hole should be wide enough for the hook to fit through. The hook should then be inserted in the earring through the hole you would have made at the back using the punch.
15. You should then close the hole with your nose pliers.

Now, your darling handmade earrings are set and ready to be used.

Bracelets

The bracelet is a project that is easy to create on your own. This project needs just a couple of materials and tools.

Materials and tools needed:

- Cricut Machine
- Leather Bracelet
- Cricut Iron-on
- EasyPress
- EasyPress Mat
- Weeding Tool
- LightGrip Cutting Mat
- Measuring Tape

The steps include:

1. Log on to your Design Space on your personal computer or iPad.
2. Once you are logged in, you can then proceed to have your SVG file downloaded. Once you have downloaded the SVG file, you should then upload it to your Design Space. Make sure you resize your design and make sure it is going to fit well on your leather bracelet.

3. You should then load your mat. Remember to have the shiny part of your Iron-on facing the mat. Your Cricut should then be set to the material "Iron-on" and then it is ready to cut.
4. Once the design has been cut-out, you should then proceed to weed with your weeding tool. You should do this with extreme care so as not to miss out on any material.
5. Your EasyPress should then be preheated to the necessary temperature. You should check online to find out what temperature the EasyPress is suitable for each material.
6. Have the weeded cut-out image positioned as you wish on the leather bracelet and then have both of them inserted in your EasyPress for about 30 seconds.
7. The transfer paper should then be peeled off.
8. This allows the unveiling of your cute handmade bracelet.

Necklaces

Necklaces are such wonderful items that can be giving out to friends, families, etc. The Cricut machine allows you the opportunity to have your own customized necklace with any material of your choice. Imagine getting to a store to purchase this nice necklace but it is not available in gold but leather. The disappointment you would feel. However, you can create your own necklace according to your taste.

Materials and tools needed:

- Cricut Machine
- Strong Grip Mat
- Transfer Tape
- Necklace (of any material of your choice)
- Jump Ring
- Pliers
- Glue

The steps include:

1. You should be logged in on your Design Space on your personal computer or iPads.
2. You can choose to download the SVG file of your choice or decide to create the design yourself.
3. You should then proceed to cut your image. You will have different options that are before you, however, you should select the option "Leather, Heavy" as this will be effective for your tooling leather.
4. There will be an on-screen instruction to guide you on how the different layers of your design can be cut.
5. The cardstock layers, Cardstock and Mod Podge should then be glued together. The safety pin should be used to make sure the glue is removed from tiny holes on each cut-out word.
6. The adhesive foil should then be applied, and to ensure it adheres well, it should be firmly pressed.
7. This should then be left to dry once the charm has been sealed.
8. You can then add jump rings through each hole in the charm to which the necklaces will be added. The jump rings are made by the jeweler pliers.
9. Your necklace is then ready for use.

Chapter 11. Other Projects Using Cricut Design Space

Night Sky Pillow

Supplies Needed:

- Black, dark blue, or dark purple fabric
- Heat transfer vinyl in gold or silver
- Cutting mat
- Polyester batting
- Weeding tool or pick
- Cricut EasyPress

Instructions:

1. Decide the shape you want for your pillow, and cut two matching shapes out of the fabric.
2. Open Cricut Design Space and create a "New Project."
3. Select the "Image" button in the lower left-hand corner and search "Start."
4. Select the stars of your choice and click "Insert."
5. Place the iron-on material on the mat.
6. Send the design to the Cricut.
7. Use the weeding tool, or pick to remove excess material.
8. Remove the material from the mat.
9. Place the iron-on material on the fabric.
10. Use the EasyPress to adhere it to the iron-on material.
11. Sew the two fabric pieces together, leaving allowance for a seam and a small space open.
12. Fill the pillow with polyester batting through the small open space.

13. Sew the pillow shut.
14. Cuddle up to your starry pillow!

Clutch Purse

Supplies Needed:

- Two fabrics, one for the exterior and one for the interior
- Fusible fleece
- Fabric cutting mat
- D-ring
- Sew-on snap
- Lace
- Zipper
- Sewing machine
- Fabric scissors
- Keychain or charm of your choice

Instructions:

1. Open Cricut Design Space and create a "New Project."
2. Select the "Image" button in the lower left-hand corner and search for "Essential Wallet."
3. Select the essential wallet template, and click "Insert."
4. Place the fabric on the mat.
5. Send the design to the Cricut.
6. Remove the fabric from the mat.
7. Attach the fusible fleecing to the wrong side of the exterior fabric.
8. Attach lace to the edges of the exterior fabric.
9. Assemble the D-ring strap.
10. Place the D-ring onto the strap and sew into place.

11. Fold the pocket pieces' wrong side out over the top of the zipper, and sew it into place.
12. Fold the pocket's wrong side in and sew the sides.
13. Sew the snap onto the pocket.
14. Lay the pocket on the right side of the main fabric lining so that the corners of the pocket's bottom are behind the curved edges of the lining fabric. Sew the lining piece to the zipper tape.
15. Fold the lining behind the pocket and iron in place.
16. Sew on the other side of the snap.
17. Trim the zipper so that it is not overhanging the edge.
18. Sew the two pocket layers to the exterior fabric across the bottom.
19. Sew around all of the layers.
20. Trim the edges with fabric scissors.
21. Turn the clutch almost completely inside out and sew the opening to close it.
22. Turn the clutch all the way inside out and press the corners into place.
23. Attach your charm or keychain to the zipper.
24. Carry your new clutch wherever you need it!

Personalized Water Bottle

Supplies Needed:

- A water bottle with a smooth surface (these are very easy to find in superstores)
- Transfer tape
- A brayer or a scraper
- Outdoor vinyl

Instructions:

1. Your first step is to open the design app. Let us say for this example that we are going to be making the name "Adam."
2. Choose a font that you like, and then use the eyeball icon in the Layers panel.
3. Create a second text box, and you can make the initial letter bigger.
4. Now, you will need to attach the two layers together so that the "Name" and the "Initial" are cut out together.
5. Resize and make it fit your water bottle.
6. To make sure that this will adhere to your bottle, you will need to use transfer tape. The brayer can help here because you can help press the transfer tape down.
7. Start in the center of the letter and work out when adhering to the bottle. Be sure to smooth all bubbles.
8. Peel off the tape very carefully, and then you are finished.

Fabric Coaster

Supplies Needed:

- The Maker
- Rotary cut and mat, or a pair of scissors
- A sewing machine
- An iron
- Cotton fabric and a coordinating thread
- Fusible fleece

Instructions:

1. Cut your fabric to the inches you need to fit on your cutting mat.
2. Open Design Space and hit the button that says "New Project."
3. Click on "Shapes" and then insert a heart shape. You will do this from the pop-up window.
4. Resize your heart to 5.5 inches. Click "Make It."
5. Change the project copies to four (left corner at the top). Then, click "Apply."
6. Click "Continue" (bottom right).
7. Set your material to medium fabrics like cotton.
8. Load your mat with the fabric attached; Cut.
9. Repeat all steps, but this time, you will place the fusible fleece on the cutting mat.
10. Change the heart shape to 5.7"
11. When you select the material, click "View More" and then type in "Fusible Fleece."
12. Cut out two fleece hearts.
13. Attach a fleece heart to the back of a fabric heart. You will use a hot iron to do this (be careful not to burn yourself).
14. Repeat with the second heart.
15. With the right sides together, sew two heart shapes together. Make sure the fleece is attached. Leave a gap in the stitches for turning.
16. Clip the curves.

17. Turn the heart's right side out, then press with the iron.
18. Fold in the edges of the opening and then press once more.
19. Stitch around the heart a quarter inch from the edge.

Glitter Tumbler

Supplies Needed:

- Painters tape
- Mod podge and paint brush
- Epoxy
- Glitter
- Stainless steel tumbler
- Spray paint
- Vinyl
- Sandpaper wet/dry
- Gloves
- Plastic cup
- Measuring cup
- Rubbing alcohol

Instructions:

1. Tape off the top and bottom of the tumbler.
2. Make sure to seal them well enough that paint will not get on either.
3. Spray paint twelve inches away from your tumbler in an area that is well ventilated.
4. Make sure that the items you used are approved and will not make you sick.
5. Once your tumbler is dry from the paint you have used you can add the glitter.
6. This will make a mess, so have something under it to catch the glitter.
7. Put the mod podge in a small container.

8. Use a flat paintbrush to put it on.
9. Take the lid off and rotate the cup adding glitter.
10. Make sure it is completely covered.
11. Make sure that an excess glitter will come off before removing the tape and letting it dry.
12. When dry take a flat brush that is clean, and stroke down the glitter to get any additional pieces not glued down.
13. Add a piece of tape above the glitter line.
14. Do the same to the bottom.
15. Get a plastic cup and gloves.
16. Use the epoxy and measure equal parts of solution A and B into measuring cups. If it is a small mug you only need about 5 ml each. Larger ones need 10 ml.
17. Pour them both in a cup and scrape down the sides using a wooden stick.
18. Stir for three minutes and pop all bubbles.
19. Your gloves should be on but if not, put them on now.
20. Add the glitter to the epoxy and stir.
21. Add the mixture to the tumbler and turn it often while you are doing this. Having a roller or something to turn it on will help and make sure it is in the air so nothing is touching it.
22. When the drugs are not coming as fast, you can slow the turning down but while it is the turning is constant.
23. Take the tape off after forty-five minutes.
24. Spin the tumbler for five hours and it should be dry, if not leave it on a foam roller overnight.
25. Sand the tumbler gently with wet sandpaper.
26. When it is all smooth from sanding clean it with rubbing alcohol.
27. Then open the Cricut design space and cut out your glitter vinyl.
28. Weed the design.
29. Add strong grip transfer tape.
30. Transfer the decal to the tumbler.

This is a very hard project that takes a lot of time and you need to make sure that children are nowhere near these products, as it will be fatal to them if they swallow them. Another thing to remember is spinning and making sure it is dry. By following these instructions, you should have a great glitter tumbler that you can take anywhere and rock a stylish look. This is a great idea for business owners as well because decorated tumblers are a hot commodity right now and everyone loves them.

Personalized Mermaid Bottle

Supplies Needed:

- You will need a water bottle with a smooth surface (these are very easy to find in dollar stores, superstores, specialty stores, or really any store you would like to go to)
- Transfer tape
- A brayer or a scraper
- Outdoor vinyl

Instructions:

1. Your first step is to open the design app. Let us say, for this example, we are going to be making a mermaid.
2. Choose a font that you like and then use the eyeball icon in the Layers panel. If you do not want to make it yourself, simply go into the design space and choose one of their ready to make projects.
3. Create a second text box, and you can make the picture bigger.
4. Now you will need to attach the two layers together so that the picture and the initials, cut together.
5. Resize and make it fit your water bottle.
6. To make sure that this will adhere to your bottle you will need to use transfer tape. The brayer can help here because you can help press the transfer tape down.

7. Start in the center of the letter and work out when adhering to the bottle. Be sure to smooth all bubbles.
8. Peel off the tape very carefully, and then you are finished
9. To make the shark, follow the same instructions.

By utilizing the tips in this book, you will be able to make some great projects and really get used to your machine and its inner workings, as well as unleash your own creativity and learn. The Cricut machines have made crafting so much easier and a lot more fun. The fact that Cricut also works with companies for you to be able to use their designs if you want to utilize them, makes this perfect for fans of pop culture.

Enjoy taking your crafting skills to the next level and learning great new projects with the Cricut machines!

Chapter 12. Other Projects Using Cricut Design Space (Part 2)

Wedding Table Plan

To make your plant wedding table plan, you will need:

- Cricut Machine
- 1 box of 25 Pollen sheets 210x297 mm
- 210g Ivory
- Extra strong double-sided adhesive tape—6mm x 10m
- High-temperature glue gun
- White metal ring 25 cm
- Straight scissors 17 cm
- 1 natural kraft string

Discover all the steps below:

STEP 1/13—Using the Cricut, cut multiple sheets using the different shades of green card stock.

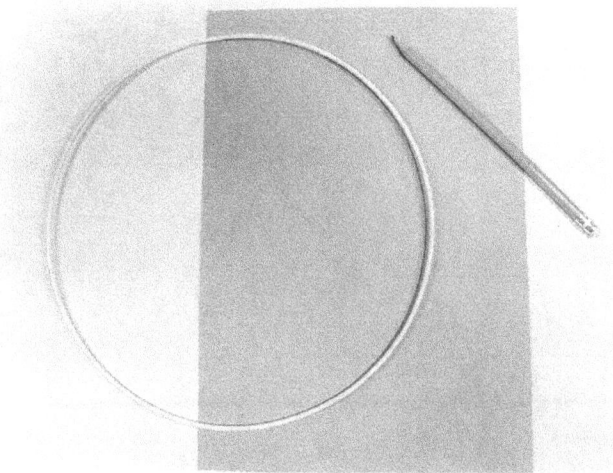

STEP 2/13—Trace the inner and outer outline of the half of the ring on green card stock with a pencil, and cut out the half-moon, leaving enough room on both sides to be able to fold it around the ring.

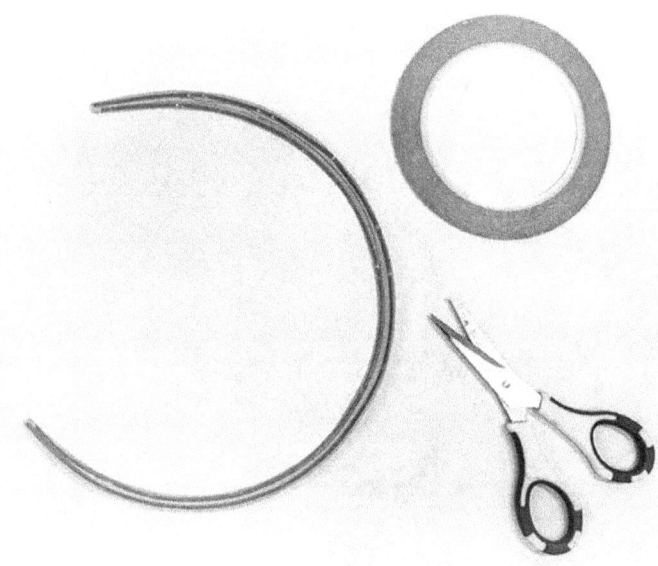

STEP 3/13—Stick the double-sided adhesive tape on the half-moon.

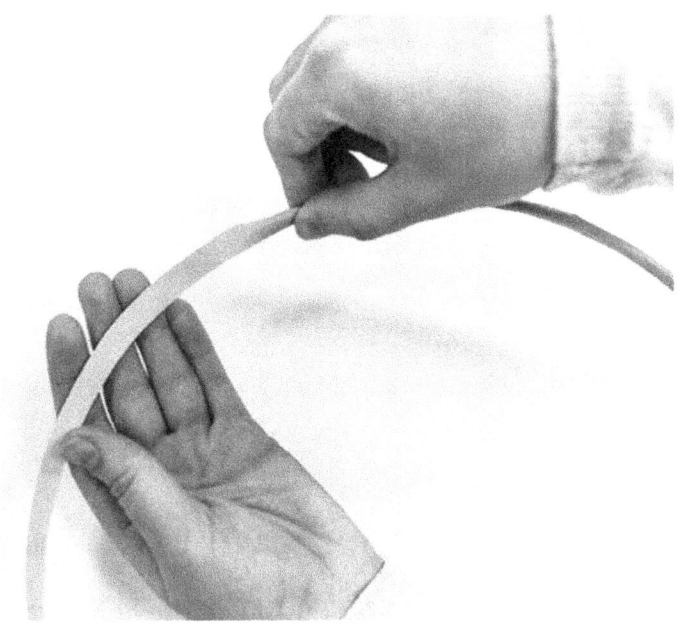

STEP 4/13—Fold it around half of the hoop, pinching the edges so that they are secure. This edge will serve as a base for easily gluing your paper sheets.

STEP 5/13—Arrange the different cut sheets on the part of the ring covered with paper and glue the elements with a glue gun.

STEP 6/13—Using the Cricut and the Natural Leaves dye, cut the berries out of the cream card stock.

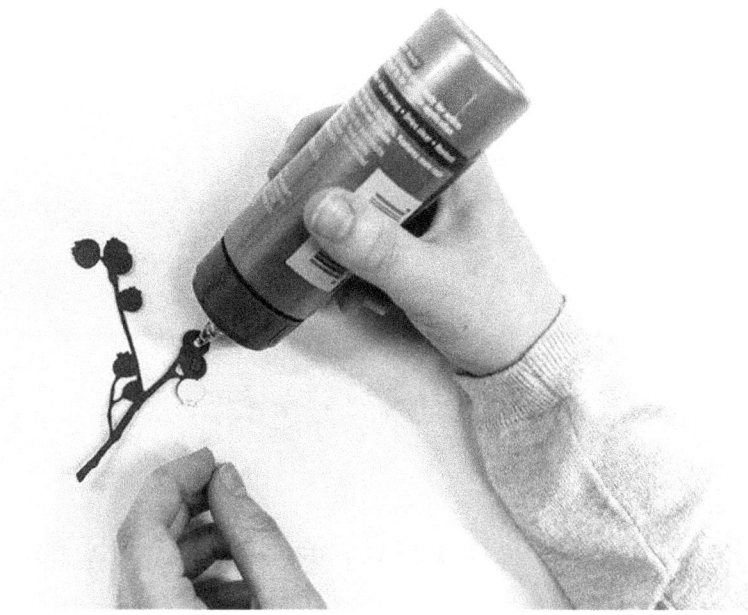

STEP 7/13—Glue the berries on the corresponding branches of the set to bring out the berries.

STEP 8/13—Insert and glue the berry branches among the other leaves where you want to add shades of color.

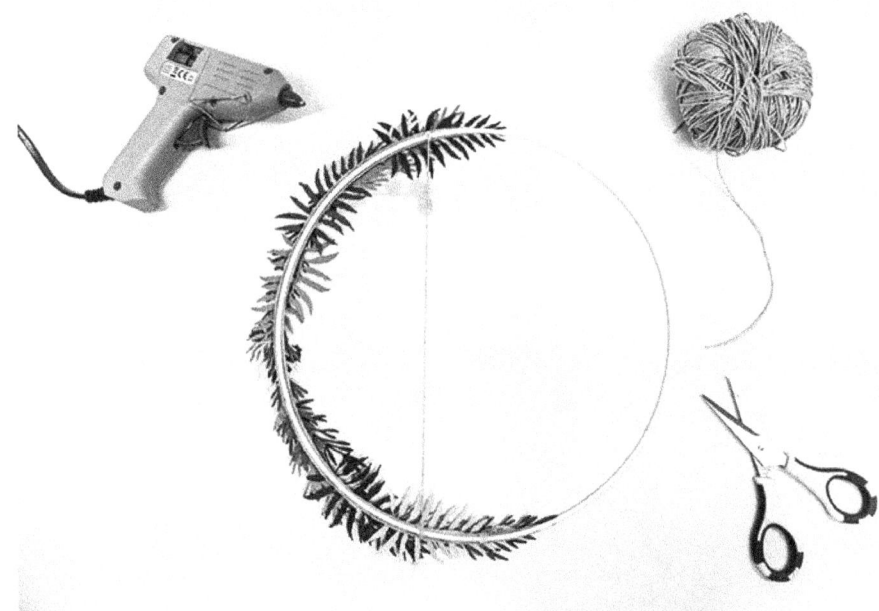

STEP 9/13—Tie the string to the back of the metal ring with the glue gun, cut off the excess if necessary

STEP 10/13—Print the table numbers on the cream card stock, cut out in a circle and glue it on the string, towards the center of the ring.

STEP 11/13—Print the names of the guests on the cream paper and cut them out with scissors, forming banners.

STEP 12/13—Create your seating plan and paste the guest names wherever you want!

STEP 13/13—Create as many rings as there are guest tables for your wedding and arrange them on a recovered wooden pallet.

Paper Decoration

To make this tropical decoration, you will need:

- Cricut
- Set of 6 Scrapbooking paper sheets
- Leaf—30.5x30.5cm—petrol blue.
- Leaf —30.5x30.5cm—menthol green
- Leaf—30.5x30.5cm—lime green
- Leaf—30.5x30.5cm—spring green
- Slate scrapbooking sheet—30x30cm
- Sheet of 34 epoxy stickers
- 8 card stock polaroid frames
- Assortment of 40 die-cuts
- 100m two-tone spool - Sky blue
- 16 mini clothespins 35 mm
- Vivaldi smooth sheet A4
- 240g—Canson—white n ° 1
- Precision cutter and 3 blades
- Blue cutting mat—2mm—A3
- Acrylic and aluminum ruler 30cm black
- Precision scissors 13.5cm blue bi-material rings
- 3D adhesive squares
- Mahé Tools—scrapbooking
- Pack of 6 HB graphite pencils

Preparation time: 2h

Techniques: Stencil, Collage, Origami, Folding, Tropical

Discover below all the steps to realize your summer decoration "Tropical Paradise":

1. Gather the materials.

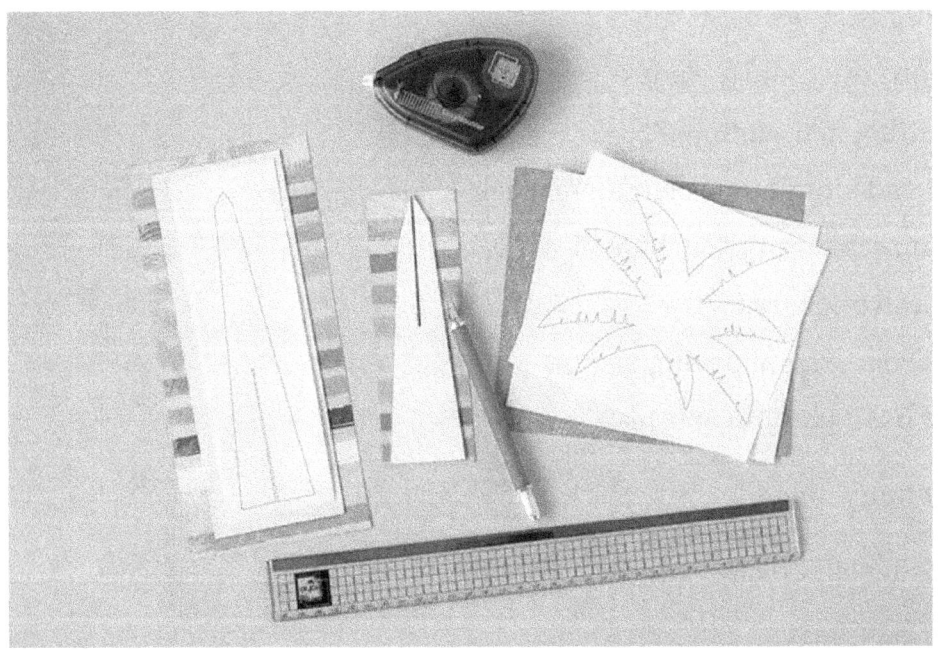

2. Using the template and a pencil, reproduce the palm tree on the papers in the collection.

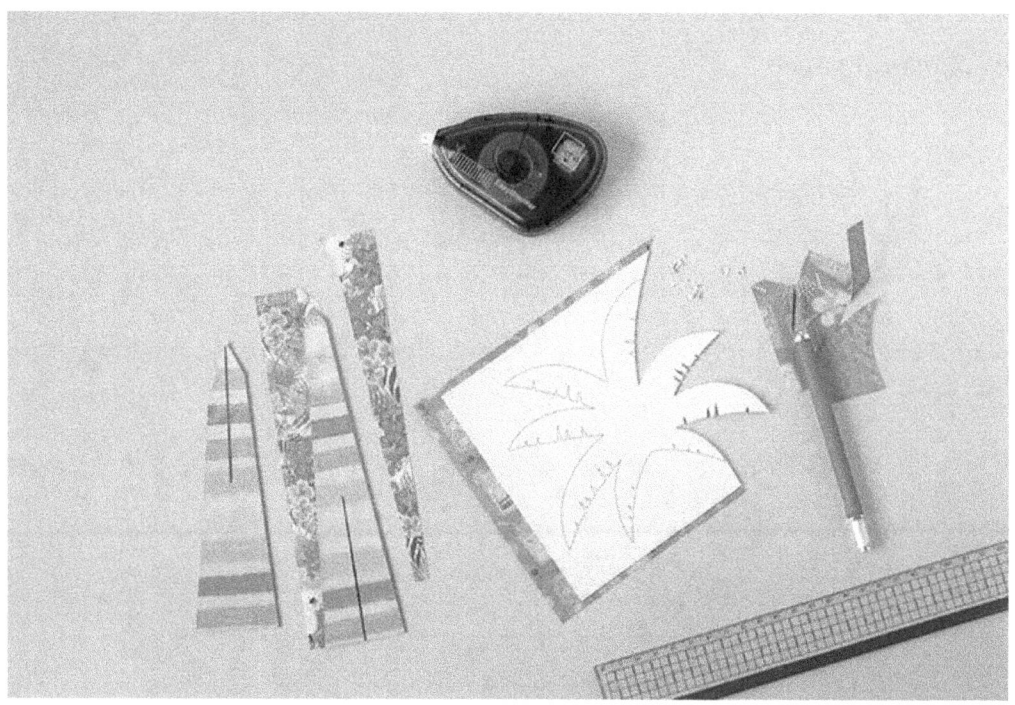

3. Cut out using Cricut.

4. Assemble the trunk of the palm tree. Glue the foliage. Using the template, reproduce the traces of the cocktail support on thin cardboard, following the dimensions indicated. Cover it with the collection paper.

5. After having cut in the slate sheet: 1 x (8.5 x 8.5 cm). Choose a Polaroid. Glue the slate sheet to the back of the Polaroid. Using a chalk pen, write "Cocktail of the day." Decorate with the stickers. Fold the support at the dotted lines.

6. Using the templates and a pencil, draw the leaves and flowers on the paper and on the collection paper. Draw.

7. Choose photos. Cut them to size: 8.5 x 8.5 cm. Stick to the back of the Polaroids.

8. Glue the leaves and flowers together. Cut the string to the desired dimensions and glue it to the back of the flowers. Glue the birds on the string and hang the photos using mini clips.

And here is a pretty summer and tropical decoration! Beautiful evenings in perspective!

Crepe Paper Flowers

Completion time: more than 2 hours

Difficulty: 1/3

To make this bouquet of crepe paper flowers, you will need:

- Assortment of 10 rolls of crepe paper, or discover our range of crepe papers
- 20 thread stems with flower 1mm x 50 cm
- Vinyl glue
- 4 pairs of multi-use scissors
- Cutout template to download, print, and cut.

Find all the detailed steps below:

1. Creation of yellow flowers:

Print the template and cut it out on Cricut. Cut 5 petals out of yellow florist crepe paper. Be sure to place the vertical template in the direction of the grooves of the crepe paper. Cut a 2.5 x 5 cm strip of orange florist crepe paper. Bisect a binding wire with a clamp cutting.

Stretch each petal by placing your thumbs in the middle of the petals. Dig with your thumbs apart. The petals become very rounded. Finely notch the orange strip. Paste up the binding wire and winding the paper to form the pistils.

Stick the pistils in the hollow of a first petal. Glue the second petal slightly offset by about 3mm. Glue all the petals until they half cover the first petal. Pinch the basis for refining.

Cut a strip of green crepe paper about 0.5 x 15 cm long. Shoot it. Glue one end to the base of the petals. Apply glue and wrap it tightly around the rod. Leave to dry. Prepare 10 yellow flowers like this.

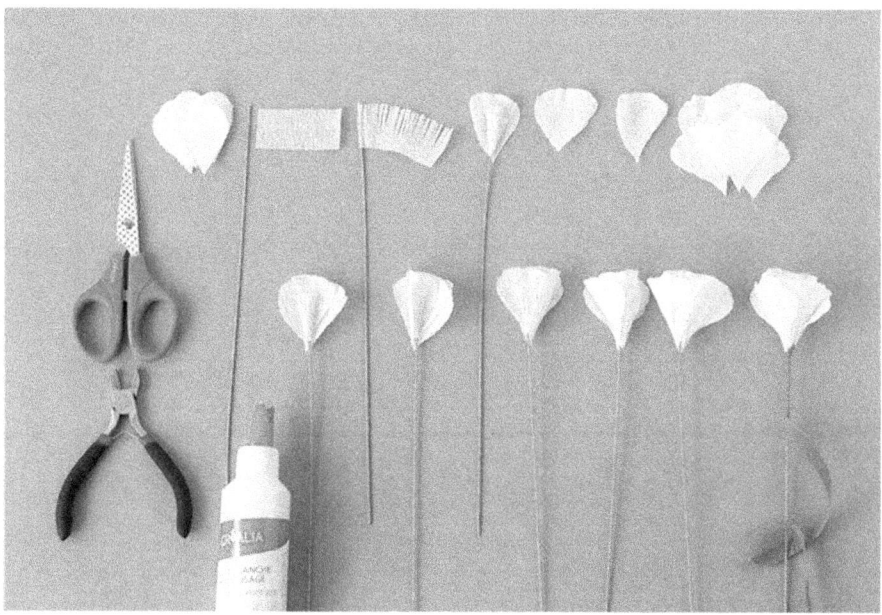

2. Creation of white:

Cut 10 petals out of white florist crepe paper. Be sure to place the vertical template in the direction of the grooves of the crepe paper. Cut a 2.5 x 5 cm strip of yellow florist crepe paper. Cut a wire to be tied in half using wire cutters.

Pinch the top edge of a petal starting from the left and spacing the inches 2 millimeters apart. Stretch the paper. Move your thumbs and repeat the operation every 5 millimeters, to form little ruffles. Do the same for each petal. Place thumbs in the middle of the petals. Dig lightly with your thumbs apart without completely stretching the paper. Finely notch the yellow strip. Stick the top of the binding wire and winding the paper to form the pistils.

Stick the pistils in the hollow of a first petal. Glue the second petal offset by about 5 millimeters. Glue all the petals by rolling the petals to surround the flower several times. Pinch the base to refine it.

Cut a strip of green crepe paper about 0.5 x 15 cm long. Shoot it. Glue one end to the base of the petals. Apply glue and wrap it tightly around the rod. Let dry. Prepare and 10 white flowers.

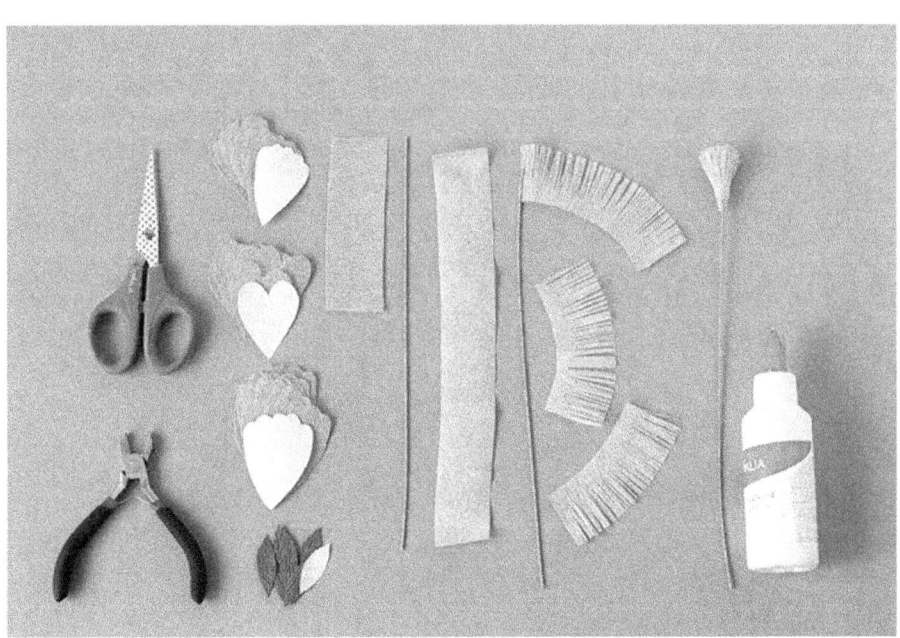

3. Creating peony flowers:

Cut 7 petals of the first template out of bright pink florist crepe paper. Prepare 7 heart-shaped petals and 6 large petals and 5 sepals in green crepe paper. Make sure to place the template vertically in the direction of the paper grooves crepe.

Cut a 3.5 x 11 cm strip of orange florist crepe paper. Cut into both a binding wire with a clamp cutting.

Stretch the orange strip. Fold it in 3 and cut. Finely notch each orange strip. Glue the first strip to the top of the wire to be bound and roll up the paper to form the pistils. Add the second, then the third strip. Spread the pistils to give them volume. Pinch the base to refine it.

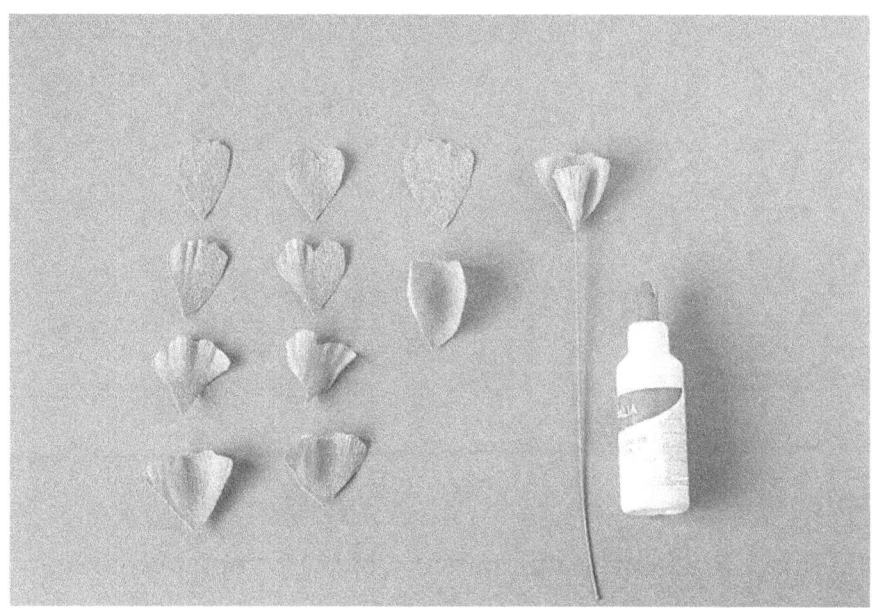

4. Give the form to the petals:

Take the first set of petals. Pinch the top edge of a petal starting from the left and spacing the inches 2 millimeters apart. Stretch the paper. Move your thumbs and repeat the operation every 5 millimeters, to form little ruffles. Do the same for each petal. Place thumbs in the middle of the petals. Widen slightly, keeping an inch without fully extend the paper.

Prepare the same way the petals in a heart shape.

For larger petals, stretch them one by one. Place thumbs in the middle of the petals. Dig with your thumbs apart. The petals become very rounded.

Stick the pistils in the hollow of a first petal.

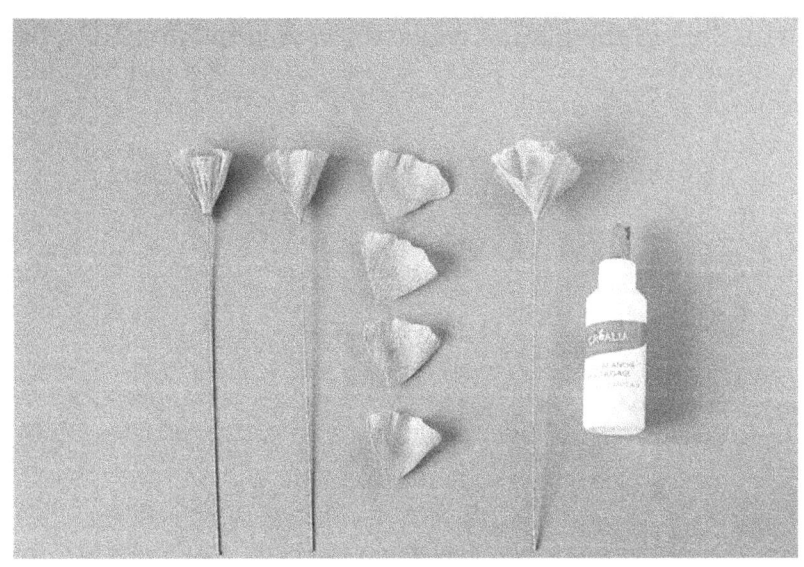

Step 5.

Glue the second petal offset by about 5 millimeters. Glue by wrapping the first 7 petals to surround the flower several times. Pinch the base to refine it.

Step 6:

Glue the second set of heart-shaped petals onto the flower. Glue each petal a little higher than the base, on the first petals to create a more garnished effect. Paste wrapping around the petals of the flower.

Finish by gluing the last set of 6 rounded petals, arranging to surround the flower only once.

Step 7.

Turn the flower over and glue the sepals starting from the stem to cover the base of the flower. Cut a strip of green crepe paper about 0.4 x 15 cm long. Shoot it. Glue it to the base of the sepals. Apply glue and wrap it tightly around the rod. Let dry. Prepare 5 hot pink peonies and 4 soft pink peonies in this way.

Step 8. The foliage.

Print the template and cut it out using Cricut. Cut 10 leaves from green florist crepe paper. Be sure to place the vertical template in the direction of the grooves of the crepe paper. Cut a wire to be tied in half using wire cutters. Paste the wire bonding at the center of the foliage. Cut a strip of green crepe paper about 0.4 x 15 cm long. Shoot it. The paste to the base of the foliage. Apply glue and wrap it tightly around the rod. Let dry. Prepare 10 green leaves in this way.

Floral Letter in Watercolor

Time: 60 minutes.

To make your floral letter in watercolor, you will need:

- Cricut Maker
- Box of 12 Aqua pencils
- 3 watercolor brushes
- Watercolor pad 25 x 25 cm
- 200 Double-sided adhesive foam squares—Cerealia
- Extra strong double-sided adhesive tape—6mm x 10m—Cerealia
- Template to download and print.

Find all the steps:

STEP 1/9—Print the templates and using the tracing paper, reproduce the letter chosen on the watercolor paper as well as the flowers.

STEP 2/9—Color the letter with watercolor pencils. Make areas darker to create contrast.

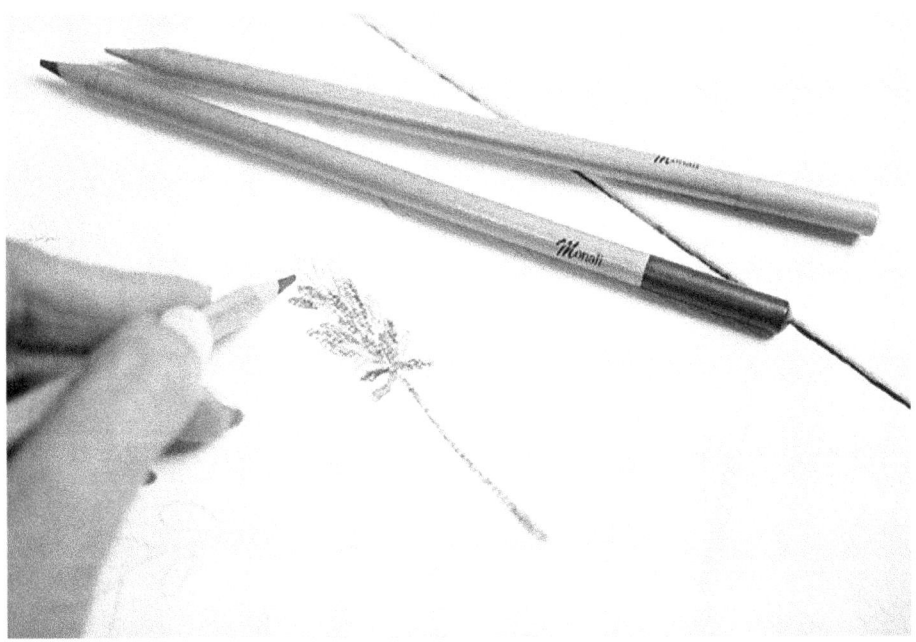

STEP 3/9—Apply water to the entire letter with a watercolor brush.

STEP 4/9—Color the plants. For flowers, put different colors on the petals.

STEP 5/9—With the watercolor brush, apply water and blend the colors together.

STEP 6/9—For the foliage, apply the first color and add lines of different colors to create nuances.

STEP 7/9—Cut out the patterns using a Cricut maker.

STEP 8/9—Glue the patterns on the letter using the foam squares. Then glue everything on the canvas with double-sided tape.

STEP 9/9—Your floral monogram is ready.

Conclusion

Thank you for making it to the end! More and more people choose to create their own materials, invitations, and holiday cards for scrapbooking. These options allow more personalization than their off-the-shelf substitutes. Not only are the home-made invitations more customized, but they are also much less expensive than stores. Cricut personal cutting machines make it possible to create a professional craft project anytime even for those with little time and even less experience.

Cricut cutting machines are locally available in craft shops and some department stores with art and craft sections. But the best deals are usually found online. The entry-level type with willingly obtainable sales prices of about 100 dollars is more than adequate for the occasional do-it-yourselfer. It can produce thousands of diverse shape groupings and needs little maintenance. More experienced craftsmen, or those managing home enterprises that create personalized paper products, may find that larger models meet their needs.

These machines are mechanized and much easier than older manual cutters to use. They can cut even heavy paper inventories, in most cases, enabling scrapbookers to create designs with a range of colors and textures. A number of sites offer advice from regular amateur users to provide guidance on how to use a new machine. They can be a valuable source of information and inspiration to illustrate the best use of the machine. While these sites are a great destination, the best feature of a Cricut home machine is the ability to create completely one-of-a-kind websites. Experiment with new shapes and color combinations to create something unique and memorable.

Cricut cutting machines are sufficiently versatile for any type of craft project. Make skilled-looking scrapbooks with personal Cricut cutting machines.

For any scrapbooker, a Cricut cutting machine is a must-have. These devices allow users to decouple paper into various interesting types, making it simple, and fun to personalize every page in a scrapbook. Designed to be small enough to take you on your journey, they will take up little space at home and can be brought with you at any scrapbooking party you attend. They are the perfect tool for anyone who wants a user-friendly way to create unique borders, inserts, and other decorating pages.

Cricut machines can produce shapes from 1" to more than 5" high anywhere. Simple to adjust metal cutting patterns, most styles of craft paper produce standardized shapes. These forms can be used to add custom letters, cheerful shapes, or thought-provoking borders that represent any page's content. While many different card stock thicknesses may be used, scrapbookers should know that paper in a heavier grade might make the blades dull faster. This means that the sharpness of the blade should always be checked and replaced if appropriate in order to ensure good performance.

A Cricut computer is not a small investment. Prices start at about $100 and some people cannot use this cutting machine. When considering, however, the costs of the production of pre-cut letters and forms, the computer will ultimately pay for itself, as are noticed by most committed enthusiasts. These may also be used for other documents, such as individual invites, gift tags, and holiday cards.

www.ingramcontent.com/pod-product-compliance
Lightning Source LLC
Chambersburg PA
CBHW081343080526
44588CB00016B/2361